W9-CMA-235

"Nolo's home page is worth bookmarking."
—WALL STREET JOURNAL

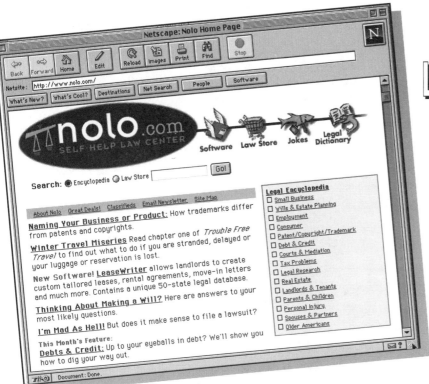

LEGAL INFORMATION ONLINE ANYTIME

www.nolo.com

24 hours a day

AT THE NOLO PRESS SELF-HELP LAW CENTER ON THE WEB, YOU'LL FIND

- Nolo's comprehensive **Legal Encyclopedia**, with links to other online resources
- **SharkTalk:** Everybody's Legal Dictionary
- **Auntie Nolo**—if you've got questions, Auntie's got answers
- **Update information** on Nolo books and software
- **The Law Store**—over 250 self-help legal products including: Downloadable Software, Books, Form Kits and E-Guides
- **Discounts** and other good deals, our hilarious Shark Talk game
- Our ever-popular **lawyer jokes**
- **NoloBriefs.com,** our monthly email newsletter

1st
Edition

QUICK & LEGAL

101

Law Forms for
Personal Use

by Attorneys Robin Leonard & Ralph Warner with the Editors of Nolo Press

NOLO PRESS BERKELEY

Your Responsibility When Using a Self-Help Law Book

We've done our best to give you useful and accurate information in this book. But laws and procedures change frequently and are subject to differing interpretations. If you want legal advice backed by a guarantee, see a lawyer. If you use this book, it's your responsibility to make sure that the facts and general advice contained in it are applicable to your situation.

Keeping Up to Date

To keep its books up to date, Nolo Press issues new printings and new editions periodically. New printings reflect minor legal changes and technical corrections. New editions contain major legal changes, major text additions or major reorganizations. To find out if a later printing or edition of any Nolo book is available, call Nolo Press at 510-549-1976 or check out our Website at www.nolo.com.

To stay current, follow the "Update" service at our Website: www.nolo.com. In another effort to help you use Nolo's latest materials, we offer a 25% discount off the purchase of the new edition of your Nolo book if you turn in the cover of an earlier edition. (See the "Special Upgrade Offer" in the back of this book.) This book was last revised in **July 1998**.

FIRST EDITION	JULY 1998
Editors	STEPHEN ELIAS
	SHAE IRVING
	JANET PORTMAN
	MARY RANDOLPH
	BARBARA KATE REPA
	MARCIA STEWART
Illustrations	MARI STEIN
Cover Design	TONI IHARA
Book Design	TERRI HEARSH
Proofreading	ROBERT WELLS
Index	SAYRE VAN YOUNG
Printing	CUSTOM PRINTING COMPANY

Leonard, Robin.
  101 law forms for personal use / by Robin Leonard & Ralph Warner. -- 1st ed.
     p.   cm.
  Includes index.
  ISBN 0-87337-412-6
  1. Forms (Law)--United States--Popular Works. I. Warner, Ralph. II. Title.
KF170.L46 1998
347.73'55--dc21   98-5035
                                     CIP

For information on bulk purchases or corporate premium sales, please contact the Special Sales Department. For academic sales or textbook adoptions, ask for Academic Sales. Call 800-955-4775 or write to Nolo Press, Inc., 950 Parker Street, Berkeley, CA 94710.

Acknowledgments

This book is a compilation and modification of some of the forms that exist in several other Nolo Press publications, plus several new ones. It couldn't have been written without the editorial assistance and support of Nolo's editorial department, particularly: Steve Elias, Shae Irving, Janet Portman, Mary Randolph, Barbara Kate Repa and Marcia Stewart. Thanks, too, to Susan Cornell for typing and retyping and retyping yet again our changes. Terri Hearsh labored long and hard to make the book both attractive and functional. Mari Stein provided the wonderful artwork.

Table of Contents

3 Things to Do After a Death

4 Renting Residential Real Estate

5 Borrowing or Lending Money

6 Buying a House

7 Buying or Selling Personal Property

8 Renting Personal Property and Storing Goods

9 Home Repairs, Maintenance or Remodeling

14 Settling Legal Disputes

15 Dealing With Direct Marketers and Telemarketers

Appendices

A Using the Forms Disk

B Tear-Out Forms

Index

Introduction

How to Use This Book

This book provides ready-to-use forms and contracts for a variety of everyday legal and practical transactions that most Americans can safely handle without formal legal help. Among the forms included are those necessary to write a short-term will, settle minor legal disputes, rent a place to live, lend money and sell a car or other property. Forms are also included to hire someone to repair, remodel or clean your house, to care for your children and for a variety of other purposes.

The Importance of Getting Contracts in Writing

The most important rule when making any business agreement is this: Get it in writing. In a few situations—such as a contract to buy or sell real estate—you must have a written agreement for it to be legally enforceable. Similarly, a contract that can't be performed within one year of when it's made must be written.

But even in the situations where an oral contract is legal, there are many practical reasons why you want to write it down. Two years from now, you and the other people involved in any transaction are likely to have significantly different recollections about what you agreed to. So putting your agreement into black and white is an important memory aid. But a well-drafted contract has several other important benefits. For one, it serves as a framework for settling disputes. If this proves impossible and a court contest ensues, it will be far easier to prove the terms of a written contract than an oral one.

Another important benefit of drafting a written agreement is that the act of putting a contract together can help you and the other parties focus on all key legal and practical issues, some of which might otherwise be overlooked. By starting this process with a well-designed form—like those in this book—you increase your chances of creating a thorough document.

Many of these forms are primarily designed for your personal use, such as the apartment-finding checklist, loan comparison worksheet and moving checklist. But other forms in the book are contracts, designed for two or more parties to create a legally enforceable agreement.

Unlike commercial contracts used to buy a house or car or even to sign up with a health maintenance organization, which almost always consist of pages full of hyped-up legalese, the contracts in this book are written in everyday (but legal) language. They are designed to describe and define a transaction, such as selling a used car or boarding your pet, with a reasonable level of specificity without sacrificing the important virtues of clarity and simplicity.

The jargon-free nature of our contracts does not jeopardize their enforceability. In general, as long as two parties—business entities or people—exchange promises to each do something of benefit for the other, a valid contract is formed. In general, a contract will be enforced unless any of the following is true:

- **The terms are too vague.** The contract must be clear and detailed enough so that an arbitrator or judge can sensibly decide who is right. For example, a house painting agreement that says "John the Painter shall paint Salli the Homeowner's house" provides so little guidance that it is next to worthless and probably would not be enforced. At the very least, to be enforceable the contract should state how much John is to be paid for his work. Of course, you'll want to go beyond creating a contract that defines who and what is involved to create one that anticipates problems likely to arise under it. To be of real value, it should include key details such as the type and color of paint to be used, the work schedule, how and when payment is to be made and what happens if John and Salli disagree about a key issue.

- **The contract involves an illegal purpose.** A contract formed to accomplish something that the law prohibits is not enforceable in a court. For instance, if two people who sign a contract to transfer an illegal gambling operation later have a falling out, the agreement will not be enforced by a judge.

- **Enforcement would be grossly unfair.** The contracts you make using this book are unlikely to be challenged on the grounds of fairness. But know that in extreme situations, if a contract is both unfair and the result of one party's superior bargaining position (such as a one-sided premarital agreement between a millionaire and an unsophisticated recent immigrant), a court might not enforce it. If you keep in mind that the best contracts substantially benefit both parties, you will have no problems.

A. Filling in the Contracts and Forms

The forms in this book are designed to be used as needed; we don't expect you to read the book from start to finish. But we do ask one thing: Read the introductory material at the beginning of any chapter from which you will use a form, as well as the material that precedes the form itself. For example, before creating a broad power of attorney, read the introductory material in Chapter 1 and the text corresponding to Form 6.

You can use the forms provided in this book in at least three ways:

- All the forms in this book are contained on the accompanying disk. If you have access to a computer, the most efficient approach is to use it to fill in and print a desired form using the computer's word processing program, customizing the form as needed.
- You can certainly get the job done the old-fashioned way—by photocopying a form out of the book and filling it in with a typewriter or pen. Although you'll be fine filling in checklists, worksheets and other forms for

your personal use by hand, we suggest that you type the contracts. Although typing is not legally required, a printed document usually carries more weight than a handwritten one and is more legible. But if convenience or cost dictate that you fill a contract in by hand, do it neatly and you should be fine.

- If someone drafts a contract and presents it to you to sign, you can use a corresponding form in this book as a checklist to make sure that the proposed contract has all the recommended ingredients. If it doesn't, have the preparer use the form in this book as a model when making modifications or additions.

Make several copies of frequently used forms. Where a form will be used repeatedly, print out or photocopy a pile of blank forms, filling them in later as needed. Especially if you don't have a computer to print out more forms, don't use the original form from the book or you'll be left without a clean copy.

1. Editing and Adding to the Forms

Some individual clauses or phrases in our contracts may not apply to your situation. If you are using the contracts on the disk, simply delete those clauses and renumber the remaining as appropriate. If you are using the tear-out contracts, draw lines through the clause and have both parties put their initials next to it. For example, a divorcing couple with no children can still use our Divorce or Separation Agreement, making the following modifications:

4. Spouse/Partner 2 agrees to pay and to indemnify and hold Spouse/Partner 1 harmless from the following debts:

_____

_____

_____

_____

RDL

5. ~~We agree to the following concerning the custody of and visitation with our minor children:~~

TH

~~_____~~

~~_____~~

~~_____~~

~~_____~~

~~_____~~

RDL

6. ~~We agree that _____~~

TH ~~*[name of parent who will pay child support]* shall pay $ _____ per month in child support~~

~~for each child until that child reaches age 18 to _____~~

~~*[name of parent who will receive child support].* We further agree that a court may increase this~~

~~amount from time to time if it is necessary and proper to do so under the child support guidelines~~

~~prescribed under state law.~~

~~We further agree that _____~~

~~*[name of parent who will obtain health insurance]* shall obtain and maintain in force a policy of health~~

~~insurance providing major medical, dental and vision coverage for each child for the duration of the~~

~~support obligation. The child's reasonable health costs that are not covered by any policy shall be paid~~

~~by _____~~

~~*[name of parent who will obtain health insurance, or names of both parents].*~~

~~We further agree that as additional child support, _____~~

~~*[name of parent who will pay child support]* shall pay to _____~~

~~*[name of parent who will receive child support]* for child care a total of $ _____ per~~

~~month, payable in advance on the _____ day of the month, beginning on~~

~~_____ and continuing as long as child care is necessary and actually being paid.~~

5

7. Alimony/Maintenance/Spousal Support

RDL ☒ We agree to a mutual waiver of any and all rights or claims that either one of us may have now or

TH   in the future to receive alimony, maintenance or spousal support from the other. We both fully

understand that by making this waiver we are forever giving up any right to receive such support.

☐ ~~We agree that _____~~

~~*[name of spouse who will pay alimony]* shall pay $ _____ per month in alimony to~~

~~_____ *[name of spouse who*~~

~~*will receive alimony]* until _____ *[date alimony obligation will end].* We further~~

~~agree that alimony will terminate on this date and will not be extended for any reason.~~

On several of our forms, you may encounter some slightly awkward language, such as "☐ Yes ☐ No" or "his/hers." Using your computer, you can easily clean this up by deleting words you don't need or substituting more appropriate language. On the tear-out forms, leaving the unneeded words in will not affect the validity of the contract. If you prefer, however, you can ink out the portion that does not apply.

If you want to change some language, delete (if you are using the contracts on the disk) or cross out (if you are using the tear-out copies) what you don't want and insert the language you want to substitute. On the tear-out forms, you must initial the changes. If the tear out form gets too messy from all the cross outs and inserts, it is best to re-type or carefully reprint the entire contract before signing it.

To add extra terms to a contract, use the space provided. If we didn't leave enough room, prepare a separate addendum sheet. Here's how:

Step 1. The first place you run out of room on a form put "Continued on Attachment 1." The second place you run out of room put "Continued on Attachment 2." Use a separate attachment each time you need more room.

Step 2. For each attachment, title a piece of 8½" by 11" paper with the word "Attachment," the proper number and the name of the form (such as "Attachment 1 to Boat Bill of Sale"). On the next line, put the word "Continuation" and the number and subject matter of the clause from the main contract which you are continuing (for example, "Continuation of Clause #4, Defects in Property").

Step 3. Type or print the additional information.

Step 4. Have both parties sign or initial the attachment sheet.

Step 5. Staple all attachments to the end of the main contract.

⚠ Be sure changes are clear and easy to understand. If you add a list of property or work specifications to a contract, your contract should still be fine. But if you delete one of our clauses, such as how disputes will be resolved, and substitute your own language, make sure your language is easy to understand, free from ambiguity and consistent with the rest of the contract.

2. Describing People, Events and Property

Some forms ask you to name people or describe events or property. Where you are asked to insert the name, address and other identifying information, such as phone number, for a person, use that person's legal name—the name on a driver's license—and home street address. If a person commonly uses two names (not including a nickname), include both, for example, "Alison Johnson aka Alison Walker-Johnson."

To identify property, be as specific as you can. There are no magic words. Your objective is simply to identify the property clearly so that no misunderstanding will arise later. Normally, this means listing the make, model, type, color, identifying number if it has one and any other identifying characteristics that come to mind. For instance, if you are selling a computer, you might say "Power Macintosh 7200, ID # 445556, 80 MB hard disk." Describe a motorcycle something like "1996 red Honda 500 Superhawk VIN # 55565433, Montana Lic. # 567891."

Take a similar approach when describing events. As long as you identify the date, time (if known) and location, and include a clear description of what happened or what is supposed to happen, your description should be adequate.

3. Selecting From Several Choices

Many of our forms contain one or more clauses which ask you to choose among several options. For instance, the following clause, taken from our simple home repairs contract, asks you to select the method of payment for the work being performed:

---

2. Payment

In exchange for the work specified in Clause 1, Homeowner agrees to pay Contractor as follows
[choose one and check appropriate boxes]:

☐ $ _____ , payable upon completion of the specified work by ☐ cash ☐ check.

☐ $ _____ , payable by ☐ cash ☐ check as follows:

_____ % payable when the following occurs: _____

_____ % payable when the following occurs: _____

_____ % payable when the following occurs: _____ .

☐ $ _____ per hour for each hour of work performed, up to a maximum of $ _____ ,

payable at the following times and in the following manner: _____

_____ .

When you see a clause like this, simply check the correct box on the tear-out form and provide any requested additional information. On the computer disk form, you can delete the inapplicable choices, delete the box before the selected choice and complete the rest of your selection. Or, you can simply keep all the options and put an "X" in the correct box. When you can choose more than one box in a sequence, we tell you to "choose one or more of the following." When we want you to only select one, we tell you to "choose one."

4. Preparing, Signing and Storing the Forms

As mentioned, before using the tear-out forms in this book, be sure to make at least two good photo-copies. For the personal checklists and forms, that's all the preparation you need before using them. These forms aren't signed and you can store them anywhere you want. For a contract with another person, you have to do a bit more work.

Step 1. Use one of your photocopies to make a rough draft.

Step 2. Prepare a final version on another photo-copy by typing or neatly printing your entries.

Step 3. Photocopy your final version.

Step 4. Sign and date both the photocopy and original. Have the other party do the same. It doesn't have to be the same day.

Step 5. Give the other party the original or a photocopy; keep the other one for your own records.

Step 6. Store your copy in a safe place.

5. Requiring a Spouse's Signature

If you'll be asked to sign a contact that makes you liable for a debt, the other person may ask that your spouse sign as well. This is most likely to happen, for example, if you're borrowing money to buy property that both spouses will use or to help finance a new business venture.

By having your spouse sign, a second person becomes legally liable for repaying the debt. Normally, if only you signed the contract and didn't repay it, the other party to the agreement could get a judgment against you but not your spouse. This means that the creditor would be able to seize property that you own in your own name, but not property that you and your spouse own in both your names or that your spouse owns in his name. (The rules are different in community property states; see the sidebar.) But if you and your spouse both sign a contract and then default, the other party can sue and get a judgment against both of you. That judgment can be enforced by seizing your joint bank account, putting a lien on your jointly owned real estate, seizing property in your name alone and seizing property in your spouse's name alone.

Who Pays the Debts in Community Property States?

Nine states follow something called the community property system: Arizona, California, Idaho, Louisiana, Nevada, New Mexico, Texas, Washington and Wisconsin. In these states, a married couple's property is generally considered community (joint) regardless of whose name it's in or who paid for it. A spouse may own separate property, but—especially in long marriages—most property tends to be community. In addition, all debts incurred during the marriage—even if only one spouse signed the loan papers—are considered community (joint) debts unless a creditor was explicitly told that only one spouse would be liable for the debt.

In most situations, the rights of creditors to seize property after getting a judgment for non-payment of a debt depend on whether the property is considered community or separate.

- **Community Property.** Usually, property earned or acquired by either spouse during the marriage—except property acquired by gift or inheritance or defined as separate under a premarital agreement—is considered community property. A creditor can go after all community property to pay for either a community debt or a separate debt.

- **Separate Property.** This is property a spouse owned before getting married, acquired during the marriage by gift or inheritance or agreed in writing to be kept separate. It's also property acquired using separate assets. For example, if you owned a house when you got married, sold it and used the proceeds to buy stock, the stock is your separate property. For community debts, a creditor can seek reimbursement from either spouse's separate property. For your separate debts, a creditor can go after your separate property and all community property, including your spouse's share. And as you might guess, on your spouse's separate debts, a creditor can go after your spouse's separate property and all community property, including your share.

6. Notaries and Witnesses

Notarization means that a person authorized as a notary public certifies in writing that:

- you're the person you claim to be, and
- you've acknowledged under oath signing the document.

Very few legal documents need to be notarized or witnessed. Notarization and witnessing are usually limited to documents that are going to be recorded at a public office charged with keeping such records, such as a county land records office or register of deeds. Occasionally—but very rarely—state laws require witnesses or notaries to sign other types of documents.

Where we suggest that you have the document notarized, we have written [Notary Seal] at the end of the form. Notarization language can vary from state to state, and you will want to use the language required in your state. You can often find a notary at a bank, lawyer's office, real estate office or title insurance office. Most charge under $20 for notarizing a document.

B. Resolving Disputes

Sadly, you may have a legal dispute involving one of the contracts in this book. One way to resolve a dispute is through a court fight. This is usually a bad way, given that trials are typically expensive, prolonged and emotionally draining. It usually makes far more sense to attempt to resolve disputes through other means, including the following:

- **Negotiation.** The parties to the dispute try to voluntarily work out their differences through open discussions which often result in each compromising a little to put the matter to rest.
- **Mediation.** The parties try to achieve a voluntary settlement with the help of a neutral third party, the mediator, who helps disputants craft their own solution. Mediation is inexpensive, quick, confidential and effective about 80% of the time.
- **Arbitration.** The parties allow a neutral third party, the arbitrator, to arrive at a binding

decision in order to resolve the dispute. Normally, the decision is solely up to the arbitrator. In some situations, however, the parties establish certain limits in advance of the arbitration—for example, if the arbitrator finds that X is liable under the contract, then Y can be awarded between $15,000 and $25,000. Where limits are set by the parties, the arbitrator is bound by them. Arbitration is almost always speedier and usually much less expensive than litigation.

Ideally, you'd like to be able to settle disputes through negotiations. Unfortunately, however, even when everyone tries in good faith, they don't always reach a compromise. Therefore, the dispute resolution approach set out below, and used in the contracts throughout this book, lets you agree in advance on a framework mandating non-court

alternatives such as mediation and arbitration for resolving disputes.

 This clause is in the file DISPUTE.

This dispute resolution system allows the parties to make one of three choices:

- **Litigation.** You go to court and let a judge or jury resolve the dispute.
- **Mediation and possible litigation.** You agree to let a mediator help you reach a voluntary settlement of the dispute. If mediation doesn't accomplish this goal, either of you can take the dispute to court. You can name the mediator when you prepare the form or agree on one when the need arises.

Disputes

[choose one]

☐ **Litigation.** If a dispute arises, any party may take the matter to court.

☐ **Mediation and Possible Litigation.** If a dispute arises, the parties will try in good faith to settle it through mediation conducted by *[choose one]:*

    ☐ _____ *[name of mediator].*

    ☐ a mediator to be mutually selected.

The parties will share the costs of the mediator equally. If the dispute is not resolved within 30 days after it is referred to the mediator, any party may take the matter to court.

☐ **Mediation and Possible Arbitration.** If a dispute arises, the parties will try in good faith to settle it through mediation conducted by *[choose one]:*

    ☐ _____ *[name of mediator].*

    ☐ a mediator to be mutually selected.

The parties will share the costs of the mediator equally. If the dispute is not resolved within 30 days after it is referred to the mediator, it will be arbitrated by *[choose one]:*

    ☐ _____ *[name of arbitrator].*

    ☐ an arbitrator to be mutually selected.

Judgment on the arbitration award may be entered in any court that has jurisdiction over the matter.

Costs of arbitration, including lawyers' fees, will be allocated by the arbitrator.

- **Mediation and possible arbitration.** You start by submitting the dispute to mediation. If mediation doesn't lead to a settlement, you submit the dispute to arbitration. The arbitrator makes a final decision which will be enforced by a court, if necessary. You can name the arbitrator when you prepare the form or agree on one when the need arises.

 For a comprehensive and practical discussion of mediation and other methods of resolving disputes, see *How to Mediate Your Dispute,* by Peter Lovenheim (Nolo Press).

C. Do You Need a Lawyer?

Most of the contracts used in this book involve relatively small and straightforward transactions. Just as you routinely negotiate deals to sell a car, paint your house or store a friend's belongings without formal legal help, you can just as safely complete the basic legal paperwork needed to record your understanding.

But like most generalizations, this one isn't always true. Creating a solid written agreement—especially where a lot of money or property is at stake—will occasionally mean obtaining the advice of a lawyer on a problematic issue. Fortunately, even when you seek a lawyer's help, the forms and information set out here will let you keep a tight rein on legal fees. You'll have gotten a running start by learning about the legal issues and perhaps drawing up a rough draft of the needed document, allowing you and your lawyer to focus on the few points that may not be routine.

Ideally, you should find a lawyer who's willing to answer a question or two, or possibly to review a completed contract draft, but who respects your ability to prepare the routine paperwork. Adopting this approach should keep the lawyer's fee to a

minimum. Bear in mind that some lawyers still subscribe to the old-fashioned notion that they and only they are the repository of legal information and expertise. In their view, you should turn every legal question and problem over to them, and your participation should be limited to promptly paying their chunky bills. It should go almost without saying that even if this were an efficient way to run your life (it isn't—you clearly need to be involved in making all key decisions), you probably couldn't afford it.

D. Icons Used in This Book

As you've read this Introduction, you no doubt encountered several icons, alerting you to specific information. Here's a complete list of the icons used in this book.

 A practical tip or good idea.

 A warning about a potential problem.

 Resources that give more information about the issue discussed in the text.

 Consider whether to skip or skim a section.

 Related topics covered in this book.

 A point about a form on the disk.

 An alert that a form needs notarization.

Delegating Authority to
Care for Children, Pets and Property

Human beings can be distinguished from the rest of the animal kingdom in one fundamental way: the ability to reason or make decisions. Many of the key decisions adults make affect the care of their minor children. And sometimes, when we know we won't be on the spot to make these decisions, we appoint a person we trust to do so.

This chapter includes several forms you can use to delegate decision-making to others in several common situations.

Be sure you choose the right person. While it's important to prepare a sound agreement authorizing someone to care for your children when you can't, even the best legal document won't be of much help if you don't choose a good caretaker. So be sure you pick someone who can be counted on to be worthy of your trust.

Form 1: Guardianship Authorization for Care of Minor

This is the form of choice when you will leave your child in the care of another adult for a few days, weeks or months. It's important to understand that by executing this form you are only establishing what the law refers to as an informal guardianship. By contrast, a formal guardianship requires court approval and is used most often when a child will be in a guardian's care for a long period of time (for example, when a young child moves in with her grandparents because her parents are deceased) and the caretaker will need to register the child at a new school and establish new arrangements for medical care.

Informal guardianships are most commonly used in these two situations:

- You will be traveling or otherwise unavailable for a short period of time (perhaps you'll be in the hospital or a rehabilitation center) and will leave your child in another adult's care.
- Your child lives with you and a stepparent who has not legally adopted him. Because you

travel frequently, the stepparent commonly functions as the primary caregiver.

Notary seal. This form contains a notary seal notice. While notarization adds a measure of legal credibility (authenticity), it isn't always necessary. For example, you probably don't need to have it notarized if you'll leave your child with a grandparent for a few days. But if you expect to be away from your child for a lengthy period of time—especially if your child will stay with a nonrelative—it's a good idea to take the time to have it notarized because, practically speaking, it is likely to enhance its acceptance.

Form 2: Authorization for Minor's Medical Treatment

This is a form to use when you want to allow another adult to authorize necessary medical care for your child during a specified activity, such as while playing on a sports team or during dance lessons. This form is useful when your child will be in the care of other adults for a short period of time, as is common for after-school sports and other recreational activities.

Notary seal. This form contains a notary seal notice. While it never hurts to have this form notarized, it's not really essential.

Form 3: Authorization for Foreign Travel With Minor

Your child may be prevented from traveling outside the U.S. with another adult unless that adult has documentation showing his legal relationship to the child and his authority to travel with the child. And if your child needs medical care while traveling, the last thing the adult she's traveling with will want to do is have to explain that the child isn't his and he has nothing showing his authority to authorize care.

When taking an unrelated minor child out of the U.S., check travel rules carefully. Start by calling the embassy or consulate for the foreign country you'll be traveling to. Ask if the country has any rules or regulations governing adults traveling in their country with an unrelated minor child. Chances are good that the country does not, but this isn't always true. When you arrive in the foreign country—especially if it's in the developing world where the communication infrastructure may be poor—it is a good idea to let the U.S. embassy or consulate know you are there with an unrelated minor child (you can even give them a copy of your authorization forms) in case any problems arise concerning your relationship to the child. That way, if you have to call for help, U.S. officials located where you are will already have knowledge of your presence in the country with an unrelated minor.

Notary seal. This form contains a notary seal notice. Because you will be traveling in a foreign country with an unrelated minor child, be sure to have the form notarized. Doing this will give the form a great degree of legitimacy, especially in the eyes of a foreign government, if anything comes up while you are traveling.

Form 4: Pet Care Agreement

Use this agreement when you need to board your animal or animals with a friend, relative or neighbor for a significant length of time. The main purpose is to specify each party's expectations, make sure the caregiver has clear and complete instructions and avoid the possibility of a misunderstanding later.

Payment for pet food and vet bills. When a friend cares for your pet while you are away, your first thought may be that it is unnecessary to reimburse him for a few dollars worth of pet food. Think again—you are already asking for a big favor, one that is only likely to be extended again if you are scrupulous about the details. Even if your friend has several animals of her own and ten bags of pet food in her garage, bring along more than enough

chow to feed your pet while you will be away. Also, if your pet is prone to illness or recovering from an illness or injury, arrange for payment of your vet bills in advance. Your vet may be willing to bill you (if you'll be away for just a few weeks). Otherwise, plan on leaving your credit card number with your vet in case your pet needs care while you are away. Finally, make sure you complete an authorization form for your vet, specifying that your pet is under the care of your friend while you are away and that this friend has the authority to arrange any necessary care decisions.

Form 5: Authorization to Drive a Motor Vehicle

Imagine the following: You're on vacation, out of the country for a few weeks. Your best friend's 19-year-old son has agreed to stay at your house, watch the dog, water the plants and generally keep an eye on things. He's a very reliable young man and you've given him use of your car. Or maybe, instead of having the 19-year-old watch your place, you arrange a month's house exchange with a family from Europe; they will stay in your house while you stay at theirs. As part of the exchange, you have use of their car and they have use of yours.

In either situation, take the scenario one step further. While driving your car, the housesitter gets pulled over for a traffic violation or becomes involved in an accident to which the police are called. The driver shows his driver's license and your car registration. The officer notes the difference in names and asks for any documentation to show your guest's legal right to operate the car. If he can't produce it, he may be detained while the police investigate whether he is driving a stolen vehicle.

Enter this form, which goes far to guarantee that the person driving your vehicle doesn't have an even worse day. In it, you clearly authorize your guest (or anyone else to whom you entrust your vehicle) to drive it. We strongly recommend you use it anytime you lend your car to someone with a different last name when you won't be easily available to verify the loan of the vehicle.

Form 6: Power of Attorney for Finances (Full Power)

A power of attorney is a legal document in which you, the principal, in legal jargon, give another person legal authority to act on your behalf. The person to whom you give this authority is called your attorney-in-fact. In this context, "attorney" refers to anyone authorized to act on another's behalf; it's most definitely not restricted to lawyers.

You can use a power of attorney to give your attorney-in-fact as much or as little authority as you choose. If you wish to give your attorney-in-fact the authority to handle all of your business and financial matters for you while you are out of town, use this form. If, as is probably more likely, you want to authorize this person to handle only a single transaction, such as selling your house, car or boat, use Form 7.

You will notice that Part 6 of the long form allows you to fill in "special instructions" for your attorney-in-fact. While the list of powers you can grant in Part 5 is comprehensive and should cover all of your basic needs, you may want to add restrictions or additions to these powers. For example, some people use the special instructions section to forbid the attorney-in-fact from selling their home, to restrict the attorney-in-fact's ability to sell or encumber a small business, to permit the attorney-in-fact to make gifts to others or to require the attorney-in-fact to make periodic financial reports to business associates or relatives. That said, however, you'll want to be judicious in your use of special instructions. If you add too many, you run the risk of making your document confusing.

⚠ Where real estate is involved, recording is necessary. If you will give your attorney-in-fact power to buy, sell or mortgage your real estate (or engage in transactions involving your probate-avoiding living trust which contains real estate), you must record the power of attorney in the county in which the real estate is located. Your local County Recorder, Land Registry or Register of Deeds office should be able to help you accomplish this.

⚠ If you live in the District of Columbia and you are granting power over your real estate, you should not use the power of attorney forms in this book. Your power of attorney must contain special language that is not included here. You can find a form including the required language for the District of Columbia in *The Financial Power of Attorney Workbook*, by Shae Irving (Nolo Press).

Our power of attorney forms are designed to be used for a preestablished period. You specify when the attorney-in-fact's authority begins and ends. In addition, you have the legal right to revoke or terminate your power of attorney at any time. If you become incapacitated while the power of attorney is in effect, your attorney-in-fact's authority automatically ends.

As you may know, there is another type of power of attorney, called a durable power of attorney, which remains in effect even if you become incapacitated and can no longer make decisions for yourself. These are very commonly signed in advance of need by older and ill people who realize that at some point they may need help managing their affairs (these "springing" durable powers of attorney only become operable upon a doctor's opinion that the person is mentally incapacitated). Because state laws vary in this legal area, if you want a durable power of attorney, you will need a resource beyond this book. Nolo publishes two excellent ones:

- *WillMaker* (software for Macintosh or Windows) lets you create a valid will, durable power of attorney for finances, healthcare directives and final arrangements document using your computer.
- *The Financial Power of Attorney Workbook*, by Shae Irving, contains all the forms and instructions you need to create a valid durable power of attorney for finances and other financial powers of attorney.

If you anticipate that your attorney-in-fact will conduct major transactions, check with your financial institutions. Many financial institutions —banks and brokerage houses, for example—have their own power of attorney forms. If yours do, you'll probably want to use their forms in addition to the broader power of attorney form in this book. Doing so will reduce hassles for your attorney-in-fact because a financial institution will know what powers its own form grants, and will have no need to quibble with your document.

Making Your Document Legal

After you've prepared your power of attorney, you must carry out just a few simple tasks to make sure the document is legally valid.

Notarization

You must sign your power of attorney in the presence of a notary public for your state. In some states, notarization is required by law to make the power of attorney valid. But even where law doesn't require it, custom does. A power of attorney that isn't notarized may not be accepted by people with whom your attorney-in-fact deals.

Witnesses

Most states don't require a power of attorney to be signed in front of witnesses. The few states that do and the number of witnesses required are listed below. Witness requirements normally consist of the following:

- Witnesses must be present when you sign the document in front of the notary.
- Witnesses must be mentally competent adults.
- The person whom you appoint as your attorney-in-fact can't be a witness.

You want to choose witnesses who will be easily available. In case they are ever needed, it's obviously a good idea to choose witnesses who live nearby and will be easy to contact.

States Requiring Witnesses	Number of Witnesses	Other Requirements
Arizona	1	Witness may not be your attorney-in-fact, the spouse or child of your attorney-in-fact or the notary public.
Arkansas	2	Neither witness may be your attorney-in-fact.
Connecticut	2	Neither witness may be your attorney-in-fact.
District of Columbia	2	Witnesses are necessary only if your power of attorney is to be recorded. Neither witness may be your attorney-in-fact.
Florida	2	Neither witness may be your attorney-in-fact.
Georgia	2	Neither witness may be your attorney-in-fact. In addition, one of your witnesses may not be your spouse or blood relative.
Michigan	2	Witnesses are necessary only if your power of attorney is to be recorded. Neither witness may be your attorney-in-fact.
Ohio	2	Neither witness may be your attorney-in-fact.
Oklahoma	2	Witnesses may not be your attorney-in-fact, or anyone who is related by blood or marriage to you or your attorney-in-fact.
Pennsylvania	2	Neither witness may be your attorney-in-fact.
South Carolina	2	Neither witness may be your attorney-in-fact.
Vermont	2	Witnesses are necessary only if your power of attorney is to be recorded. Neither witness may be your attorney-in-fact.

Form 7: Power of Attorney for Finances (Limited Power)

Use Form 7 if you want your attorney-in-fact to handle only one transaction—such as refinancing your real estate, selling your car or negotiating with creditors on your behalf. If your needs really are definable in this way, it makes good sense to use the restricted document rather than the broader power of attorney set out in Form 6. Even though the longer document is just as legal, it's not wise to clutter your power of attorney with a lot of unnecessary language or to give your attorney-in-fact unnecessary powers.

To make your document legally valid, follow the instructions that accompany Form 6. They explain the requirements for notarizing your document and, if necessary, having it witnessed.

And remember, if your attorney-in-fact will have the power to buy, sell or encumber your real estate, you must record the document at the County Recorder's, Land Registry or Register of Deeds office in the county in which the real estate is located.

Form 8: Notice of Revocation of Power of Attorney

You can use a Notice of Revocation of Power of Attorney form in two situations:
- You want to revoke your power of attorney prior to the termination date set out in the document.
- Your power of attorney has ended as specified in the document, but you want to be absolutely sure that all people and institutions who have received it know that it is no longer in force.

⚠️ **If you recorded your Power of Attorney, record the Notice of Revocation.** If you put your power of attorney on file in the public records and it hasn't expired on its own, you should also record your Notice of Revocation. Otherwise, people who don't actually know of your revocation are entitled to continue to deal with your attorney-in-fact on your behalf. ∎

Basic Estate Planning

Making plans for what will happen to your property after you die is called estate planning. Generally, if you die without a will or other legal means for transferring property, your property will be distributed to certain close relatives—your spouse, children, parents and siblings—under state "intestacy" laws.

Making a will is an important estate planning step. For many people, coupled with naming beneficiaries for retirement plans, insurance policies and other investments, it's the only one they need. Whether or not that is true for you depends on your circumstances. Generally speaking, the more wealth you possess, the more you'll want to consider legal issues beyond the scope of a will, such as avoiding probate—the court-supervised process of gathering and distributing a deceased person's assets—and reducing death taxes. And, depending on your situation, you may want to provide for a disabled child, establish a fund for grandchildren or make charitable gifts.

This chapter introduces the concept of estate planning and provides some bare-bones will forms. Resources listed throughout the chapter explain where to go for more extensive information.

Form 9:   Property Worksheet

Before you write a will or other estate planning document, you may find it helpful to make an inventory of your property. Filling out the Property Worksheet can jog your memory to make sure you don't overlook important items.

Even if you haven't made a will, you may have already named someone to get some of your property at your death. For example, if you have a retirement account (such as an IRA or 401(k)) or insurance policy, you have probably named a beneficiary and alternate beneficiary. If you own real estate, you may hold it in joint tenancy with right of survivorship, meaning that the other joint owner will automatically inherit your share at your death.

Nolo Press publishes *Personal RecordKeeper*, a comprehensive software program designed to keep track of all your property (investments, memorabilia), key addresses (friends, business contacts) and the location of important items (safe deposit box key, family pictures, old tax returns). It can both help to organize your life and provide a roadmap to the final arrangements you have made after your death.

Form 10: Beneficiary Worksheet

If you plan to leave all your property to one or a very few people (for example, "all property to my spouse, or if she predeceases me, to my children in equal shares"), there is no need to complete this form. You already know who will get your property at your death, and you can turn to Forms 11 and 12.

Like the Property Worksheet, the Beneficiary Worksheet is a tool that can help you get ready to draft your estate planning documents. On the Beneficiary Worksheet, list each item of property you want to leave as a distinct gift. Then list the beneficiary or beneficiaries you want to get each item. If you name more than one beneficiary to share a specific gift, state the percentage share each is to receive. It is also highly advisable to name an alternate beneficiary or beneficiaries for each gift, in case your first choice dies before you do.

In addition to naming beneficiaries, list all debts you want to forgive at your death. For example, if you loaned your best friend $10,000 and he pays you back with interest $100 a month, it will take him many years to pay off the debt. If he still owes you money when you die, you can forgive or waive the balance due. This means that your heirs cannot go after him for the rest.

Be sure to include the property for which you've already named a beneficiary. As noted in the discussion for Form 9, you may have already planned the eventual disposition of much of your property before you prepare a will. Common property that may already have beneficiaries includes:

- bank accounts, naming (on a form provided by the bank) a payable-on-death beneficiary
- real estate, holding it with someone else in joint tenancy, in tenancy by the entirety or (in community property states) in community property with your spouse
- securities, registering them in transfer-on-death form if your state law allows it
- retirement accounts, naming a beneficiary (on a form provided by the account custodian) to take whatever is still in the account at your death, and
- life insurance policies, naming a beneficiary (on a form provided by the company) to receive the proceeds at your death.

If you've already taken care of property in one of these ways, check the box in the margin on the Beneficiary Worksheet.

Finally, list a "residuary" beneficiary or beneficiaries. This is one or more people or organizations who will get everything you don't leave to a specific beneficiary. Do this even if you are sure you have identified all your property and named a beneficiary to receive it; there is always a chance that between the date you make your will and your death, you'll acquire additional property.

Forms 11 and 12: Bare-Bones Wills

A simple or "bare-bones" will:
- is easy to make
- lets you leave your property to anyone you wish, and
- is easy to change or revoke; you're not stuck with it if you change your mind later.

Anyone who is 18 or older (19 if you live in Wyoming) and of sound mind can make a valid will. You have to be very far gone before your will can be invalidated on the grounds that you were mentally incompetent. Or put another way, if you're reading and understanding this book, your mind is sound enough.

In addition to designating who will receive your property, your will is also where you appoint the person you want to supervise its distribution after your death (your executor). And if you have minor children, a principal purpose of your will may be to name a guardian for them—someone to raise your children in the event you die and the other parent isn't available to raise the children.

This book contains two bare-bones forms, which can be used by residents of all states except Louisiana. These wills are a good choice if you suddenly want a will on the eve of a long trip or don't want to spend much time on estate planning right now. Unless you have a very simple estate plan for leaving your property, however, you'll probably want to draft a more extensive will for the long term. Precisely because these bare-bones forms are short, simple and easy to use, they do not include a lot of options. For example, they do not let you create a trust to hold property that may be left to children or young adults.

If you have children, use Form 12. Otherwise, use Form 11.

Nolo Press publishes several books and software products containing more sophisticated—but still easy-to-use—information on wills and living trusts. A living trust is the document used most often to avoid probate, the process of distributing a person's property under court supervision.

- *Plan Your Estate*, by Denis Clifford and Cora Jordan, is a comprehensive estate planning book, covering everything from basic estate planning (wills and living trusts) to sophisticated tax-saving strategies (AB trusts and much more). If you haven't yet decided how to approach your estate planning tasks, this is Nolo's best resource.
- *WillMaker* interactive software lets you make a more sophisticated will than the ones contained here. For example, with *WillMaker* you can choose among three ways to provide property management for children should you die

before they are competent to handle property themselves. In addition, *WillMaker* allows you to express your last wishes for your funeral and burial and contains both a healthcare directive (living will) and durable power of attorney for finances valid in your state. With over 600,000 copies sold, *WillMaker* has drafted more wills than any one lawyer—or law firm—in history. To see how *WillMaker* works, check out the "try and buy" version available at the Nolo web site, www.nolo.com.

- *Living Trust Maker* software lets you create a revocable living trust to avoid probate. The program creates an individual trust or a trust for a married couple. Especially if you haven't taken advantage of other probate-avoidance techniques, a living trust may offer a safe and efficient way to save your survivors many thousands of dollars.

- *Nolo's Will Book*, by Denis Clifford, provides step-by-step instructions and forms to create a detailed will. Its will is similar in scope and sophistication to *WillMaker*'s. The book comes with a disk, which you can use with any standard word processing program to make drafting and printing out the will easy.

- *8 Ways to Avoid Probate*, by Mary Randolph, explains important and often overlooked ways to avoid probate. It is now possible to avoid probate for many kinds of property without creating a living trust. If you vaguely know you should be paying attention to probate avoidance, but dread thinking about it, start with this small but thorough book.

These are not tear-out forms. Unlike the forms in the rest of this book, will forms should not just be torn out, filled in and signed. Instead, use the disk that comes with this book (or a typewriter, if you don't have access to a computer) to print out a fresh will which eliminates all the clauses you don't need, and then sign it in front of witnesses following the instructions below. If you simply fill in the blanks and sign it, your will may not be valid.

Leaving property. Use Part 3 of the will, "Specific Gifts," to leave specific items of property. When you list the items in your will, describe them so that your executor—and anyone else—will know exactly what you meant. There is no need to use formal legal descriptions unless they are really necessary to identify the property. Here are some examples of good property descriptions:

- "my house at 435 76th Avenue, Chicago, Illinois"
- "all household furnishings and possessions in my house at 435 76th Avenue, Chicago, Illinois"
- "$10,000 from my savings account, No. 44444, at First National Bank, Chicago, Illinois."

When you leave property, any encumbrances on it—for example, a mortgage—pass with the property. In other words, the beneficiary takes the debt as well as the property.

If you want to leave everything to just one beneficiary, or a group of them—your spouse or your three children, for example—leave the "Specific Gifts" part of the will blank. Instead, use "Part 4, Residuary Estate." Since "residuary" simply refers to the rest of your estate and you have made no gifts, it's easy to see that everything will go to the person or persons you name as your residuary beneficiary(ies). Similarly, if you wish to leave a few small specific gifts (for example, family memorabilia or $10,000) to named individuals, with everything else going to one or several persons (for example, to be divided among your three children), use Section 3 to make your specific gifts and Clause 4 to leave everything else to your children.

Naming your executor. In your will, you must name the person you want to be in charge of winding up your affairs after your death. This person is called your executor (the term "personal representative" is used in some states). The executor must shepherd your property through probate, the court process of distributing the property of a deceased person, if it's necessary, and must see that your property is distributed according to the wishes expressed in your will.

Many people name their spouse or a grown child as executor. The executor usually doesn't need special financial or legal expertise. The important thing is that the person you choose is completely trustworthy and will deal fairly with other beneficiaries.

Signing your will. Your signature on your will must witnessed. When you are ready to sign it, gather together three adults who aren't beneficiaries of your will. Your witnesses do not need to read your will. You simply state, "This is my will." The witnesses (in unison or individually) respond, "She says it's her will." Then you sign your will while the witnesses watch. Finally, each witness signs while the other witnesses watch.

⚠️ **If you're married, your spouse may be able to claim a share of your estate.** In most states (all except Arizona, California, Idaho, Louisiana, Nevada, New Mexico, Texas, Washington and Wisconsin), a surviving spouse has the right to reject what he or she might take through a will and instead claim a share of the deceased spouse's entire estate. In most states, that share is from one-third to one-half of the estate. The details get tricky fast. The point is, if you plan to leave your spouse at least half of your property, you don't need to worry about it. But if you don't, see a lawyer and don't try to use the forms in this book.

Form 11: Simple Will (If You Have No Children)

This is the will to use if you don't have children. Use Form 12 if you do. Remember, these forms can be used by residents of all states except Louisiana.

Read the introduction to Forms 11 and 12 for brief but important instructions on filling out the form correctly, so that you will create a legally valid will that accomplishes what you want.

⚠️ **Do not just fill in and sign this form.** As mentioned above, to be legally valid, your will must be printed out (using the disk that comes with this book) or typed, eliminating all items that don't apply to you. *Do not* just fill in the blanks of this form and try to use the completed form as your will.

Form 12: Simple Will (If You Have Children)

If you have young children, you obviously have some special issues to consider before you make your will. Here is some information to help you.

Custody of minor children. If you have minor children, use your will (Part 8) to name the person you want to raise the children if you die and the other parent is unavailable to raise them. This person is called their "personal guardian." It is also wise to nominate an alternate personal guardian, in case the first choice can't serve.

If you and the other legal parent die (or are otherwise out of the parenting picture) before your kids reach 18, meaning a guardian must be appointed, a judge will review your choice. If no one objects, the person you name will be routinely appointed. But in an unusual situation, a judge who is convinced that naming a different personal guardian is in the best interests of the child has the authority to do so.

⚠️ **You cannot name different guardians for different kids.** The bare-bones will form in this book requires that you name the same personal guardian for all of your minor children. If for some reason you want to name a different person as guardian for different children, use *Nolo's Will Book* (with disk) or *WillMaker* software program.

Property left to your children. Minors cannot legally own property outright, free of supervision, beyond a minimal amount—up to about $3,000 in most states. By law, an adult must be legally responsible for managing any significant amount of property owned by a minor child. So if your children might eventually take property through your will—even if they're only alternate beneficiaries—you should arrange for an adult to supervise any property they might own. You can do this easily in your will.

Form 12 gives you a choice of two methods to provide for adult supervision for gifts to your children:

- **Name a custodian for each child.** The custodian will manage any property slated for the child until the child turns 21 (in most states). A custodian is authorized under your state's Uniform Transfers to Minors Act (UTMA). (See Part 10 of the will.)

- **Name a property guardian.** You should always name a property guardian and successor property guardian in your will, even if you appoint a custodian under the Uniform Transfers to Minors Act. The property guardian will be formally appointed by a court and will manage any property not left through your will (and so not covered by the UTMA custodianship)—for example, property the minor gets from someone else.

Uniform Transfers to Minors Act. All states except Michigan, South Carolina and Vermont have adopted the Uniform Transfers to Minors Act (UTMA). This law authorizes you to appoint an adult custodian and successor custodian in your will to supervise property you leave to a minor. The custodianship ends, and any remaining property must be turned over to the child outright, at the age the UTMA specifies. In most states, this is either 18 or 21, but a few, including California and Alaska, allow you to choose 25. Our form sets the ending age at the oldest age allowed in your state, which in the majority is 21.

Because the custodian has almost complete discretion over management of the property, it is essential that you name someone who is both totally honest and has good financial management skills. The custodian also has a legal duty to act prudently, and always in the best interests of the child. Normally, no court supervision is required.

You can name UTMA custodians for as many children as you wish. In addition, you can name different custodians for different children. When preparing your will, you'll first list all gifts you leave, including gifts to your minor or young adult children. Then you'll complete a separate UTMA clause for each child.

Other Property Management Options

Form 12 does not offer two other fairly common— but legally more complicated—ways to arrange for a minor's property to be managed by an adult:

- A family pot trust that will hold property left to all your minor children, allowing the trustee you name to spend it as needed. For example, if one child had an expensive medical problem, the trustee could spend more for that child and less for others.
- A trust for each child. This option is primarily of value for people with larger estates who do not want adult children to take control of money outright until they are in their middle or late twenties. It gets around the fact that in most states a custodianship under the terms of the Uniform Transfers to Minors Act ends at age 21.

These options are available in *WillMaker* and *Nolo's Will Book*.

Do not just fill in and sign this form. To be legally valid, your will must be printed out (using the disk that comes with this book) or typed, eliminating all items that don't apply to you. *Do not* just fill in the blanks of this form and try to use the completed form as your will.

Form 13: Codicil for a Simple Will

A codicil is sort of a legal "P.S." to a will. In a codicil, you can revoke a clause in your will and then substitute a new clause. Or you can simply add a new provision, such as a new gift of an item of property.

A codicil must be executed with all of the formalities of a will. It must be typed or computer-printed (start with "First Codicil to the Will of _____," leaving off our title), then dated and signed by you in front of three witnesses. You don't have to use the same witnesses who signed your will, but none of the witnesses should be people named as a beneficiary in your will or codicil.

Today codicils are less commonly used than they were in the days when wills were laboriously copied by hand or typed on a typewriter. With almost universal access to computers, it's usually easier—and less likely to confuse—to prepare a whole new will. Nevertheless, codicils can still be sensibly used to make limited changes to a will—for example, when you want to change who receives one item.

⚠ Do not just fill in and sign this form. To be legally valid, your codicil must be printed out (using the disk that comes with this book) or typed, eliminating all items that don't apply to you. *Do not* just fill in the blanks of this form and try to use the completed form as a codicil. ■

Things to Do After a Death

After a death, someone must step in and wind up the deceased person's affairs. Dealing with a welter of details can seem hard and intrusive at a time of grief, but taking concrete steps to provide for family members and carry out the deceased person's wishes can also be a therapeutic activity. The following simple forms and letters can help you take some of the first steps necessary after a death in the family.

How to Probate an Estate, by Julia Nissley, gives California residents step-by-step instructions for handing an estate after someone has died.

These forms are not applicable in all situations. Use the forms in this chapter to notify the deceased's creditors, such as credit card companies, the Social Security Administration and other companies with whom the deceased conducted business, such as magazine and newspaper publishers (to cancel subscriptions), utility companies (to cancel service or to put it in the name of someone else), alumni associations and charities to which the deceased contributed. Do not use these forms to claim benefits under an insurance policy or retirement plan. You will need to contact those companies to complete their forms in order to request benefits.

Form 14: Request for Death Certificate

If you are named in a will or appointed by a court to handle the estate of someone who has died, you are normally called the executor, administrator or personal representative. If you're the spouse or partner, adult child or other family member, you may be taking care of body disposition, such as a cremation or burial, and handling other after-death matters. No matter what your role, if you will be contacting agencies or organizations about the death, you will need certified copies of the death certificate, obtained from the county in which the deceased person died. Before you send in a request, call the local office that provides certificates and get its address and the cost of each certificate. The local health department should be able to advise you on where to go for more information.

Form 15: Notice to Creditor of Death

After a death, you will want to notify creditors, such as card issuers, department stores, banks, mortgage companies and other businesses from which the deceased bought on credit or had an account. This might include a local pharmacy or furniture store. If a formal probate court proceeding is conducted, you'll also probably have to publish a notice to creditors in a local newspaper. Call the newspaper and ask to speak with someone familiar with this process.

Form 16: Notice to Social Security Administration of Death

If the person who died was receiving monthly Social Security benefits, you should promptly notify the Social Security Administration (SSA) of the death. To do so, call the SSA at 800-772-1213.

You must also return benefits for the month in which the person died. If you have an actual check, take it in person your local SSA office and get a receipt, or send it to the SSA via certified mail, return receipt requested. If, as is more likely, the check was deposited directly into the deceased person's bank account, instruct the bank to send it back. And remember to send this notice so that the SSA doesn't deposit further checks.

Form 17: Notice to Other Interested Organizations

You may want to notify businesses and organizations that aren't creditors of the deceased person—that is, they aren't owed any money—but that may need to know of the death. For example, you might want to send a simple notice to alumni or other membership associations, charities to which the deceased person donated regularly, magazine publishers and mail-order businesses that regularly send catalogs. It's easier to send a form, like the one in Appendix B, than to write individual letters to each. ∎

4

Renting Residential Real Estate

ealing with a landlord or property manager can be challenging, to say the least. Doing it successfully requires not only knowing your rights under landlord-tenant law, but also, if necessary, asserting them. It also means coping with your landlord's business policies and idiosyncrasies.

Whether you rent (or own) property, you doubtless understand just how bad a failed landlord-tenant relationship can be. But there is an excellent way to get any landlord-tenant relationship off to a good start and minimize the possibility of future misunderstandings and legal problems: putting all agreements and concerns in writing. This chapter includes the principal forms you'll need to do this. Most are geared toward tenants, although we indicate when conscientious landlords will also find them useful.

 To learn the details of landlord-tenant law, see the following Nolo books and software:

From the landlord's point of view:

- *Every Landlord's Legal Guide*, by Marcia Stewart, Ralph Warner and Janet Portman. This 50-state book provides extensive legal and practical information on leases, tenant screening, rent, security deposits, privacy, repairs, property managers, discrimination, roommates, liability, tenancy termination and much more. It includes more than 25 legal forms and agreements as tear-outs and on disk.
- *Lease Writer* (CD-ROM for Windows/Macintosh). This full stand-alone software program generates a customized legal residential lease or rental agreement, plus more than 20 key documents and forms every landlord or property manager needs. It includes a database to track tenants, rental preferences and policies; instant access to state-specific landlord-tenant information and extensive online legal help.

From the tenant's point of view:

- *Every Tenant's Legal Guide*, by Janet Portman and Marcia Stewart. This book gives tenants in all 50 states the legal and practical information they need to deal with their landlords and protect their rights when things go wrong. It covers all important issues of renting, including signing a lease, getting a landlord to make

needed repairs, fighting illegal discrimination, protecting privacy rights, dealing with roommates, getting the security deposit returned fairly, moving out and much more.

Form 18: Apartment-Finding Service Checklist

Many landlords list their rental property with a homefinders' service that provides a centralized listing of rental units for a particular geographic area. Using one of these services can be an efficient way for a tenant to search for a place to live, especially in metropolitan areas. Prices of apartment-finding services vary, but typically tenants pay a flat fee, such as $50 to $100 for a one-month "membership." In some tight rental markets, you may also have to pay the service a percentage of your monthly rent if you find an apartment through them. Check newspaper ads or look in the Yellow Pages under "Apartment-Finding and Rental Service."

Many homefinding services do a good job of helping people to find a place to rent, but some are sloppy and a few are actually crooked. Unscrupulous companies have been caught selling either outdated rental lists—most or all of the apartments have already been rented—or lists no different from what is in a newspaper. So before you sign up with an apartment-finding service, check with a local consumer organization to be sure it's reputable and worth the money. Also, especially in urban areas, pay close attention to the geographical scope of any service you are considering. Some may be excellent in one area but not others.

Form 18, the Apartment-Finding Service Checklist, offers you a good way to organize and collect the information you need before pulling out your checkbook.

Form 19: Rental Application

Landlords routinely use rental applications to screen potential tenants and select those who are likely to pay the rent on time, keep the unit in good condition and not cause problems. Conscientious landlords will insist on checking references and credit history before signing a lease or rental agreement.

If you own or manage rental property, you can use Form 19 to help screen potential tenants. Before doing so, be sure all applicants sign the rental application authorizing you to verify the information and references and to run a credit check. Also, use the "Notes" section at the end of the application to write down legal reasons for refusing an individual— for example, negative credit history, insufficient income or your inability to verify information. You will want this kind of record in order to survive a fair housing challenge if a disappointed applicant files a discrimination complaint.

Make sure you understand how discrimination laws work. Many types of discrimination are illegal, including race, religion, national origin, sex, familial status, disability and, in some states, sexual orientation or marital status. For more information on legal and illegal reasons to reject a tenant, see the resources listed at the end of this chapter.

Savvy tenants will also find Form 19 useful when looking for a new place to live. We suggest you complete this rental application in advance—providing information about your employment, income, credit background and rental housing history—and take a copy along when you see a potential rental unit. This is almost guaranteed to impress a landlord or his rental agent.

Form 20: Fixed-Term Residential Lease

Leases and rental agreements often look so similar they can be hard to tell apart. That's because both cover nitty-gritty issues, such as the amount of rent and deposits you must pay and the number of people who can live in the rental unit. The big difference is the length of the tenancy. A rental agreement typically lasts only from one month to the next (although week-to-week agreements are possible in many states), and self-renews unless terminated by either the landlord or tenant. By contrast, a lease almost always covers a longer, fixed term, such as one year. Form 20 is a fixed-

term lease. Form 21 is a month-to-month rental agreement. We believe both are fair and balanced from both the landlord and tenant viewpoint.

Several blanks of these forms have legal implications:

Clause 15, Landlord's Right to Access. This tries to balance the tenant's right of privacy against the landlord's right to enter the rental unit to make repairs or for other reasons. A landlord always has the right to enter a rental unit in case of genuine emergency, such as fire. But to show the unit to prospective tenants or to make repairs, many states require 24 hours' written notice. Some states have no notice requirements or simply require the landlord to give the tenant "reasonable notice." Arizona, Delaware, Hawaii, Kentucky, Rhode Island, Vermont and Washington require two days' notice of landlord's entry. In all other states, we believe 24 hours' notice is a workable standard, and therefore recommend that you adopt it in completing Clause 15.

Clause 19, Payment of Court Costs and Attorney Fees in a Lawsuit. Under the law of many states, a clause providing that a landlord will be entitled to attorney fees and court costs in a legal dispute will be read by a court to go both ways. This means that if the tenant wins, she will be entitled to attorney fees and court costs, even if the lease or rental agreement doesn't specifically say so.

For tenants, a landlord's attorney fees clause often makes it easier to find a lawyer willing to take a case that does not have the potential for a hefty money judgment. That's because with an attorney fees clause, a winning lawyer will get paid by the landlord, rather than rely on the tenant's pocketbook. On the other hand, tenants who are confident about representing themselves may prefer not to have an attorney fees clause, reasoning that a landlord who can't recover attorney fees in a lawsuit may be more willing to compromise, rather than go to court.

Landlords usually prefer to include an attorney fees clause unless they intend to do all or most of their own legal work in any potential eviction or other lawsuit. In that situation, if a tenant wins, the landlord will have to pay the tenant's legal fees; if the landlord wins, the tenant will owe nothing because the landlord didn't hire an attorney.

All states have laws regulating residential landlord-tenant relationships. Typically, these laws include establishing the maximum amount allowed for a security deposit, the deadline for returning it, the amount of notice required to change or end a month-to-month tenancy, tenants' privacy rights, late rent charges, a tenant's right to install locks and disclosures regarding the condition of property.

Some states require that leases include certain language. Alaska, Florida, Georgia, Kentucky, Maryland, Michigan, North Carolina, Tennessee and Washington require landlords to give tenants written information on various aspects of the security deposit, such as where it is held, interest payments and when the deposit may be withheld. Even if it's not required, you may want to provide details on security deposits in the space provided in Clause 18 of Forms 20 and 21.

Federal law requires landlords to disclose known lead-based paint hazards in the rental premises. In addition, some states require landlords to make other disclosures about the property, such as flood hazards, before a new tenant signs a lease or rental agreement. Clause 20 is the place to make these kinds of disclosures.

Form 21: Month-to-Month Residential Rental Agreement

Remember, a rental agreement lasts from one month to the next, but automatically self-renews unless the tenant or landlord terminates it in writing. By contrast, a lease almost always covers a longer, fixed term—often one year. Otherwise these agreements are almost identical.

Read the introductory language with Form 20 for a brief discussion of how to complete Clauses 15 and 19, and a summary of how landlord-tenant laws often vary from one state to the next.

Form 22: Cancellation of Lease

Ideally, you'll sign a lease for just the amount of time you need a rental. But despite your best efforts to plan ahead, you may want to move before your lease is up.

One option is to simply move out without sweating the legalities. Leaving before a fixed-term lease expires, without paying the remainder of the rent due under the lease, is called breaking the lease. With a little luck, it may not cost you much—in most states, the landlord is required to re-rent the property reasonably quickly. If the landlord does so (and doesn't attempt to hide the fact that he has a new rent-paying tenant), your financial liability will be limited to paying the rent for the brief time the unit was vacant.

Nevertheless, if you plan to leave early, you don't just have to move out and hope your landlord plays fair and gets a new tenant quickly. For a variety of reasons, he may drag his feet, claim he couldn't find a new tenant or rent the unit to a tenant who pays less rent than you did—meaning you're liable for the difference. Fortunately, there are steps you can take to minimize your financial responsibility—as well as help avoid receiving a bad reference from the landlord next time you're apartment hunting.

First, consider simply asking the landlord to cancel the lease using Form 22. If you and the landlord both sign and date this form, your obligations for rent beyond the termination date end. (You are still responsible for unpaid back rent and any damage you've caused beyond normal wear and tear.) Why would a landlord voluntarily agree to let you off the hook? If you have been a steady and considerate tenant, it's possible that you'll be treated in kind, especially if the landlord has a new tenant standing by who will pay a higher rent. If the landlord initially balks at canceling the lease, you might bring her around by offering to pay an extra month's rent in exchange for the lease cancellation.

In addition, in some states, landlords must allow early termination of a lease under certain conditions. For example, in Delaware you need give only 30 days' notice to end a long-term lease if you must move because your present employer has relocated or because of health problems—yours or a family member's. In New Jersey, a tenant who has suffered a disabling illness or accident can break a lease and leave after 40 days' notice. Some states, such as Georgia, allow members of the military to break a lease because of a change in orders. If you have a good reason for a sudden move, check your state's law.

If you can't get the landlord to cancel the lease outright, your best approach is usually to find a new tenant to sign a new lease at the same or higher rent and be ready to move in as soon as you leave. If you follow this approach, you should owe nothing additional since the landlord won't be able to argue that a suitable replacement tenant couldn't be found. If the landlord accepts the new tenant, you and the landlord should cancel your lease by completing Form 22. The landlord and the new tenant can sign their own lease, and you won't be in the picture.

If the landlord won't accept the tenant you find: Keep careful records of all prospective tenants you find, especially their credit histories—you can use Form 19. If the landlord sues you for back rent, present these to the judge as proof the landlord failed in her responsibility to limit (mitigate) your damages by accepting a suitable replacement tenant.

Form 23: Consent to Assignment of Lease

If the landlord won't cancel your lease or sign a new lease with a tenant you find, your next best option may be to "assign" your lease to a new tenant (called an "assignee") who is acceptable to the landlord. With an assignment, you turn over the remainder of your lease to someone else. You can do this with Form 23. Unless the landlord agrees

otherwise, you remain in the picture as a guarantor of rent payments in case the new occupant (the assignee) fails to pay. Having a second source for the rent is one reason a savvy landlord might agree to an assignment but not a cancellation.

A landlord can voluntarily waive his right to look to you as the guarantor of the assignee's rent, something that is not uncommon when the new tenant has excellent credit. Clause 4 of Form 23 releases you from this worrisome obligation, essentially putting you in the position of someone who has terminated the lease. If the landlord balks at the release, and you are reasonably sure of your replacement's ability to pay the rent, you may not be risking much if you cross out Clause 4 and remain theoretically responsible for the rent.

Form 24: Landlord-Tenant Checklist

Legal disputes between tenants and landlords have justly gained a reputation for having the potential to be almost as nasty as a bad divorce. And like a failed marriage, disputes often continue after the legal relationship is over. This is most likely to occur when a landlord keeps all or part of a tenant's security deposit, claiming the place was left filthy or damaged.

Fortunately, using Form 24, a landlord and tenant can work together to minimize deposit-related disputes by jointly inspecting the rental unit at both the start and end of the tenancy. The idea is to identify damage, dirt, mildew and obvious wear and tear before the tenant moves in (use column 1) and inspect the unit again in the company of the landlord or property manager just before the tenant moves out (use columns 2 and 3).

In the additional explanation section at the end of the form, note any areas of disagreement. Incidentally, to avoid a court battle over security deposit deductions, many wise landlords and tenants try to compromise any disputed damage claims when doing the final inspection.

 Take photos at move-in and move-out to avoid disputes. You'll be able to compare "before" and "after" pictures, rather than just have landlord's word against tenant's. If you end up in court fighting over the security deposit, documenting your point of view with photos will be invaluable visual proof. Or consider taking along a friend or colleague as a potential witness to the condition of the rental unit at move-in or move-out time—someone who will be available to testify in court on your behalf if necessary.

Form 25: Notice of Needed Repairs

The law is plain: Landlords are legally required to offer their tenants livable premises when they originally rent a unit and to maintain their rental property in decent condition throughout the rental term. In most states, the legal jargon used to describe this obligation is the "landlord's legal duty to adhere to the implied warranty of habitability."

Tenants have the right to a decent place to live even if they move into a place that's clearly substandard (below reasonable habitability standards), or even if the lease comes right out and says that the landlord doesn't have to provide a habitable unit. Or put another way, almost all courts have rejected the sleazy argument that a tenant waives the right to a livable place because he is so desperate for a place to live that he accepts a substandard rental unit.

If there's a problem with the physical condition of your rental unit, you'll want to notify your landlord or manager as soon as possible so that it can be promptly fixed. The best approach is to put every repair and maintenance request in writing, using Form 25, keeping a copy for yourself. You may find it easier to call your landlord first, particularly in urgent cases, but be sure to follow up with a written repair request.

Be as specific as possible regarding the problem, its effect on you, what you want done and when. For example, if the thermostat on your heater is always finicky and sometimes doesn't function at all, explain how long you've been without heat and how low the temperature has dipped—don't simply say "the heater needs to be fixed." Be sure to note the date of the request and how many requests, if

any, have preceded this one; keep records of all repair requests.

If your landlord ignores your requests and your rental is unlivable, you'll have to undertake stronger measures, such as calling state or local building or health inspectors, moving out, withholding the rent or repairing the problem yourself. These remedies, available only in certain situations according to your state's laws, are thoroughly discussed in the Nolo books listed at the beginning of this chapter.

If you are a landlord, it's a good idea to give tenants copies of Form 25 and encourage them to immediately report plumbing, heating, weatherproofing or other defects or safety problems. Be sure to note details as to how and when the problem was fixed, including reasons for any delay, on the bottom of the tenant's repair request form. Keep copies of all completed forms in your tenant files.

Form 26: Tenant's Notice of Intent to Move Out

If you have a month-to-month tenancy, in most states and for most rentals you must provide 30 days' notice to your landlord if you want to move out. In some states, if you pay rent weekly or twice a month, you can give written notice to terminate that matches your rent payment interval. For example, if you pay rent every two weeks, you need give only 14 days' notice.

In most states, you can give notice at any time during the month. If you pay your rent on the first, you don't have to give notice on that date so that your tenancy will end on the last day of the month. For example, if you pay rent on the first of the month but give notice on the tenth, you will be obliged to pay for only ten days' rent for the next month, even if you move out earlier. To calculate the amount, prorate the monthly rent.

If you give oral notice, follow up in writing. If you know your landlord or manager well, you may wish to tell him that you'll be moving. Fine, but immediately follow up with written confirmation. The law almost always requires written notice. You can use Form 26 for this purpose. ∎

Borrowing or Lending Money

This chapter contains several forms you can use when you borrow money from or lend money to a friend, relative or someone else who isn't a commercial customer. (Banks and other institutional lenders follow many legal rules and must use forms with far more fine print.)

Form 27: Loan Comparison Worksheet

A good consumer shops around before making a significant purchase. There is no reason to act otherwise when you are looking to borrow money. A bank loan from one bank may come with very different terms than a loan from a credit union or finance company—or even from a different bank across town. And a loan from your former college roommate or your Aunt Charlotte may be very different still.

The cost of a loan doesn't only depend on how much interest you pay. Although long-term loans will carry a higher rate of interest than will short-term loans (the lender runs the risk that inflation will erode the real value of the interest it receives for a longer period, so it passes some of this risk on to you in the form of a higher interest rate), short-term loans are not necessarily cheaper. That's because application and other up-front fees, which can vary considerably from one lender to the next, also must be taken into consideration to compute the cost of a loan. Fortunately, this isn't true of all short-term loans, so be sure to shop around. When you apply for a loan, you must be told the annual cost of the loan. This is stated as the annual percentage rate, or APR. You can use that figure to compare the annual cost of the loan, which includes the annual interest and finance charges, as well as non-interest fees.

APR isn't the entire story, especially for adjustable rate loans or loans with a balloon payment or other feature. For a full comparison, use Form 27 to record the terms of any loans you are considering, whether to buy a car or computer system, pay down your credit cards or just take a well-deserved vacation. Because mortgage loans involve far more considerations than these loans, use Form 48:

Mortgage Rates and Terms Comparison in Chapter 5, when shopping around for a mortgage.

Form 28: Authorization to Conduct Credit Check

Commercial lenders—banks, credit unions and finance companies—will always check a loan applicant's credit before agreeing to lend money. If you're thinking of lending someone money, it makes good sense to do the same. Doing a credit check to learn whether or not the person is likely to repay you in full and on time puts you in a good position to say "no" to someone with poor credit. While checking a person's credit and saying "no" may put a strain on a personal relationship, making a loan to someone who can't handle it is more likely to cause long-term problems. When a personal loan isn't repaid, the result is often the loss of a friendship or a serious family tension.

Form 29: Monthly Payment Record

Especially if a loan will be repaid over many months or years, it's easy to forget if and when every payment has been made. Of course, this is especially likely if the debtor misses several payments because of an emergency and then makes them up a little at a time. Use Form 29, Monthly Payment Record, to keep track of payments made under installment notes.

Forms 30-34: Promissory Notes

A promissory note is nothing more than legal jargon for a written promise to pay money to someone. As with all legal documents, promissory notes often contain loads of needless hyped-up legalese. Because the notes in this book are designed to be used primarily between family and friends—and because, lawyers notwithstanding, there is no law against using plain English—we prefer to keep the language simple.

Basic Loan Terms Explained

To be able to understand your loan agreement, you'll need to know the meaning of a few terms.

Adjustable rate

The interest rate charged by the lender that is set initially, usually fairly low, and then fluctuates (usually meaning it increases) every several months.

Balloon payment

A lump sum payment made at the end of a loan to cover the remaining balance. For example, you borrow $10,000 for five years at 6% interest. The monthly payments are $193.33. You can only afford to pay about half that amount. So the lender lets you pay $100 a month. At the end of five years, you owe a balloon payment of $6,511.53.

Cap

On an adjustable rate loan, the cap refers both to the maximum amount the interest rate can increase each year and the ultimate maximum a interest rate can reach. For example, an adjustable rate loan that begins at 4% may have an annual cap of $1/2$% and a lifetime cap of 7%. This means that at the beginning of the second year, the rate will be $4^1/2$%. If the loan continues to increase $1/2$% each year, it will reach its lifetime cap or 7% at six years, and never go up again.

Collateral

Property you pledge as security for repayment of a loan. Sometimes it's the item being purchased, such as when you finance the purchase of your car. Other times the collateral is property you already own that you pledge as security on a new loan. If you default, a lender can take the collateral without first suing you and obtaining a judgment.

Cosigner

A creditworthy person who agrees to be fully liable for repayment of a loan if you default.

Credit check

A lender obtaining a copy of your credit report from a credit reporting agency in order to verify your creditworthiness.

Credit insurance

Insurance coverage required by some lenders to pay off your loan in the event you become disabled or die.

Fixed rate

The interest rate charged by the lender that is established at the outset and will never change.

Grace period

The number of days you have after your loan payment is due to make the payment without being charged a late fee. For example if your loan payments are due on the 1st of the month, you may have a grace period until the 10th, meaning that the lender will accept your payment until that date without penalizing you.

Late fee

The fee a lender charges when you pay late. See Grace period.

Loan application fee

Nuisance fees charged by lenders for the privilege of lending you money. These include credit checks, appraisals on collateral and loan processing fees.

Loan discounts

Incentives offered by a lender to reduce your loan interest rate. For example, you might be offered a $1/2$% discount if you set up a direct payment from your checking account or if you maintain a checking account with the lender with a minimum balance of $1,000.

Prepayment penalty

A penalty imposed on you for paying off a loan early. It's usually expressed as a flat fee or a percentage of the interest the lender lost by your prepaying.

The primary function of a promissory note is to serve as written evidence of the amount of a debt and the terms under which it will be repaid. One is typically signed when money is borrowed or something is bought on credit. Perhaps in the best of all possible worlds, such evidence would not be needed. One friend would lend another $1,000, the two people would shake hands, and that would be it. But because the "best possible world" and the "real world" are often barely on speaking terms when it comes to loan repayment, here are several important reasons why all promissory notes should be put in writing:

- You are assured that the borrower and lender have agreed to the same terms, including the repayment schedule and interest rate.
- You specify exactly what those terms are.
- Both parties have a written document with which to refresh their memories if need be.

This chapter contains five promissory notes, each designed to deal with a somewhat different repayment scenario:

- Form 30: Promissory Note—Installment Payments With Interest
- Form 31: Promissory Note—Installment Payments With Interest and Balloon Payment
- Form 32: Promissory Note—Installment Payments Without Interest
- Form 33: Promissory Note—Lump Sum Payment With Interest
- Form 34: Promissory Note—Lump Sum Payment Without Interest.

All of these notes are for unsecured loans— meaning that the borrower does not pledge any property, such as a house or car, as collateral to guarantee repayment. This means if the borrower doesn't repay the loan, the lender must sue in court to get a judgment, which then makes her eligible to collect by use of wage or property attachments. You can add a security provision using Form 36, which would give the lender the right to force the sale of property pledged as collateral, such as a house or car, if the borrower doesn't repay.

If the borrower's credit is questionable. If you want to lend money to someone with questionable credit, consider requiring a cosigner. You can add a cosigner clause to your promissory note by using Form 35.

Form 30: Promissory Note— Installment Payments With Interest

Form 30 allows for repayment in installments rather than all at once, and charges interest. Charging a friend or family member interest strikes some people as being ungenerous. In our opinion, this view is based on a misconception as to the function of interest, which is to fairly compensate the lender for the use of his money. Think of it this way. Suppose Joan lends Harry $5,000 for a year, interest-free. If Joan had put the money in a certificate of deposit, she would have earned the going rate of interest. By giving Harry the money interest-free, Joan ends up paying for the privilege of lending the money to Harry.

Interest charged on money lent to friends and relatives tends to run between 5% and 10%. If you wish to charge a higher rate of interest, check your state law to see if the rate is legal; it may constitute the crime of usury.

How much interest is appropriate? In an effort to be generous to a relative or friend, many lenders charge interest at somewhat less than the market rate, sometimes as little as—or just slightly more than—they would receive if they purchased a bank certificate of deposit for the same time period. This is a great deal for the borrower; after all, even if Harry qualified to borrow from a bank or other commercial lender, he would have to pay a much higher rate of interest than Joan would receive if she put the money in a CD.

Charging interest adds a level of complication when it comes to figuring out the amount of the monthly payments. For this, you will need an amortization calculator or software program.

Fortunately, several financial sites on the Internet have free calculators you can use for this purpose:

- TimeValue Software at http://timevalue.com/tools.htm
- FinanCenter at http://financenter.com/calcs.html
- First Source Bank at http://1stsrce.com/phtml/finance/financl.htm, and
- Credit Union One at http://www.cuone.com.

You plug in the loan amount, interest rate and number of months the borrower will take to repay the loan. The calculator gives you the monthly payment amount.

If the borrower decides to pay off the principal sooner than the note calls for under the installment plan, you will have to recalculate the payments based on the new outstanding balance. Again, this is easy to do with the right calculator.

Now let's translate some legal terminology into English.

Acceleration. Our promissory notes accelerate the borrower's responsibility to make all necessary loan payments if he misses one or more regularly scheduled payments. You specify the number of days—typically 30 or 60—the borrower has to pay before you exercise this option. Without this provision you can't sue for loan installments not yet due, even though the borrower has missed several payments and it is obvious he has no plans to repay.

Attorney fees. Under the laws of many states, a clause providing that a lender will be entitled to attorney fees and court costs in a legal dispute will be read by a court to go both ways. This means that if the borrower wins, she will be entitled to attorney fees and court costs, even if the loan papers don't specifically say so.

Buyer in due course. This is a person who buys or otherwise legally receives a promissory note from a lender. The borrower's obligation to repay the note doesn't change just because the lender sells the note to someone else.

Joint and several liability. This means that if there is more than one borrower, all borrowers are liable for repaying 100% of the loan. If Chuck and Laura borrow $5,000 from Miguel and default, Miguel can go after either Chuck or Laura for the full $5,000. Neither can claim that he or she is liable for only $2,500.

Form 31: Promissory Note—Installment Payments With Interest and Balloon Payment

Form 31 is similar to Form 30 in that the loan is required to be repaid in installments with interest. But there's an additional twist; individual payments are lower than they otherwise would be, with the shortfall made up by one large balloon payment at the end of the loan term. To see how this works, let's take a look at an example. You lend a friend $10,000 at 7% and want it paid back in three years. Using an amortization calculator, you discover that your friend would have to pay you $308.78 each month to pay it back over that time.

Your friend can't afford to pay that amount each month now, but knows he will receive some money in about three years when a trust matures. So you propose the following: Your friend can borrow $10,000 from you at 7% and repay it over three years. But to make his payments affordable now, you agree to amortize the loan as though it were to be paid off in ten years, meaning your friend's monthly payments are only $116.11, far less than $308.78. You agree to take these low payments for 36 months and at the end, your friend will make you one large payment, called a balloon payment, of the remaining principal. That amount is $7,693.

Form 32: Promissory Note—Installment Payments Without Interest

Use Form 32 if the borrower will repay you in installments, but you won't charge interest. When the parties involved in the transaction are family members or close friends, the amount borrowed is relatively small and the probability of repayment is high, lenders sometimes prefer to use an interest-free installment note.

Be aware that if the IRS learns of an interest-free loan, it can impute interest. This means that the lender will be assumed to have earned interest and will be required to report that interest as income on her tax return. For most personal loans, this won't be a problem because uncharged interest can be treated as a tax-free gift, as long as the total amount given to the borrower in a calendar year is $10,000 or less.

Form 33: Promissory Note— Lump Sum Payment With Interest

This note is normally used when the borrower won't be able to repay the loan for a period of months or years. For example, you might borrow money from a friend to help you open a small business. You aren't likely to have the cash-flow for at least six months or a year to repay the loan. In such a situation, your friend might agree to be repaid in a lump sum in a year.

The easiest way to determine the amount of annual interest which will be due on the loan is to use simple, not compound, interest. Multiply the amount of the loan by the annual interest rate. For instance, if the loan is for $4,000, and your annual interest rate is 10%, the annual amount of interest on the loan is $400. To determine the total amount of interest due, multiply the annual interest amount by the time period of the loan. In our example, if the loan is for two years, the interest due would be $800.

If you need to compute the interest for a period of months rather than years, compute the interest for one year, divide by 12, and then multiply the result by the number of months. For example, assume the $4,000 loan is for an 18-month period. Take the annual interest amount ($400), divide by 12 ($33.33) and multiply by 18 ($600).

If the loan is paid back before it is due, Clause 2 gives you two choices:

- Charge the full interest. This is not unreasonable, given that you committed yourself to

being without the amount of the entire loan for the time indicated.

- Prorate the interest to correspond to the actual period of time the loan was outstanding. Returning to the $4,000 loan example, if you originally figured interest at 10% for two years ($800) but the loan was paid back in 18 months, simply charge the 18-month figure ($600) instead.

Form 34: Promissory Note— Lump Sum Payment Without Interest

This promissory note, which calls for a lump sum loan repayment and no interest, is about as basic as you can get. This sort of note is normally used by people with a close personal relationship when the person lending the money is primarily interested in helping out the borrower and expects nothing in return except, eventually, the return of the amount borrowed.

If the IRS learns of the loan, it can impute interest. This means that the lender will be assumed to have earned interest and will be required to report that interest as income on her tax return. For most personal loans, this won't be a problem because uncharged interest can be treated as a tax-free gift, as long as the total given to the borrower by the lender is $10,000 or less in a calendar year.

Form 35: Cosigner Provision

A cosigner is someone who promises to repay a loan if the primary debtor defaults. If you'll be lending money to someone with a questionable credit history, no credit history or a background of sporadic employment, you might require one or more cosigners, such as a parent or friend. (If there is more than one cosigner, each is 100% liable to repay the note if the borrower fails to.) If you will require a cosigner, staple this form to the promissory note and then have the cosigner complete it.

Federal law requires that commercial lenders give cosigners a notice of their potential liability when they agree to cosign a debt. Although this is not required for personal loans between friends and relatives, we believe full disclosure of the risks of cosigning is a good idea and so we incorporate much of that notice language in Form 35.

Security Agreements

If you lend money to someone who does not repay it, in general, your only recourse to get paid is to sue the person, obtain a court judgment and then take property that can legally be seized to satisfy a debt.

There is an easier way: You can attach a security agreement to the promissory note. In a security agreement, property belonging to the borrower, such as a car or computer, is specified as collateral for repayment of the loan. If the borrower doesn't repay the loan, you can take the property, sell it and use the proceeds to satisfy what is owed. You don't have to go to court.

Sometimes, a dishonest borrower will try to use the same piece of collateral to secure more than one debt. The result is that if the unscrupulous borrower later defaults on these secured loans, the lenders will find themselves competing to sell the collateral and use the proceeds to satisfy their debts. This raises the legal question of how secured creditors can protect themselves. The answer is that they must be the first to file evidence of their claim with the correct recording agency.

This chapter includes four different forms relating to security interests:

- Form 36, Security Agreement Provision for Promissory Note
- Form 37, Uniform Commercial Code (U.C.C.) Financing Statement
- Form 38, Release of U.C.C. Financing Statement
- Form 39, Release of Security Interest.

Creating a security interest is a multistep process. First you must add Form 36 to your promissory note. If the collateral is personal property, such as a

car, the security agreement must be filed with your state's agency using Form 37. If the collateral is real property, the borrower must sign a mortgage or deed of trust before a notary public. You then must record it with the county land records office.

The Difference Between a Mortgage and a Deed of Trust

When the borrower execute a deed of trust, he gives the trustee (often a title company) the right to sell the property, with no court approval, if he fails to pay the lender on time. By contrast, a mortgage normally involves only a borrower and a lender, and depending on the laws of the state where the property is located, often requires a more complicated judicial foreclosure proceeding if payments aren't made.

Here is deed of trust language translated into English.

Beneficiary. The lender is the beneficiary of the deed of trust; if the borrower defaults and the trustee sells the house, the beneficiary is paid from the proceeds.

Trustee. The trustee, usually a title insurance company, doesn't exercise any control over the house as long as the borrower keeps payments current. If he defaults, however, the trustee can sell the house and use the proceeds to pay off the trust beneficiary (the lender).

Trustor. The trustor is the borrower. As trustor, the borrower signs a deed of trust giving the trustee the power to sell the house and turn the proceeds over to the beneficiary (the lender) if the borrower defaults on the loan.

Form 36: Security Agreement Provision for Promissory Note

You can use Form 36 to identify the security interest as a part of your contract.

Form 37: U.C.C. Financing Statement

Use Form 37, the U.C.C. Financing Statement, to record your security interest if the collateral identified in your security agreement is personal property. Once you have completed the security agreement, contact the appropriate state agency—most likely the motor vehicles department if the collateral is a car, boat or similar vehicle, or the Secretary of State for most other property, such as electronics equipment or a computer system. Ask to be sent a copy of the state's rules for filing a U.C.C. statement, and ask if the state has any special form you must use.

Complete the state form, or Form 37 if the state doesn't have one, and attach the promissory note with security interest. Then file them with the appropriate state office.

If the collateral identified in your security agreement is real property, you will need to get a mortgage or deed of trust form used in your state. These should be available at most office supply stores and are not difficult to fill out. If you need help, anyone in the real estate business should be able to provide it.

Form 38: Release of U.C.C. Financing Statement

When a borrower pays off a loan, she obviously wants the public record to reflect that her property is no longer encumbered (held hostage) in favor of the lender. You will want to file Form 38 with any public agency where you filed a U.C.C. Financing Statement when the borrower pays off the loan. That will let prospective lawyers, creditors and credit rating agencies know that the lender no longer claims an interest in the borrower's collateral.

This form should correspond to your original U.C.C. Financing Statement. Therefore, make sure the property description is identical and the other information makes it clear which U.C.C. Financing Statement is being released.

Form 39: Release of Security Interest

If the collateral for your loan is real, not personal, property and so you filed a mortgage or deed of trust, not a U.C.C. Financing Statement, you must file a Release of Security Interest when the borrower pays off the loan. That will let prospective lawyers, creditors and credit rating agencies know that the lender no longer claims an interest in the borrower's collateral.

This form should correspond to your original mortgage or deed of trust. Make sure the property description is identical and the other information makes it clear which mortgage or deed of trust is being released.

Form 40: Agreement to Modify Promissory Note

If someone who borrows money from you falls behind on repayment, give a call to find out what's wrong. Offer whatever help you can to get the person back on track. Sometimes this will require no more than being willing to extend the repayment period for a few months. In other instances you might take interest-only payments or rewrite the loan at a lower interest rate. Whatever you agree on, you must put it in writing. You can use Form 40 for that purpose.

Form 41: Overdue Payment Demand

If a couple of phone calls or personal conversations fail to work out a new agreement or get the borrower back on track with payments, your next step is to send the borrower a formal letter. You can use Form 41 in such a situation. Send it to all borrowers and all cosigners.

Form 42: Demand to Make Good on Bad Check

This form is similar to Form 41 in that it's used when someone who owes you money is not meeting her obligation to pay you and has ignored all your efforts to resolve the problem informally. The difference is that this form is for use when the person who owes you money writes you a bad check, a slightly more complicated legal situation.

Although writing a bad check is a crime in every state, rarely is a person prosecuted for writing bad checks. Even in the unlikely event that a district attorney is willing to bring charges, there's a good chance the person would avoid a trial by agreeing to attend a diversion program for bad check writers and making restitution—that is, paying up.

In most states, you'll want to deal with getting a bad check in a civil, not criminal, manner. The person who receives a bad check can sue for extra damages (above and beyond the amount of the check) if she isn't paid within 30 days of making a formal written demand for payment. See the chart below for the amount authorized in your state. If your state is not listed, you can still sue for the amount of the check, but you will not be entitled to extra damages.

You can use Form 42 to make a formal written demand for payment on a bad check.

State	Damages permitted (above the amount of the check)
Alabama	Actual and punitive damages; reasonable attorneys' fees.
Alaska	Three times the amount of the check or $100, whichever is greater, not to exceed the amount of the check by $1,000.
Arizona	Twice the amount of the check or $50, whichever is greater, plus reasonable attorneys' fees.
Arkansas	Twice the amount of the check, but in no case less than $50.
California	Three times the amount of the check, not less than $100 nor more than $1,500.
Colorado	Three times the amount of the check, but in no case less than $100.
Connecticut	For checks written on closed accounts, the amount of the check or $750, whichever is greater. For checks written with insufficient funds, the amount of the check or $400, whichever is greater.
Florida	Three times the amount of the check or $50, whichever is greater, plus reasonable attorneys' fees.
Georgia	Twice the amount of the check, not to exceed $500.
Hawaii	Three times the amount of the check or $100, whichever is greater, not to exceed $500.
Illinois	Three times the amount of the check or $100, whichever is greater, not to exceed $500.

State	Damages permitted (above the amount of the check)
Indiana	Three times the amount of the check, not to exceed $500.
Iowa	Three times the amount of the check, not to exceed $500.
Kansas	Three times the amount of the check or $100, whichever is greater, not to exceed $500.
Louisiana	Twice the amount of the check or $100, whichever is greater, plus reasonable attorneys' fees.
Maine	Face value of the check or costs to collect it, whichever is less, not to exceed $40.
Maryland	Twice the amount of the check, not to exceed $1,000.
Massachusetts	Damages set by the court, not less than $100 nor more than $500.
Michigan	Twice the amount of the check or $500, whichever is greater, not to exceed $500.
Minnesota	$100, plus reasonable attorneys' fees.
Mississippi	Face amount of the check, if $25 or less. One-half of the amount of the check, if between $26 and $200, but not less than $25 nor more than $50. One-quarter of the amount of the check, if over $200.
Missouri	Three times the amount of the check or $100, whichever is greater, not to exceed $500.
Montana	Three times the amount of the check or $100, whichever is greater, not to exceed $500.

State	Damages permitted (above the amount of the check)
Nevada	Three times the amount of the check, not less than $100 nor more than $500.
New Hampshire	$10 per business day the bad check writer fails to pay the judgment, up to $500.
New Mexico	Three times the amount of the check or $100, whichever is greater, not to exceed $500.
New York	For checks written on closed accounts, twice the amount of the check or $750, whichever is greater. For checks written with insufficient funds, twice the amount of the check or $400, whichever is greater.
North Carolina	Three times the amount of the check or $500, whichever is less, but not less than $100.
North Dakota	Three times the amount of the check or $100, whichever is less.
Oregon	Three times the amount of the check or $100, whichever is greater, not to exceed $500, plus attorneys' fees.
Pennsylvania	Three times the amount of the check or $100, whichever is greater, not to exceed $500.
Rhode Island	Three times the amount of the check, not less than $200 nor more than $1,000.
South Carolina	Three times the amount of the check, not to exceed $500.
Tennessee	Three times the amount of the check, not to exceed $500.

Buying a House

No doubt about it—buying a house is one of the largest and most important investments you'll ever make. And as with any big investment, good careful planning and organization are necessary to get the best house for your money. The forms in this chapter help you accomplish this by providing:

- an efficient method to help you consider a wide range of features, establish your priorities and compare potential houses (Forms 43, 44 and 45)
- a systematic procedure for determining how much house you can afford—in terms of both the down payment and monthly mortgage payments (Forms 46 and 47), and
- a simple way to keep track of information you collect on different loans and efficiently compare features such as interest rate and loan costs (Form 48).

This chapter also includes several other useful real estate forms, including a moving checklist and a lease option contract (Forms 49 and 50).

Getting Started

When you're looking for a house, it's easy to become confused by the huge array of choices. This is understandable, given that houses themselves are so different. Then, there's the issue of location—houses come in all sorts of neighborhoods, school districts and potential hazard zones (fire, earthquake and flood, to name a few). And, of course, price and purchase terms are crucial considerations for most homebuyers. To cope with all these and at least a dozen other variables you'll want to consider so you end up with a house you really want to live in, it's essential to establish your priorities in advance and stick to them.

Forms 43, 44 and 45 will help simplify house hunting, by first helping you identify house features most important to you and then allowing you to systematically evaluate and record relevant information about each house you see. Most important, this approach will help you make good compromises

should affordability problems result in your lowering your sights and considering houses that don't have all the features you'd like.

Nolo Press publishes *How to Buy a House in California*, by Ralph Warner, Ira Serkes and George Devine, an excellent resource on all aspects of house buying. Although it's written specifically for Californians, who have the benefit of many laws concerning disclosure of defects, the information on all other topics, including looking for a house, negotiating with a seller, financing the purchase and closing escrow, apply to anyone buying.

You can find other house-buying resources on the Web:

- **Homebuyer's Fair**, http://www.homefair.com, offers lots of information to help you buy or sell a home or relocate to a new area. Especially useful if you're trying to decide where to live based on home prices, schools, crime, salaries and other factors.
- **International Real Estate Digest**, http://www.ired.com, answers over 1,000 real estate questions and lists hundreds of real estate Websites all over the world.
- **Realty Locator**, http://www.realtylocator.com, provides over 100,000 real estate links nationwide, including property listings, agents, lenders and information resources.
- **E-Loan**, http://www.eloan.com, **HomeShark**, http://www.homeshark.com and **Intuit**, http://www.quickenmortgage.com, allow you to compare rates from various lenders, prequalify and apply for a loan.

Form 43: Ideal House Profile

Form 43 lists all major house features such as number of bedrooms, type of yard, sales price and location. Use it to identify the essential items you're looking for (must have) in a house. For example, under *Upper Price Limit*, you might note $300,000 in the "must have" column. And if you have two kids, you might note that three bedrooms and excellent public schools are also mandatory priorities. Once you've run through your list of "must haves," jot down features that you'd like but that aren't crucial to your decision of whether or not to buy. For example, under *Yards and Grounds*, you might note patio and flat back yard in the "hope to have" column.

Be sure to list your "absolute no ways" (you will not buy a house that has any of these features) at the bottom of the form. Avoiding things you'll always hate, such as a house in a flood zone, in a poor school district or too far from where you work can be even more important than finding a house which contains all your mandatory priorities.

Be sensitive to your spouse's (partner's) major concerns. If you're buying with another person, prepare your list of priorities together, so that each person's strong likes and dislikes are respected.

After you've completed Form 43, you might feel depressed, wondering how you'll ever afford a house with all the features you've listed as "must haves." If so, you might even need to change a couple of "must haves" to "hope to haves."

Can any of your priority items be added after you move in? Decks, patios and sometimes even an extra room can also be added a few years down the road. Of course, replacing a small dark yard with a large sunny one can't be done.

Once you've completed Form 43, you're ready for Form 44, which will help you see how each house stacks up with your priorities.

Getting more neighborhood information: If you're moving to a new area, you may not have a good sense of what particular cities and neighborhoods are like. Before finalizing a decision to buy, you'll want to take steps to get more information. For example, if under your "must have" column you've written "excellent public schools," you need in-depth information about the school system in each community you are considering. It's fine to ask a real estate agent, but she is probably anxious for you to make a purchase and may not

be objective. Instead, take the time to talk to people in the area whose kids currently attend its schools, or ask for help from a reference librarian at an area public library.

Form 44: House Priorities Worksheet

Now it's time to use the information collected in Form 43 to create a House Priorities Worksheet for each house you visit. Start by making several copies to allow for mistakes or the eventual scaling back of your priority list if it turns out you can't afford all the features you would like. Then, enter relevant information on a master copy of Form 44 under each major category—"must have," "hope to have" and "no way."

Once you have completed your Form 44 to your (and your partner's) satisfaction, make a small pile of copies (or install the Form 44 on your laptop computer if you'll be taking it house hunting). Take one with you each time you visit a house.

For each house you see, fill in the top of the Form 44. Enter the address, asking price, name and phone number of the contact person (listing agent or seller, if it's for sale by owner) and the date you saw the house. As you walk around each house and talk to the owner or agent, enter a checkmark if the house has a desirable or undesirable feature. Also make notes next to a particular feature if it can be changed to meet your needs (an okay kitchen could be modernized for $25,000). Add comments at the bottom, such as "potential undeveloped lot next door" or "neighbors seem very friendly." If you look at a lot of houses, taking notes such as these will help make sure you don't forget important information.

Set up a good filing system. As the list of houses you look at grows, you will need a method to keep track of the information you collect. Failing to adopt a good system may lead to revisiting houses you've already seen and rejected or making decisions based on half-remembered facts.

For each house that seems like a possible prospect, make a file that includes a completed House Priorities Worksheet, the information sheet provided at the open house, the Multiple Listing Service information, if available, ads and your notes. Or if you are more digitally inclined, use your computer to set up a simple database with key details on each house you see.

Form 45: House Comparison Worksheet

If, like many people, you look at a considerable number of houses over an extended period of time, you may soon have trouble distinguishing or comparing their features. That's where Form 45, House Comparison Worksheet, comes in. Across the top of the form list the addresses of the three or four houses you like best. Then in the left column, fill in your list of priorities and "no ways" from Forms 43 and 44. Then put a check on the line under each house that has that feature to allow for a quick comparison.

Form 46: Family Financial Statement

When planning to buy a house, one of your most important tasks is to determine how much you can afford to pay. To do this, begin by preparing a thorough family financial statement, which includes:

- your monthly income
- your monthly expenses, and
- your net worth (your assets minus your liabilities).

We use the word "family" as shorthand for the economic unit that will buy a house. For these purposes, an unmarried couple or a single person is just as much a family as is a married couple with three kids.

Preparing a family financial statement begins the process of learning how much house you can afford—in terms of both the down payment and

monthly mortgage payments. It also gives real estate people and potential lenders a good sense of your general financial situation. And if you haven't prequalified for a mortgage loan when you make a purchase offer, a financial statement can be extremely helpful to convince the seller that you're a serious bidder. This may be crucial, especially if there's more than one prospective buyer. That's because the person who can best convince the seller she's financially able to swing the deal with no glitches often prevails.

⚠ **Don't list incorrect or incomplete information on your Family Financial Statement.** A lender will surely check with credit reporting agencies, and usually with employers and banks, to verify your information, meaning that listing bogus or exaggerated information is likely to be discovered and held against you. If necessary, a far better approach is to take the time to clean up a bad or erroneous credit file (see Chapter 10) before you start house hunting.

Form 47: Monthly Carrying Costs Worksheet

Your next step in determining how much house you can afford is to complete the Monthly Carrying Costs Worksheet. To use the worksheet, you will need to provide the following information:

Estimated purchase price. How much money you'll need to spend on a house likely to have at least most of the "must have" features listed on your Ideal House Profile (Form 43).

Down payment. Enter the down payment you plan to make. Figure you'll probably need to put down 20% of the house purchase price, unless you qualify for a government loan or other low down payment loan. If you have a relatively high monthly income and few debts, you may find a lender who will allow you to put down less—but if so, the interest rate is almost sure to be higher.

Interest rate. Check mortgage interest tables printed in the Sunday newspaper real estate section and online Websites featuring mortgage information (listed in resources at the beginning of this chapter). Loan brokers can also be a valuable resource when it comes to determining how much interest you'll need to pay. Use Form 48 to shop for a mortgage.

Principal and mortgage interest payment factor per $1,000 over the length of the loan. You can find this using the amortization chart below.

Monthly mortgage payment. Multiply the factor from the amortization chart by the loan amount you need to borrow. For example, if you estimate the house you want to buy will cost $260,000, a 20% down payment of $52,000 leaves you with a $208,000 mortgage loan. Your research shows you can get a 7% interest rate for a fixed-rate loan. The monthly factor per $1,000 for a 30-year loan at a 7% rate is 6.65. So your monthly mortgage payments will be 208 x 6.65, or $1,383.

Homeowner's insurance. You can get exact quotes in advance from insurance agents. Very roughly, expect to spend $200-$400 per $100,000 of house value, depending on where you live and other factors.

Property taxes. These vary tremendously depending on where you live. You'll need to get an estimate from a local tax assessor's office.

Long-term debts. These are items such as monthly payments on a car or student loan.

Private mortgage insurance (PMI). Your lender may require this if you're making a down payment of less than 20%. PMI is often about ½% of the loan.

Homeowners' association fee. You may have to pay this monthly fee if you're looking at a condo or a house in a development.

Lender qualification. Other things being equal (which they rarely are), lenders normally want you to make all monthly payments with 28%-38% of your monthly income. Whether you qualify at the bottom or top of this range depends on the amount of your down payment, the interest rate on the type of mortgage you want, your credit history and the level of your other long-term debts.

Mortgage Principal and Interest Payment Factors (Per $1,000)

Interest rates (%)	15-year mortgage	20-year mortgage	25-year mortgage	30-year mortgage
5.00	7.91	6.60	5.85	5.37
5.25	8.04	6.74	5.99	5.52
5.50	8.17	6.88	6.14	5.68
5.75	8.30	7.02	6.29	5.84
6.00	8.44	7.16	6.44	6.00
6.25	8.57	7.31	6.60	6.16
6.50	8.71	7.46	6.75	6.32
6.75	8.85	7.60	6.91	6.49
7.00	8.99	7.75	7.07	6.65
7.25	9.13	7.90	7.23	6.82
7.50	9.27	8.06	7.39	6.99
7.75	9.41	8.21	7.55	7.16
8.00	9.56	8.36	7.72	7.34
8.25	9.70	8.52	7.88	7.51
8.50	9.85	8.68	8.05	7.69
8.75	9.99	8.84	8.22	7.87
9.00	10.14	9.00	8.39	8.05
9.25	10.29	9.16	8.56	8.23
9.50	10.44	9.32	8.74	8.41
9.75	10.59	9.49	8.91	8.59
10.00	10.75	9.65	9.09	8.78
10.25	10.90	9.82	9.26	8.96
10.50	11.05	9.98	9.44	9.15
10.75	11.21	10.15	9.62	9.33
11.00	11.37	10.32	9.80	9.52
11.25	11.52	10.49	9.98	9.71
11.50	11.68	10.66	10.16	9.90
11.75	11.84	10.84	10.35	10.09
12.00	12.00	11.01	10.53	10.29
12.25	12.16	11.19	10.72	10.48
12.50	12.33	11.36	10.90	10.67
12.75	12.49	11.54	11.09	10.87
13.00	12.65	11.72	11.28	11.06

Form 48: Mortgage Rates and Terms Worksheet

As with any other consumer product, significant savings can be achieved by carefully shopping for a mortgage. But because of the wide variety of mortgages on the market (fixed, adjustable, hybrid) and the fact that fine-print terms can significantly influence how much you'll really have to pay, it's essential that you carefully compare the total cost of different deals.

Form 48 is a Mortgage Rates and Terms Worksheet you can use to keep track of information you collect on different loans. You can use it whether you'll be working with a loan broker, a person who specializes in matching house buyers and appropriate mortgage lenders, or shopping for a mortgage on your own.

This form is important for three primary reasons:

- Filling it out all but requires that you really understand the fine-print details of every loan you consider.
- Having this information will be an invaluable aid to your memory; days or weeks later you can check what you've been offered.
- Assuming you get information about more than one loan, it will let you efficiently compare features.

Begin by entering the lender's name, the name of the loan agent you met or spoke with, her phone number and the date of your meeting or telephone conversation. Then, for all loans complete sections 1-5. Finally, if applicable, complete one of the remaining sections.

See the table below for a brief description of key mortgage terms. For more information, check the resources at the beginning of this chapter.

Key Mortgage Terms

Fixed rate mortgage

The interest rate and the amount you pay each month remain the same over the entire mortgage term, which is traditionally between 15 and 30 years. There are several variations of fixed rate loans. **Two-step loans** start at a very low rate and automatically jump up to a higher rate after several years. **Fixed rate balloon payment loans** run for a shorter term (such as five or seven years) and then end with one large (balloon) payment which needs to be paid off or, more likely, refinanced at then-current interest rates. Some **hybrid loans** start out fixed rate for the first few years and then become adjustable.

Adjustable rate mortgage (ARM)

The interest rates on these mortgages fluctuate according to interest rates in the economy. ARM rates are linked to a market-sensitive financial yardstick (called an **index**), such as one-year U.S. Treasury bills. Initial "teaser" interest rates are usually lower for ARMs than for fixed rate mortgages. Then after a year or two, these rates take a good-sized jump, at which point they track interest rates in the general economy—going up if interest rates increase and down if they fall. A **margin** is the factor or percentage a lender adds to the index rate to arrive at the interest rate you pay over the market rate. All ARMs have caps, which come in various forms. A **life-of-the-loan** or **overall cap** is the maximum (such as five or six percentage points) your interest rate can go up or down over the term of your mortgage. A **periodic cap** limits the amount your interest rate can go up or down at each adjustment period, such as going up 2% annually, with your payments increasing accordingly.

Key Mortgage Terms (continued)

Negative amortization

Fortunately, many high-quality mortgages don't use this consumer unfriendly (not to mention confusing) system. Sometimes called "deferred interest" or "interest advances," this negative amortization takes away many of the advantages provided by periodic caps on ARMs. That's because with negative amortization, if interest rates rise, your **payment cap** only works to limit the amount your monthly payment can go up (not the total you owe, which is not capped). The extra money over the cap is simply added onto the mortgage total you owe, often with the result that you'll owe larger payments in the future or a large balloon payment at the end of the mortgage.

Convertible loan

This mortgage begins as an ARM and can be changed to a fixed rate mortgage after a certain period of time (such as two years), and then only during a specified **conversion window** such as two weeks.

PMI and impound account

Lenders may require private mortgage insurance (PMI) if you're making a down payment of less than 20%. Some PMI policies require that you set up an impound account, where you deposit up to a year's payments of PMI when the house purchase closes. In addition, you make monthly payments into the impound account for property taxes and homeowner's insurance. which in turn are paid by the lender or company that services the loan.

Assumable

A loan which a credit-worthy buyer can take over (assume) from a seller.

Prepayment penalty

A charge for paying off your mortgage early. Most high-quality commercial mortgages don't charge a prepayment penalty.

Rate lock-in

A lender's guarantee to make a loan at a particular interest rate, even if the market changes within a specific time period, such as three to six weeks.

Debt-to-income ratios

The ratio of your monthly mortgage payments (including insurance and property taxes) plus long-term debts to your income; also called lender qualification.

Monthly carrying costs

The sum of your monthly payments for your mortgage, homeowner's insurance and property taxes.

Points and loan costs

The fees associated with getting a mortgage, which usually add up to 2%-5% of the cost of the mortgage. Points make up the largest part of lender fees, with one point equaling 1% of the loan principal. Often, loans charging more points have a slightly lower interest rate. If you will own a house for many years, paying relatively high points to get a lower fixed rate of interest is usually a good idea—you have years in which to enjoy the lower interest payments and amortize the cost of the points. But the reverse is also true—if you will move in three to five years or less, try to pay as few points as possible even if you pay a little more interest.

Time limits

How long it takes to process your loan application, including the time required to run a credit check, appraise the property, get your loan approved and come up with the money ("fund the loan").

Form 49: Moving Checklist

Congratulations! If you are looking at this form, chances are you found a good house, closed escrow and are getting ready to move in. Use Form 49 to help you plan your move.

Form 50: Lease Option Contract

A lease option is a contract where an owner leases her house, usually from one to five years, to a tenant for a specific monthly rent and simultaneously gives the tenant the right to buy the house, usually for a price established in advance. The tenant typically pays a fee for the option—often a lump sum payment at the start of the contract, or sometimes, periodic payments tacked on to the rent. Depending on the contract, the potential buyer normally can exercise the option to purchase at any time during the lease period, or at a date specified. From the tenant/buyer's point of view, you obviously want to have as much flexibility as possible when it comes to how and when you exercise the option.

A lease option is often a good arrangement for a potential buyer because it lets you move into a house you may buy without having to come up with a down payment or financing. Even better, it allows you the luxury of waiting to see if the value of the house reaches or surpasses the amount of the option price before deciding whether to purchase. If the value does increase, the house will be easier to finance, as you will already have equity—the difference between the sales price and the then-current market value. If the market value rises

significantly, this equity may even cover the down payment. In addition, if your contract allows the up-front option payment or a small portion of the rent to be applied towards the down payment, this amount would become a credit in escrow from the seller to the buyer that could be transferred to the lender as part of your down payment.

Buyers want all extra payments credited toward the purchase price. A prospective purchaser who pays a flat fee in exchange for an option to purchase, or agrees to a higher monthly rent to achieve this benefit, only makes a good deal if all money over and above a reasonable rent will be credited towards the purchase price if the option is exercised.

If you choose not to exercise your option, you ideally want to be able to sell or assign that right to someone else, if possible, for cash or a share of the house's equity; that's the purpose of Clause 19. Many landlords won't accept this clause, however, because it means that even if you don't purchase, it will be you, not the seller, who stands to benefit from an increase in the house value. Typically, landlords will want to be able to pocket the option payment(s) if you decide not to purchase.

For more information on the legal implication of leases, read the discussion of Form 20 (Fixed-Term Residential Lease) in Chapter 4, Renting Residential Real Estate. Also, see Chapter 4 for other forms useful to landlords and tenants.

Finally, unless you're experienced in the field of lease options, have your final contract checked by someone who is. ■

CHAPTER

7

Buying or Selling Personal Property

This chapter contains forms for use when you sell used personal property, such as a car, boat, appliance, furniture or computer. These simple bills of sale are designed to be used to record the terms of sale of all types of property, with the exception of real estate and securities, which are closely regulated by law.

A bill of sale is a written document which at a minimum includes:

- a statement that a sale has taken place
- a description of the item sold
- a statement of the amount paid, and
- the signature of the person selling the property and the date of the signing.

In addition, bills of sale often include:

- a promise by the seller that she owns or otherwise has the right to sell the item
- a written warranty or guarantee that the item is in good condition and will be repaired or replaced if it fails within a certain period
- an "as is" statement making it clear that no warranty is included
- disclosures of any major defects known to the seller, and
- a statement that the item has been inspected by an expert and that the expert's report is attached.

Use a well-drafted bill of sale to head off future legal trouble. When used cars, boats and other items of property are sold without a written bill of sale, the chances of future legal problems—maybe even a court battle—go way up. Far better to define in advance all key terms of the sale, including, most important, the condition of the goods being sold, and whether the sale includes any seller's warranty (for example, 30 days on parts and labor) or is made "as is."

Form 51: Joint Ownership Agreement

The forms in this chapter are designed for use either by individual or joint buyers. When there are two buyers, both names go on the bill of sale and both must sign. From the seller's perspective, this is all that needs to happen. But this is not the end of the matter for the buyers. They will have to decide on the form of their joint ownership.

For certain types of property—for example, automobiles, mobile homes and large boats—the form of ownership can be designated on the ownership certificate of title (slip) provided by the Department of Motor Vehicles or other state licensing agency. For property that doesn't carry a certificate of title, however, the joint buyers may want to execute a separate agreement specifying the form of ownership. Form 51 can be used for this purpose.

There are several different ways of jointly owning property, each with its own legal consequences. The owners can be tenants in common, joint tenants, tenants by the entirety or owners of community property. Here is what these terms mean.

Vehicles, boats and planes—check your state's rules. When states issue ownership documents, as they do for motor vehicles, planes and many boats, they also set up detailed ownership rules. For example, in some states, separating owners' names by "or" means either can sell the vehicle without the other's consent, while using the word "and" means all owners must sign. In other states, the opposite is true.

Tenants in common. Two or more people can own property as tenants in common, each owning a share of the entire property. The shares may be equal or unequal. This fact need not be reflected in the bill of sale, but if ownership is unequal, it should definitely be spelled out in a separate contract. The key legal attribute of a tenancy in common is that each tenant's share is her separate property, which she can sell or leave to her heirs in her will. If the owners do not make an agreement to the contrary, the property is assumed to be owned in equal shares by the owners as tenants in common.

Joint tenants with right of survivorship. Two or more people can own property as joint tenants with right of survivorship, each owning an equal share of the entire property. (In some states, "joint tenancy" is all you need—the words "with right of survivorship" aren't required.) Each owner may transfer his share to another, but this automatically destroys the joint tenancy and changes it into a tenancy in common. Under joint tenancy, each owner's share passes to the other joint tenants at the owner's death, even if a will or living trust says differently.

Tenants by the entirety. This is a form of joint ownership available only to married couples, and even then it is only recognized by about one-third of the states. It operates similarly to joint tenancy, in that at death, the deceased spouse's share automatically passes to the surviving spouse. The one difference, however, is that a spouse cannot unilaterally sever a tenancy by the entirety arrangement.

Community property. In California, Nevada, Arizona, New Mexico, Idaho, Texas, Louisiana, Washington and Wisconsin, most property acquired by a couple in the course of their marriage is considered community property and owned equally by both. This usually means that neither spouse may dispose of the property without the consent of the other, and that the property is equally divided between the spouses (or their estates) in the event of death or divorce, unless they agree in writing to a different plan.

Form 52: Motor Vehicle Bill of Sale

This bill of sale is for vehicles that must be registered with your state's motor vehicles department. This typically includes cars, trucks, motorcycles, recreational vehicles and motor homes. It does not include stationary non-registered mobile homes that are designed to be used semi-permanently at a fixed location such as a mobile home park. Such homes are commonly treated as real property—just as if they were houses—and as such are covered by special transfer, financing and recording rules not discussed here. The category of motor vehicle also doesn't include off-road farm machinery—for that use Form 55—unless it can be registered in your state as a motor vehicle.

Describe the vehicle in detail, including the vehicle identification number (VIN), and indicate the price paid. (Your state motor vehicles depart-

ment wants the price to compute the sales tax.) A buyer who doesn't know and thoroughly trust the seller is advised to check with the motor vehicles department where the vehicle is registered to be sure that no one else claims an ownership interest (lien) in the vehicle, as would be the case if the seller hadn't yet repaid a purchase loan.

Clauses 4 and 5, aimed at providing the buyer full disclosure regarding any mechanical problems with the vehicle, give the seller his best chance to avoid future legal problems. If the vehicle is inspected by a mechanic who prepares a written report which is given to the buyer, and the seller conscientiously lists all known defects, it's highly unlikely that an unsatisfied buyer can later get a judge to agree that the seller was guilty of misrepresentation.

We include a general disclaimer of the implied warranty of merchantability and other implied warranties (see Chapter 14, the text accompanying Form 89) to help protect the seller against later claims by the buyer that the vehicle didn't measure up to the seller's representations or the buyer's expectations. You can substitute a short warranty covering parts or labor or both for this disclaimer.

Be sure to contact your state motor vehicles department for any special requirements when selling a motor vehicle, such as successfully qualifying for a smog certificate. If these exist, include them in Clause 8.

Form 53: Boat Bill of Sale

This form is similar in content to the bill of sale for a motor vehicle (Form 52). Carefully read the discussion that accompanies that form, especially the advice about arranging for an inspection by a third party and the wisdom of the seller bending over backwards to list (disclose) all defects, so a buyer has no grounds to later claim that the condition of the boat was misrepresented.

This form includes a number of entries unique to boat sales. But because there are so many sizes and types of boats, you must fill in the details key to your sale. One way to do this is to add necessary attachments to this contract (see the Introduction for instructions). For example, Attachment 1 might contain a thorough list of all personal property items included in the sale, while Attachment 2 contains the maintenance history of the boat.

Form 54: Computer System Bill of Sale

This bill of sale should be used for computers, computer peripherals and software, especially where a whole system is being sold. If only one or two components are being sold, Form 55, which is a bit simpler, should be adequate. Before using this form, review the material that precedes Form 52, which discusses a number of the key clauses in this agreement.

Form 55: General Bill of Sale for Miscellaneous Personal Property

Form 55, the General Bill of Sale, should be used for items which don't fall into one of the other categories specifically covered previously in this chapter. Examples of items for which this form is appropriate are jewelry, art works, sports equipment, rare books, furniture, collections, appliances, tools, photographic equipment and electronic items. Before using this form, read the brief discussion that precedes Form 52.

Form 56: Notice to Cancel Certain Contracts

Under federal law, you have the right to cancel certain types of consumer contracts you enter into, as long as you act quickly—most laws require that you cancel a contract within three days of signing. The contracts you can cancel anywhere in the U.S., under a rule issued by the Federal Trade Commission, are:

- door-to-door sales contracts for more than $25, and

- a contract for more than $25 made anywhere other than the seller's normal place of business —for instance, at a sales presentation at a friend's house, hotel or restaurant, outdoor exhibit, computer show or trade show; public car auctions and craft fairs—are exempted from coverage.

To take advantage of your right to cancel, you have until midnight of the third business day following the day you signed the contract to cancel it either in person or by mail. You must be given notice of this right and a cancellation form when you sign the contract. (If you simply pay cash and don't sign anything, you are probably out of luck if you later change your mind.) If you were not given a cancellation form, you still have only three days to cancel. You just need to use your own form, such as our Form 56.

After canceling, the seller must refund your money within ten days. Then, the seller must either pick up the items purchased or reimburse you within 20 days for your expense of mailing the goods back to the seller (many states give the seller 40 days). If the seller doesn't come for the goods or make an arrangement for you to mail them back, you can keep them.

In addition to door-to-door, a second federal law, called the federal Truth in Lending Act, lets you cancel a home improvement loan, second mortgage or other loan where you pledge your home as security (except for a first mortgage or first deed of trust). Again, you have until midnight of the third business day after you signed the contract to cancel it.

In addition, most states have enacted their own laws that allow consumers to cancel, within a few days of signing, written contracts for a number of other types of goods and services. Specifically, state laws typically allow cancellation of contracts to join a health club, purchase a time-share or membership camping property, buy a hearing aid, join a dating service or sign up for dance or martial arts lessons. To find out which contracts may be canceled in your state, contact your state's attorney general, consumer affairs office. (Call directory assistance for your state's capital.)

To cancel a contract, first call the seller and orally state that you want to cancel. Next, immediately submit the written cancellation notice you were given when you made the purchase. Sign, date and send it by certified mail, return receipt requested, so you have proof of the date you mailed it. For immediate notice, fax it. (Fax machines usually date faxes when sent.) If you were not given a form (which is often the case) or have misplaced it, use Form 56 to cancel the contract. Don't worry, our form is just as legal as the seller's. ■

Renting Personal Property and Storing Goods

People frequently rent tools, equipment and other personal property. While this is often done from commercial companies which have their own forms, it is also common to rent objects from a neighbor or friend as an informal way of helping your friend or neighbor with the purchase cost. Many rented items are used to perform a certain task, as would be the case if you rented a rototiller and weight drum to lay sod, or power saw and sander to do a small remodeling job around your home. In other situations, you might rent property for a recreational purpose—for example, if you're assigned to bring a volleyball net and badminton set to the company picnic. The type of contract you need will depend greatly on the type of property, its value and how long you need to rent it for.

This chapter includes a form for renting personal property, a notice to end a rental agreement and a contract for the storage of property.

Form 57: Personal Property Rental Agreement

You can use this form for a short-term rental (30 days or less) of relatively inexpensive personal (non-real estate) property. Because not a great deal is at stake, this form doesn't deal with the many potentially complex issues that can arise when property is rented for an extended period. But it does a great job of covering the basics, including the names of the parties, a description of the property, the amount of rent and length of the rental period.

Form 58: Notice of Termination of Rental Agreement

Either the owner or renter can use Form 58 to end any rental agreement that is not made for a specific period.

Form 59: Storage Contract

It is common to store property with friends and relatives—everything from bikes, beds and books to washing machines, weights and walking sticks. Sometimes, this amounts to nothing more than leaving a few small objects for a short time. On other occasions, however, it means storing a household or garage full of goods for a year or more. In many situations involving friends and family, money isn't charged for storage, although payment certainly can be appropriate when bulky or valuable objects are stored for a considerable period of time. This is especially true when the goods are stored in a place (for example, a garage or spare room) that might otherwise be rented or used.

Especially when a fee is charged for storage or when valuable property is to be stored for an extended period, it makes sense to write down your understanding of key issues, such as the length of the storage and who will be responsible if the stored property is damaged. If any problem comes up, such as the owner's delay in picking up the goods, having a simple written storage contract will enhance efforts to arrive at a fair settlement and help preserve relations between the parties.

Carefully identify property. One common cause of disputes concerns a property owner claiming that a valuable item is missing, while the custodian says it was never present in the first place. The best way to prevent this is to make a thorough list of the items to be stored. Clause 1 may not provide enough space to do this, meaning you'll need to add an Attachment. (Instructions for doing so are in the Introduction.) Identify each item as thoroughly as possible, including the make, model, year, color and condition. ■

Home Repairs, Maintenance or Remodeling

This chapter includes three agreements that cover home maintenance, repairs, remodeling and other work you plan to have done at your residence, such as painting or gardening. To assure yourself of a good job, your most important task is to find a contractor who has done excellent work for a number of other people in your community. But even with a highly recommended person, it's hardly a secret that serious misunderstandings between a homeowner and contractor can easily arise if the key job specifications and payment details haven't been carefully worked out and written down before the work begins. Failing this, there is often little you can do if a kitchen remodeling, roof, painting or other job ends up taking twice as long and costs twice as much as you originally anticipated.

God really is in the details. When drafting a house remodeling contract, the more specific you are about the details of the job, the more assured you will be of getting the work done right, on time and within your budget.

The forms in this chapter can be used in several different ways:

- **To analyze a contract proposed by a contractor.** A large firm, especially one doing major home repairs and remodeling, will usually present you with its own contract. If you insist on using one of our forms, the contractor may even refuse to work with you. But it is certainly appropriate to carefully study how our contracts differ from the one you are given by the contractor and, based on what you learn, suggest desired changes to the contractor's agreement.
- **As the actual contract.** Smaller contractors often use brief cursory contracts that provide few details of how the job will be done and when it will be completed. If so, the contractor may be happy to use one of the forms in this chapter.
- **Instead of an oral contract.** A small contractor may not plan to work under a written contract at all—perhaps because of an aversion to

formality. If so, red flags should be flying, because without a written agreement the possibilities for future misunderstandings are legion. Although oral agreements are common for very simple jobs such as garbage hauling, handyman repairs, touch-up painting or a day's yard cleanup, it's far better, even in these situations, to take the time to prepare a brief written agreement.

Some states require people who do home repair and remodeling work to register with the state. Registration usually does not require any demonstration of experience or training. It is primarily designed to keep track of people offering contractor services so that homeowners can locate them if something goes wrong during or after the job is done.

Almost all states have licensing requirements for certain categories of highly skilled home improvement and construction work. For example, most states license people who do residential electrical and plumbing work or who build new structures. By contrast, there is less uniformity among the states as to whether licensing is required for contractors who do general repair and remodeling work, such as framing, dryboard installation, paneling, deck construction, siding and painting.

Among the states that require a license for general repair and remodeling tasks, requirements for the license vary. But most require some experience and skills training, and some evidence of financial responsibility or effective customer recourse policy. For details, call your state Consumer Protection Office to find out if your state regulates contractors, and if so, the name and phone number of the agency that does the regulating, such as the State Contractors' Licensing Board. Then contact the agency directly for information. Many state agencies publish and distribute free consumer pamphlets.

License and registration requirements are often tied to:

- Size of the job—for example, a license may be required for work on any job over $5,000.
- Type of job—some states require a license for plumbing or electrical work but not for painting.

• Location of contractor—most states regulate contracting work of any type that is done by out-of-state contractors.

Also keep in mind that as a general rule, a homeowner must obtain a permit from a city or county agency before major home repairs can begin. Building permits are usually required for jobs that involve structural alterations, additions (a new room), substantial remodeling (a kitchen or bathroom) or new electrical wiring or plumbing installations. Permits, however, are usually not required for casual carpentry, minor plumbing and electrical repairs or adding a new window or door. In addition, if the house is part of a condominium complex or planned unit development, formal approval of the work by a homeowner's association or "architectural review committee" will be necessary if the work affects the home's exterior appearance. Homeowner association approval is usually necessary for new windows, exterior painting, roofing and additions.

Either you or the contractor must be responsible for getting information about the necessary permits. If the job requires a permit or approval, but none is obtained, the homeowner may have to redo all or a portion of the work if a later inspection reveals deficiencies. Also, the value of the home may be adversely affected when it comes to resale if the buyer learns of the non-permit work.

Beware of unlicensed contractors. Even where licenses are required, you can always find someone unlicensed who will do the work, usually promising a "cheap" price. Be wary about accepting these offers—unlicensed contractors are not bonded and in some states can't be sued. And, of course, an unlicensed contractor is almost sure to work without getting a building permit. Even if your "illegal" job is done decently and not discovered by a building inspector—who might require that you tear it out if it is discovered—the fact that you used an unlicensed contractor will probably emerge when you sell your house. This means you'll probably receive a lower price than you would have if you had had the work done by a licensed contractor working under a proper permit.

A word about independent contractors. Our contracts treat the person who will come to your house as an independent contractor, not your employee. As long as the contractor is doing one job or occasional work, this is legal. If the person will work for you regularly (an everyday gardener, for example), the law probably requires that you treat her as an employee. See Chapter 11 for a discussion of employees and independent contractors and why, where legally possible, it makes sense for you to treat any person you hire to do work around your house as an independent contractor.

Form 60: Home Maintenance Agreement

Form 60 is intended for unskilled labor on a one-time job that isn't expected to last for more than a day or two and doesn't involve the need for a significant amount of materials. Typical jobs that fall into this category are hauling refuse, cleaning a garage or house, washing windows, gardening and other work. Such jobs are usually performed by one person who supplies her own tools.

Our contract may not provide enough room. If you want to be highly specific about the work to be done—for example, specifying the cleaning products to be used or precise amount of trimming to be done—you will probably need to include an Attachment. See the Introduction for information on how to prepare one.

Form 61: Home Repairs Agreement (Simple)

Form 61 covers home repairs done by skilled labor for a job that isn't expected to take more than a few days, such as installing new locks or windows, non-structural carpentry repairs, touch-up painting, masonry work and roofing repairs. Work like this probably won't require a contractor's license or permit, but this won't always be true. To cover situations where permits and licenses are required, we include Clauses 5 and 7. If you don't need them, follow the instructions in the Introduction for crossing off or deleting unnecessary contract clauses.

➡ If the job is a major one where the contractor will have to replace or install significant materials, skip ahead to Form 62.

Form 62: Home Repairs Agreement (Detailed)

Use Form 62 for more complicated jobs that involve both labor and materials. The types of jobs for which you may appropriately use this form range from a major landscaping job, building a deck or balcony, remodeling a kitchen, adding a room, putting on a new roof or painting the complete exterior or interior.

Again, after picking a good contractor, the biggest key to the success of this type project is to prepare a contract with highly detailed specifications. For major construction jobs, often it's a good idea to hire an architect to do preliminary drawings and then have the contractor go over them carefully before they are made part of the contract. For small jobs such as remodeling a room, you may be able to dispense with the architect, but it is still a good idea to prepare detailed specifications and drawings. You can include your specifications and drawings as an Attachment to this agreement. See the Introduction for information on preparing an Attachment.

Space does not permit us to provide examples of detailed specifications for the wide variety of house remodel jobs. Fortunately, there are some good products on the market that can help you, including:

- *A Consumer's Guide to Home Improvement, Renovation and Repair,* by Robert M. Santucci, Brooke C. Stoddard and Peter Werworth (John Wiley & Sons, Inc.)
- *The Home Remodeling Organizer,* by Robert Irwin (Dearborn Financial Publishing), and
- *3D Home Architect Deluxe* (Windows software, Broderbund).

Liens and Lien Waivers

A lien is a notice to the world that someone claims a financial interest in your property. The most common type of a lien is a consensual one, that is one you agree to, such as a mortgage or deed of trust on your house. In it, your lender's interest in your home is clearly stated and the lien (evidenced in the mortgage or deed of trust note) is recorded at your county land record's office. Anyone who wants to know if someone claims an interest in your house can do a title search at the land record's office and the lien will show up.

Other types of liens are nonconsensual, that is, they are filed at the property recorder's office against your will. A common example is an income tax lien filed by the IRS. Similarly, a contractor who works on your home without getting paid, or someone who the contractor hires to do subcontracting work or buys supplies from but does not pay, has the legal right to place a "mechanic's lien" against your house. Lien problems are particularly likely to develop where you dutifully pay the contractor, who pockets the money instead of paying his subcontractors, who in turn file liens against your house.

To help reduce the possibility that your job will end in this sort of disaster, our contract contains Clause 8, which provides you with assurance against liens being filed against your house by the contractor, a subcontractor or a materials provider.

💡 **Only pay the contractor what he deserves or has earned.** Don't pay too much up front— just enough to let the contractor purchase the materials he needs to get started. In addition, it is usually best to agree to make periodic payments which are tied to measurable, easy to define goals and insist that the contractor really meet each goal before you make the payment that is tied to it. ∎

Handling Personal Finances

You probably don't think too much about monthly budgets, joint accounts or stopping payment on a check unless you are having financial problems. But by being proactive—reviewing your finances in advance and knowing your legal rights—you can often avoid legal and money problems. The forms in this chapter are designed for you to get a handle on your personal finances—budgeting, dealing with debts and debt collectors and reviewing your credit report—whether you're trying to avoid problems or you're in the midst of a crisis.

Form 63: Daily Expenses

Creating a budget—comparing your average monthly expenses to your total monthly income—is a first step to putting your financial house in order. Although it's not hard to do, it is a three-step process. Step one is to get a clear picture of how you spend your money. You can do that using Form 63, on which you record everything you spend over the course of a week. Step two is to total up your income. You can do that using Form 64. The final step is comparing the two. For that you can use Form 65.

Here's how to use Form 63:

1. Make nine copies of the form. You will use eight to record your expenses for about two months. By using your figures for two months, you'll avoid creating a budget based on a week or a month of unusually high or low expenses. If you and another adult (such as a spouse or partner) share finances, make eight copies each. You will use the ninth to record other expenses.

2. Select a Sunday to begin recording your expenses; record that Sunday's date in the blank at the top of one copy of the form.

3. Record every expense you pay for by cash or cash equivalent—check, ATM or debit card or automatic bank withdrawal—on that week's form. Include deposits into savings accounts, certificates of deposit or money market accounts and purchases of investments.

Do not record credit card charges. When you make a payment on a credit card bill, however, list the amount of your payment and the items covered by the payment. If you don't pay the entire bill, list the older charges that total the amount paid less that month's finance charge, and attribute the balance to the finance charges.

4. At the end of the week, put away the form, take out another copy and fill it out according to step 3. Repeat for eight weeks.

5. At the end of the eight weeks, take out the ninth sheet. Anywhere on it, list seasonal, annual, semi-annual or quarterly expenses you incur each year, but which did not come due during your two-month recording period. The most common are property taxes, car registration, charitable gift, magazine subscriptions, tax preparation fees and auto and house insurance payments. Divide the annual cost of these items by 365 to get the "daily expense."

Use Form 64 together with Form 63 to help you create a budget. On Form 64, you total up your monthly income. Be sure to include income information for both people if you and another adult share finances.

Part A is for jobs for which you receive a salary or wages. Part B is for self-employment income, including farm income and sales commissions. Part C is for investment income and Part D is for other sources of income, such as bonus pay, alimony or child support, pension or retirement income and public assistance.

When you are done listing the amount of all sources of income, total up Column 4. This is your total monthly income.

 Don't include your income that is automatically reinvested. As you list your income, you may be inclined to list your interest and dividends that are automatically reinvested, such as retirement plan income and stock dividends, to get a true sense of your income. But the purpose of creating a budget is to keep track of your actual expenses and the income you have available to pay those expenses. By including income you don't actually receive, you will be left with the impression that you have more income to cover on your expenses each month than you actually receive.

Form 64: Monthly Income

Use Form 64 together with Form 63 to help you create a budget. On Form 64, you total up your monthly income. Be sure to include income information for both people if you and another adult share finances.

Part A is for jobs for which you receive a salary or wages. Part B is for self-employment income, including farm income and sales commissions. Part C is for investment income and Part D is for other sources of income, such as bonus pay, alimony or child support, pension or retirement income and public assistance.

When you are done listing the amount of all sources of income, total up Column 4. This is your total monthly income.

 Don't include your income that is automatically reinvested. As you list your income, you may be inclined to list your interest and dividends that are automatically reinvested, such as retirement plan income and stock dividends, to get a true sense of your income. But the purpose of creating a budget is to keep track of your actual expenses and the income you have available to pay those expenses. By including income you don't actually receive, you will be left with the impression that you have more income to cover on your expenses each month than you actually receive.

Form 65: Monthly Budget

After you've kept track of your expenses (Form 63) and income (Form 64) for a couple of months, you're ready to create a budget using Form 65. Follow these steps:

1. Using your total actual expenses, project your monthly expenses for the categories relevant to you on Form 65. To find your projected monthly expenses, divide the total of your actual two months' expenses by two. Be sure to include the daily equivalent of any quarterly, semi-annual or annual expenses that you noted on your ninth sheet.

2. Enter your projected monthly expenses into the projected column on Form 65. Remember, this is just an estimate based on two months of recordkeeping. Enter the total near the bottom of the column.

3. Enter your projected monthly income (bottom line of Form 64) below your total projected expenses on Form 65.

4. Figure out the difference. If your expenses exceed your income, you will have to cut your projected expenses or increase your income.

5. During each month, use a pencil to write down your actual expenses in each category. Do this as accurately as possible—remember, creating a budget is really designed to help you adopt a sound spending plan, not to fill in the "correct" numbers. Check your actual monthly expenditures periodically to help you keep an eye on how you're doing. Are you keeping close to your projected figures? If you are not, you will need to change the projected amount for those categories.

When a large payment comes due. While you have included one-twelfth of your quarterly, semi-annual and annual expenses in each month's projection, those expenses and other unanticipated ones don't arise every month. Ideally, your budget provides for a cushion each month—that is, your income exceeds your expenses—so you'll be able to handle the large payments when they come due by using that month's cushion or the savings you've built up from the excess each month. If you don't have the cash on hand to pay the large payment, you will have to cut back in other expense categories.

Form 66: Statement of Assets and Liabilities

Subtracting what you owe (liabilities) from what you own (assets) reveals your net worth. A net worth statement can help you and any lenders analyze your eligibility for a mortgage, business loan or other type of loan.

To find your net worth, use Form 66, Statement of Assets and Liabilities. Fill in as much information as you can. Don't worry about listing every asset or debt, as the information on this form changes daily as your assets change value and the balances on your debts rise or fall.

What values should you use for your assets? As best you can come up with them, you will want to include an asset's market value—the amount you could get if you sold the item on the open market. This means you are not looking at what you could get in a forced sale—such as a repossession or foreclosure, or if you had to sell all your personal belongings at a garage sale. Instead, you're looking at what your home could bring in under normal selling conditions, how much you could get for your car by selling it through the paper or to a dealer and how much your household goods are worth, considering they generally depreciate about 20% a year.

Form 67: Estimate of Income Tax Liability

There are many reasons why you may want to estimate your tax liability in advance. You may be setting up a budget for the upcoming year (or month) and want to know if you'll owe Uncle Sam, or if you can look forward to a refund. You may be planning a major purchase and hope to put your tax refund toward the purchase price. Or you may be in the process of divorcing and attempting to allocate marital debts, including any tax obligations. Whatever your reason, you can use Form 67 to estimate your federal income tax liability.

Tax Rate

Form 67 asks for your estimated tax. Use the rates below to estimate.

Single

Income over	but less than	This amt.	plus	%		of income over
$0	$24,650	$0	+	15%	x	$0
$24,650	$59,750	$3,697	+	28%	x	24,650
$59,650	$124,650	13,525	+	31%	x	59,750
$124,650	$271,050	33,644	+	36%	x	124,650
$271,050	and over	86,348	+	39.6%	x	271,050

Married filing jointly

Income over	but less than	This amt.	plus	%		of income over
$0	$41,200	$0	+	15%	x	$0
$41,200	$99,600	6,180	+	28%	x	41,200
$99,600	$151,750	22,532	+	31%	x	99,600
$151,750	$271,050	38,699	+	36%	x	151,750
271,050	and over	40,823	+	39.6%	x	135,525

Married/separately

Income over	but less than	This amt.	plus	%		of income over
$0	20,600	$0	+	15%	x	$0
20,600	49,800	3,090	+	28%	x	20,600
49,800	75,875	11,266	+	31%	x	49,800
75,875	135,525	19,349	+	36%	x	75,875
135,525	and over	40,823	+	39.6%	x	135,525

Head of household

Income over	but less than	This amt.	plus	%		of income over
$0	$33,050	$0	+	15%	x	$0
33,050	85,350	4,957	+	28%	x	33,050
85,350	138,200	19,602	+	31%	x	85,350
38,200	271,050	35,985	+	36%	x	138,200
271,050	and over	83, 811	+	39.6%	x	271,050

There are three steps involved. First, enter your income, deduction and exemption information onto Form 67 to total up your estimated tax liability. Next, consult the tax value chart to figure out how much the IRS will claim you owe this year. Finally, figure out the difference. A positive number represents the amount you may owe the IRS. A negative number is your likely refund.

Don't sweat the details. Use last year's figures unless you know they have changed. You can even make estimates.

Form 68: Assignment of Rights

An assignment is a legal transfer of property or money, or the right to receive property or money, to another person. Assignments are most economically used to transfer rights under a contract, such as the right to receive payments or the right to file a lawsuit. This is the type of assignment this form is designed to handle. For example, you might assign the right to receive income from a book contract to your 15-year-old so that the money would be taxed in her bracket, not yours.

Tax implications of assignments. If you assign money to another person and receive something of equal value in return, there should be no tax implication. If, however, you assign your right to receive money to another person as a gift and the IRS learns of the assignment, it will treat it as a taxable transaction. For most assignments, this won't be a problem because the gift can be treated as tax-free, as long as the total amount given through the assignment in a calendar year is $10,000 or less.

One note of terminology: A person making an assignment is called the assignor. The person receiving the transfer is called the assignee.

Form 69: Notice to Terminate Joint Accounts

As part of a breakup or divorce, you will want to promptly close credit accounts you hold jointly with a spouse or partner. To do so, write your creditors—use the customer service address on the back of a billing statement—and ask them to close your accounts immediately. Request that the company advise you of any outstanding charges, and state that you refuse to be responsible for any charges made after the date of your letter. Send all mail by certified mail, receipt requested, and keep a copy for your files. While such a letter may not fully protect you, it is better than doing nothing, and you put the burden on the creditor.

Most of the time, the creditor will do a "soft close" of the account, especially if there is an outstanding balance. This means that the account is only sort of closed. If you or your ex charges, the creditor will re-open the account. The only way to avoid this is to insist that the creditor do a "hard close." You'll have to pay off the outstanding balance, but there is still no guarantee that the creditor will hard close the account. Some simply keep the account in soft close status for six months or so after you request the closure, supposedly to save you the embarrassment of your accidentally using the card and being turned down.

Don't overlook home equity lines of credit. You and your ex may have applied for a home equity line of credit a while ago and forgotten about it. Equity credit lines which supply a checkbook can be used just like a joint checking account. Whoever has the checkbook has access to the money. Unless you have the checkbook, be sure to pay a visit to your banker. Request that the account be closed or frozen. Even if you have the checkbook, request that the account be closed so that your ex can't request more checks. By leaving an equity line of credit open, you risk losing your home.

Form 70: Notice to Stop Payment of Check

It's not unusual to write a check, hand it over or mail it to the recipient and then change your mind and want to stop payment. For example, you might not notice that delivered goods were defective until after the delivery person was paid and left. Many other situations give rise to the need to put a stop payment on a check.

The first thing to do is call your bank, savings and loan, credit union or other financial institution where your account is located to make an oral request to stop payment. Most financial institutions will charge you for this. Then immediately send or, better yet, drop by a written confirmation, Form 70. In many situations, the stop payment notice lasts only six months or a year, and if you fear the person to whom you wrote the check will try to cash it much later, you may need to renew your stop payment notice. Don't just assume that checks get stale after six months and that you won't need to renew your stop payment notice. Banks, savings and loans, credit unions and other financial institutions have the option of rejecting checks they deem too old, often six months or older, but usually don't exercise this right. In fact, most people who work in a bank or other such institution never look at the date of the check. They simply post it to the account. If the money is there to cover it, the check is paid.

Form 71: Request for Credit Report

If you want to repair your credit or establish credit, your first step is to get a copy of your credit report. This is a file maintained by a credit reporting company that sells information to banks, lenders, landlords and others who routinely evaluate customers' credit-worthiness. Credit reports contain:

- personal information about you
- accounts reported monthly, usually credit card accounts, department store accounts, bank loans, car loans, student loans and most mortgages

- accounts reported when in default, such as medical bills, utility payments, subscriptions and some mortgages
- public records, such as lawsuits, judgments and liens, and
- requests by creditors for a copy of your report (inquiries).

You can get your credit report by requesting a copy from one of the three major national credit bureaus:

- Equifax, P.O. Box 740241, Atlanta, GA 30374-0241; 800-685-1111
- Experian, National Consumers Assistance Center, P.O. Box 949, Allen, TX 75013; 800-682-7654
- Trans Union, P.O. Box 390, Springfield, PA 19064; 800-916-8800.

If you call for your credit report, you will most likely be able (via a voice mail system) to order your report over the phone. If you can't get through or want to put your request in writing, use Form 71.

You are entitled to a copy of your credit report for free if:

- You've been denied credit because of information in your credit file. You must request your copy within 60 days of being denied credit.
- You are unemployed and planning to apply for a job within 60 days following your request for your credit report.
- You receive public assistance.
- You believe your credit file contains errors due to someone's fraud, such as opening up accounts by using your name or Social Security number.
- In some states, you haven't requested a copy in the last year. You can get a free copy of your credit report once a year if you live in Colorado, Georgia, Maryland, Massachusetts, New Jersey or Vermont.

If you don't qualify for a free copy, you'll have to pay a fee of $8, except in Connecticut ($5 for the first report requested in a year and $7.50 for subsequent reports) and Maine ($2-$3).

Form 72: Challenge Incorrect Credit Report Entry

Once you receive your credit report, review it carefully. Sometimes credit bureaus confuse names, addresses, Social Security numbers or employers. If you have a common name, say John Brown, your file may contain information on other John Browns, John Brownes or Jon Browns. Your file may contain information on family members with similar names.

As you read through your credit report, make a list of everything that is incorrect, out-of-date or misleading, such as:

- incorrect or incomplete name, address or phone number
- incorrect Social Security number or birthdate
- incorrect, missing or outdated employment information
- incorrect marital status
- bankruptcies older than ten years or not identified by the specific chapter of the bankruptcy code
- lawsuits or judgments reported beyond seven years
- paid tax liens, criminal records or delinquent accounts older than seven years
- credit inquiries older than two years
- commingled accounts—credit histories for someone with a similar or the same name
- duplicate accounts—for example, a debt is listed twice, once under the creditor and a second time under a collection agency
- premarital debts of your current spouse attributed to you
- lawsuits you were not involved in
- incorrect account histories—such as a late payment notation when you've paid on time
- paid tax, judgment, mechanic's or other liens listed as unpaid
- a missing notation when you disputed a charge on a credit card bill
- closed accounts incorrectly listed as open, and
- accounts you closed that don't indicate "closed by consumer."

Once you've compiled a list of all information you want changed or removed, complete the "request for reinvestigation" form which was enclosed with your credit report. If the bureau did not enclose such a form, use our Form 72.

Form 73: Dispute Credit Card Charge

If you use a credit or charge card but don't receive the product you purchased or you receive a defective item, you can legally refuse to pay if all of the following are true:

- You attempt in good faith to resolve the dispute with the merchant, who refuses to replace, repair or otherwise correct the problem.
- Your credit card or charge card was not issued by the seller—for example, you used a Visa, MasterCard, American Express or Discover card, not a Sears or Chevron card.
- The purchase was for more than $50 and was made within the state in which you live or within 100 miles of your home.

If you are entitled to withhold payment, promptly write to the credit card company at the billing address and explain why you aren't paying. The credit card issuer must receive your letter within 60 days of the statement date on your bill. Detail how you tried to resolve the problem with the merchant. Use Form 73. Keep a copy for your own records.

Form 74: Demand Collection Agency Cease Contact

Many people don't understand that they have the legal right to tell a bill collector who works for a collection agency to leave them alone. To do this you must put your demand in writing and send it to the collection agency—you can use Form 74. By law, all collectors from the agency must then cease all phone calls, letters and other communications with you, unless they are contacting you to notify you that:

- collection efforts against you have ended, or
- the collection agency or the creditor will invoke a specific remedy against you, such as suing you.

⚠️ **This law applies only to bill collectors working for a collection agency.** You do not have the right to demand that the in-house collectors at a bank, department store, hospital or other creditor end their contacts with you.

Form 75: Complaint Letter

Every state and the federal government prohibit unfair or deceptive trade acts or practices. This means that a seller can't deceive, abuse, mislead, defraud or otherwise cheat you.

If you think you've been cheated by someone selling a service or product, let the appropriate federal, state and county government offices know. Although law enforcement in the area of consumer fraud is not uniformly great, many hardworking investigators do their jobs superbly. The more agencies you notify, the more likely someone will take notice of your complaint and act on it— especially if more than one consumer has registered a complaint about the same company.

Your first step is to draft a complaint letter. Do this by using Form 75. Next, compile a list of agencies and their addresses where you will send your letter. Consider the following:

- U.S. Office of Consumer Affairs, 800-664-4435, which provides free help with referring consumer complaints to the appropriate agency.
- Federal Trade Commission, 6th & Pennsylvania Avenues, NW, Washington, DC 20580, 202-326-2222 (voice) or 202-326-2050 (fax), which oversees advertisers, door-to-door sellers, mail-order companies, credit bureaus and most retailers.
- Your state consumer protection office. (See addresses and phone numbers below.)
- Your state's licensing boards for licensed professionals, such as contractors, lawyers, funeral directors, doctors, insurance companies, car dealers and car repair outfits.
- Your local district attorney's consumer fraud division.

- The customer service department for the company you're complaining about.
- A local Better Business Bureau office.

Attach copies (never the originals) of all receipts, contracts, warranties, service contracts, advertisements and other documents relating to your purchase. Keep a copy of your letter for your records.

How to Word a Complaint

Here are two examples of language to include in a complaint letter:

I wish to complain about the abuse I received by R. Green at the Drone Collection Agency. R. Greene called me six times a day for two weeks, using profanity. R. Greene also called my 76-year-old father and threatened to sue him, even though he has nothing to do with this debt.

I wish to complain about a business located in your state called Celebrity Cards. About three months ago, I received a package of cards from this company unsolicited. I received a second package two months ago. Last month, I received a bill from the company for $50 plus shipping and handling. I never ordered these cards and wrote to the company to say so. I also stated that I considered the unsolicited items sent to my home to be a gift. Just this week I received a second bill and a threat to send this debt to a collection agency and report it to a credit bureau.

State	Phone & Fax	State Consumer Protection Offices
Alabama	334-242-7334, 800-392-5658 334-242-7458 (fax)	Consumer Assistance, Office of Attorney General, 11 South Union Street, Montgomery, AL 36130 (collection agencies, credit bureaus, general consumer complaints)
Alaska	907-465-3600 907-465-2075 (fax) http://www.law.state. ak.us/ (Internet)	Office of the Attorney General, P.O. Box K—State Capitol, Juneau, AK 99811-0300 (the Consumer Protection Section was eliminated in 1989; if you write or call this office, you can be sent a four-page letter listing various state, federal and private consumer protection agencies and organizations which may be of assistance)
Arizona	602-255-4421 800-544-0708 602-381-1225 (fax)	State Banking Department, Consumer Affairs, 2910 North 44th Street, Suite 310, Phoenix, AZ 85018 (collection agencies)
	602-542-5763 800-352-8431 602-542-1275 (fax) 602-542-5002 (TTY)	Consumer Information and Complaints, Office of Attorney General, 1275 West Washington Street, Phoenix, AZ 85007 (credit bureaus, general consumer complaints)
Arkansas	501-682-2007 800-482-8982 501-682-8084 (fax) 501-682-6073 (TTY)	Advocacy Division of Attorney General's Office, 200 Tower Building, 323 Center Street, Little Rock, AR 72201 (collection agencies, credit bureaus, general consumer complaints)
California	916-445-1254 800-952-5210 916-324-4298 (fax)	Department of Consumer Affairs, Consumer Assistance Office, 400 R Street, Suite 3000, Sacramento, CA 95814 (general consumer complaints)
	202-326-2222 202-326-2050 (fax)	Federal Trade Commission, Consumer Protection, 6th & Pennsylvania Avenue, NW, Washington, DC 20580 (collection agencies, credit bureaus)
Colorado	303-866-5304 800-332-2071	Collection Agency Board, Office of Attorney General, 1525 Sherman Street, 5th Floor, Denver, CO 80203 (collection agencies)
	303-866-5189 800-332-2071 303-866-3955 (fax)	Consumer Protection Unit, Office of Attorney General, 1525 Sherman Street, 5th Floor, Denver, CO 80203 (credit bureaus, general consumer complaints)
Connecticut	860-240-8200 860-240-8178 (fax) http://www.state.ct. us/dob/ (Internet)	Department of Banking, Consumer Credit Division, 260 Constitution Plaza, Hartford, CT 06106 (collection agencies, credit bureaus)
	860-566-4999 860-566-1531 (fax)	Department of Consumer Protection, 165 Capitol Avenue, Hartford, CT 06106 (general consumer complaints)
Delaware	302-577-3250 302-577-2610 (fax)	Department of Justice, Consumer Protection Unit, 820 North French Street, 4th Fl., Wilmington, DE 19801 (collection agencies, credit bureaus, general consumer complaints)
District of Columbia	202- 727-7170 202-727-8073 (fax)	Department of Consumer and Regulatory Affairs, 614 H Street, NW, Room 1120, Washington, DC 20001 (collection agencies, credit bureaus, general consumer complaints)

State	Phone & Fax	State Consumer Protection Offices
Florida	904-922-2966 800-435-7352 904-487-4177 (fax)	Division of Consumer Services, Department of Agriculture and Consumer Services, 235 Mayo Building, Tallahassee, FL 32399 (collection agencies, credit bureaus, general consumer complaints)
Georgia	404-656-3383 404-651-9148 (fax)	Consumer Affairs Division, Office of the Attorney General, 40 Capitol Square, SW, Atlanta, GA 30334-1300 (collection agencies, credit bureaus, general consumer complaints)
Hawaii	808-586-2820 808-586-2818 (fax)	Financial Institutions Division, P.O. Box 2054, Honolulu, HI 96805 (collection agencies)
	808-586-2630 808-586-2640 (fax)	Office of Consumer Protection, Dept. of Commerce and Consumer Affairs, 235 S. Beretania St, 8th Floor, Honolulu, HI 96812 (credit bureaus, general consumer complaints)
Idaho	208-332-8000 208-332-8098 (fax)	State Department of Finance, 700 West State Street, Statehouse Mail, Boise, ID 83720-0031 (collection agencies)
	208-334-2424 800-432-3545 208-334-2530 (fax)	Consumer Protection Division, Office of Attorney General, 210 Statehouse, Boise, ID 83720-1000 (credit bureaus, general consumer complaints)
Illinois	217-782-1090 800-252-8666 217-782-7046 (fax) 217-785-2771 (TTY)	Consumer Protection Division, Office of Attorney General, 500 South Second Street, Springfield, IL 62706 (collection agencies, credit bureaus, general consumer complaints)
Indiana	317-232-6690 317-233-3283 (fax)	Securities Division, Secretary of State, 302 West Washington, Room E-111, Indianapolis, IN 46204-2270 (collection agencies)
	317-232-6205 800-382-5516 317-232-7979 (fax)	Consumer Protection Division, Office of Attorney General, Indiana Gov't Center South, 5th Floor, 402 West Washington, Indianapolis, IN 46204-2270 (general consumer complaints)
	202-326-2222 202-326-2050 (fax)	Federal Trade Commission, Consumer Protection, 6th & Pennsylvania Avenue, NW, Washington, DC 20580 (credit bureaus)
Iowa	515-281-5926 515-281-4209 (fax) http://www.state.ia/ government/ag/ (Internet)	Consumer Protection Division, Office of Attorney General, Hoover State Office Building, Des Moines, IA 50319 (collection agencies, credit bureaus, general consumer complaints)
Kansas	913-296-3751 800-432-2310 913-296-6296 (fax)	Consumer Protection Division, Office of Attorney General, Kansas Judicial Center, 2nd Floor, Topeka, KS 66612 (collection agencies, credit bureaus, general consumer complaints)
Kentucky	502-564-4002 800-432-9257 502-564-8310 (fax)	Consumer Protection Division, Office of Attorney General, P.O. Box 2000, Frankfort, KY 40602-2000 (collection agencies, credit bureaus, general consumer complaints)
Louisiana	504-342-7013 504-342-7335 (fax)	Consumer Protection Section, Office of Attorney General, P.O. Box 94095, Baton Rouge, LA 70804-9095 (collection agencies, credit bureaus, general consumer complaints)

State	Phone & Fax	State Consumer Protection Offices
Maine	207-624-8527 800-332-8529 207-624-8690 (fax)	Bureau of Consumer Credit Protection, State House, Station No. 35, Augusta, ME 04333-0035 (collection agencies, credit bureaus, general consumer complaints)
Maryland	410-333-6330	Complaint Department, Commissioner of Consumer Credit, 501 St. Paul Place, 13th Floor, Baltimore, MD 21202 (collection agencies)
	410-576-6550 410-576-7003 (fax)	Consumer Protection Division, Office of Attorney General, 200 St. Paul Pl., Baltimore, MD 21202-2022 (credit bureaus, general consumer complaints)
Massachusetts	617-727-2200 617-727-5762 (fax)	Consumer Protection Division, Dept. of Attorney General, 1 Ashburton Place, Boston, MA 02111 (collection agencies, credit bureaus, general consumer complaints)
Michigan	517-373-7233 517-335-0908 (fax)	Department of Commerce-BOP, Financial Institutions Bureau, P.O. Box 30224, Lansing, MI 48909 (collection agencies)
	517-335-0855 517-373-4916 (fax)	Consumer Protection Division, Office of Attorney General, P.O. Box 30213, Lansing, MI 48909 (credit bureaus, general consumer complaints)
Minnesota	612-296-2488 800-657-3602 612-296-4328 (fax)	State Commerce Department, Enforcement Division, 133 East 7th Street, St. Paul, MN 55101 (collection agencies)
	612-296-4519 612-297-4193 (fax)	Consumer Mediation Services, Office of Attorney General, 1400 NCL Tower, 445 Minnesota Street, St. Paul, MN 55101-2130 (credit bureaus, general consumer complaints)
Mississippi	601-359-4230 800-281-4418 601-359-4231 (fax)	Consumer Protection Division, Office of Attorney General, P.O. Box 220, Jackson, MS 39225-2947 (collection agencies, credit bureaus, general consumer complaints)
Missouri	573-751-3463 800-722-3321 573-751-9192 (fax)	Division of Finance, P.O. Box 716, Jefferson City, MO 65102 (collection agencies)
	573-751-3321 800-392-8222 573-751-0774 (fax)	Consumer Protection Division, Office of Attorney General, P.O. Box 899, Jefferson City, MO 65102 (credit bureaus, general consumer complaints)
Montana	406-444-3553 406-444-2903 (fax)	Consumer Affairs Unit, Dept. of Commerce, 1424 Ninth Avenue, Helena, MT 59620 (collection agencies, credit bureaus, general consumer complaints)
Nebraska	402-471-2008 402-471-3237 (fax)	Secretary of State, Collection Agency Board, 2300 State Capitol Lincoln, NB 68509-4608 (collection agencies)
	402-471-2682 402-471-3297 (fax)	Consumer Protection Division, Office of Attorney General, 2115 State Capitol Building, P.O. Box 98920, Lincoln, NB 68509-8920 (credit bureaus, general consumer complaints)

State	Phone & Fax	State Consumer Protection Offices
Nevada	702-486-4120 702-687-6909 (fax)	Financial Institution Division, 406 East 2nd street, Carson City, NV 89710 (collection agencies)
	702-486-7370 702-486-7371 (fax)	Consumer Affairs Division, 1850 E. Sahara Ave., Suite 204, Las Vegas, NV 89104 (credit bureaus, general consumer complaints)
New Hampshire	603-271-3641 603-271-2110 (fax)	Consumer Protection Bureau, Office of Attorney General, 33 Capitol Street, Concord, NH 03301 (collection agencies, credit bureaus, general consumer complaints)
New Jersey	201-504-6200 201-648-3538 (fax)	Consumer Protection Office, P.O. Box 45025, Newark, NJ 07101 (credit bureaus, general consumer complaints)
	202-326-2222 202-326-2050 (fax)	Federal Trade Commission, Consumer Protection, 6th & Pennsylvania Avenue, NW, Washington, DC 20580 (collection agencies)
New Mexico	505-827-6060 800-827-5826 505-827-6685 (fax)	Consumer Protection Division, Office of Attorney General, P.O. Drawer 1508, Santa Fe, NM 87504 (collection agencies, credit bureaus, general consumer complaints)
New York	518-474-1471 518-474-2474 (fax)	Consumer Protection Board, 5 Empire State Plaza, Suite 2101, Albany, NY 12223-1556 (collection agencies, credit bureaus, general consumer complaints)
North Carolina	919-733-4723 919-733-7491 (fax)	Consumer Protection Section, Office of Attorney General, Department of Justice, P.O. Box 629, Raleigh, NC 27602 (collection agencies, credit bureaus, general consumer complaints)
North Dakota	701-328-3404 701-328-2226 (fax)	Consumer Protection Division, Office of Attorney General, 600 East Boulevard, Bismarck, ND 58505-0400 (collection agencies, credit bureaus, general consumer complaints)
Ohio	614-466-3376 800-282-0515 614-466-5087 (fax)	Consumer Protection Division, Office of Attorney General, State Office Tower, 30 East Broad Street, 25th Floor, Columbus, OH 43215-3428 (collection agencies, credit bureaus, general consumer complaints)
Oklahoma	405-521-4274 405-521-6246 (fax)	Consumer Affairs Division, Office of Attorney General, 2300 N. Lincoln Blvd., Oklahoma City, OK 73105-3498 (collection agencies, credit bureaus, general consumer complaints)
Oregon	503-378-4320 503-378-3784 (fax)	Financial Fraud, Department of Justice, 1162 Court Street, NE, Salem, OR 97310 (collection agencies, credit bureaus, general consumer complaints)
Pennsylvania	717-783-5048 800-441-2555 717-787-1190 (fax)	Bureau of Consumer Protection, Office of Attorney General, Strawberry Square, 14th Floor, Harrisburg, PA 17120 (collection agencies, credit bureaus, general consumer complaints)
Rhode Island	401-274-4400 401-277-1331 (fax)	Consumer Protection Division, Department of Attorney General, 150 S. Main Street, Providence, RI 02903 (collection agencies, credit bureaus, general consumer complaints)

State	Phone & Fax	State Consumer Protection Offices
South Carolina	803-737-2080 800-922-1594 803-734-2192 (fax)	Department of Consumer Affairs, 1101 Williams St., Columbia, SC 29211 (collection agencies, credit bureaus, general consumer complaints)
South Dakota	605-773-4400 605-773-4106 (fax)	Division of Consumer Affairs, Office of Attorney General, State Capitol Building, 500 East Capitol, Pierre, SD 57501 (collection agencies, credit bureaus, general consumer complaints)
Tennessee	615-741-4737 800-342-8385 615-532-6934 (fax)	Division of Consumer Affairs, Department of Commerce and Insurance, 500 James Robertson Parkway, 5th Floor, Nashville, TN 37243-0600 (collection agencies, credit bureaus, general consumer complaints)
Texas	512-463-2185 512-463-2063 (fax)	Consumer Protection Division, Office of Attorney General, P.O. Box 12548, Austin, TX 78711 (collection agencies, credit bureaus, general consumer complaints)
Utah	801-538-1015 801-538-1121 (fax)	Consumer Rights Division, Office of Attorney General, 236 State Capitol, Salt Lake City, UT 84114 (collection agencies, credit bureaus, general consumer complaints)
Vermont	802-828-3171 800-649-2424 802-828-2154 (fax)	Consumer Assistance, Office of Attorney General, 109 State St., Montpelier, VT 05609-1001 (collection agencies, credit bureaus, general consumer complaints)
Virginia	804-786-2042 800-552-9963 804- 371-2945 (fax)	Office of Consumer Affairs, Department of Agriculture and Consumer Services, 1100 Bank St., Richmond, VA 23219 (collection agencies, credit bureaus, general consumer complaints)
Washington	360-733-6200 800-551-4636 360-664-0228 (fax)	Consumer Resource Center, Office of Attorney General, P.O. Box 40100, Olympia, WA 98504-0100 (collection agencies, credit bureaus, general consumer complaints)
West Virginia	304-558-8986 800-368-8808 304-588-0140 (fax)	Consumer Protection Division, Office of Attorney General, 1900 Kanawha Blvd. E., Building 1, Charleston, WV 25305-0220 (collection agencies, credit bureaus, general consumer complaints)
Wisconsin	608-224-4920 608-224-5045 (fax)	Consumer Protection Bureau, Department of Agriculture, Trade and Consumer Protection, P.O. Box 8911, Madison, WI 53707 (credit bureaus, general consumer complaints)
	608-261-9555 800-425-3328 608- 267-6889 (fax)	Office of Commissioner of Banking, P.O. Box 7876, Madison, WI 53707 (collection agencies)
Wyoming	307-777-7891 307-777-6869 (fax)	Consumer Affairs Division, Office of Attorney General, 123 State Capitol Building, Cheyenne, WY 82002 (collection agencies, credit bureaus, general consumer complaints)

Form 76: Notice of Insurance Claim

If you're planning to make a claim against an insurance company—you were in a car accident, a victim of a slip and fall or something similar—you can use Form 76 to notify the appropriate company or companies. Depending on the circumstances, send your letter to the insurance company of the person or company you believe was at fault, such as the owner and driver of a vehicle if you were in a car accident or the landlord (building owner) and tenant (company that rents) if you were in a slip and fall. In addition, if you are covered by your own auto, homeowner's, business or other policy, be sure to notify your own insurer. You can begin by contacting your agent or broker by phone, but it's nevertheless a good idea to mail or fax in a written claim as well, keeping a copy for yourself.

Your notification should be a simple typed letter giving only basic information and asking for a written response. It should not discuss fault or responsibility, or the details of your injuries. Make sure the letter includes the following:

- Your name and address. You do not have to include your phone number if you do not wish.
- The date, approximate time of day and general location of the accident or incident.
- A request that the insurance company confirm by return letter whom it represents and whether it is aware of anyone else who might be responsible for the accident.
- When writing to your own automobile insurance company, include basic information about the other driver and vehicle—name, address, telephone number, license number, insurance policy.

If the insurance company does not feel you provided sufficient information, it may send you its own form to complete.

Additional information and forms on dealing with debts, planning a budget, rebuilding your credit and other similar topics can be found in *Money Troubles: Legal Strategies to Cope With Your Debts* and *Credit Repair*, both written by Robin Leonard and published by Nolo Press. ∎

Hiring Household Help and Child and Elder Care

Many people hire others to work regularly in their homes—for example, to take care of their children during the work-day, care for elderly parents or clean their houses. These relationships are often set up informally, with no written agreement. But informal arrangements can be fraught with problems. If you don't have a written agreement clearly defining responsibilities and benefits, you and your help are all too likely to have different expectations about the job. This can lead to serious disputes—even to either or both of you bitterly backing out of the arrangement. Far better to draft a clear written understanding of what the job entails and when you expect the work to be done.

In addition, there is the serious legal issue of whether the person you hire is an independent con-tractor or your employee for whom you are legally required to pay Social Security and other benefits. Legally, most household workers who work for you on a regular basis are considered employees—but especially where a person runs his own business and works for you only occasionally, you can and should use a written contract to define the person as an independent contractor.

Here are some of the main ways an independent contractor and an employee differ:

Independent Contractor vs. Employee		
Factor	**Independent Contractor**	**Employee**
Supervision	Works free from supervision of the person paying for the services, re-sponsible only for the final result. For example, a dishwasher repair person.	The employer provides instructions on what work must be done and how to do the work. For example, a weekly house cleaner.
Benefits	Typically does not receive benefits, such as medical insurance, sick leave and vacations. Responsible for paying his or her own Social Security and taxes.	Employer is responsible for Social Security (which is split with employee), workers' compensation, unemploy-ment and, in some states, disability insurance. Employer may give other benefits as well.
Number of Employers	Offers services to the public at large, not to just one person or company— for example, advertises services to the masses.	Usually works regularly for one or a few employers.
Method of Payment	Paid a set amount for a particular job or an hourly rate for a particular job.	Typically paid a salary or hourly wage for work done on a regular schedule established by employer.
Equipment and Supplies	Provides own equipment and supplies and has own business at a definite location.	Employer provides equipment and supplies and a place to work. Employee does not maintain a discrete business office or location.

In general, the main factor that determines whether a person is an employee or an independent contractor is whether you, the person doing the hiring, has the right to control the work and how it gets done. The people you hire are considered employees when you set the hours, responsibilities, benefits and pay rate. They are considered independent contractors when they own their own businesses and use their own supplies.

You can usually treat a household worker, especially one who works part-time, as an independent contractor for employment tax purposes regardless of whether he or she qualifies as such under the normal IRS tests if the following are true:

- You have consistently treated all workers performing substantially similar duties as independent contractors for federal tax purposes since 1977.
- You have a good reason for treating the workers as independent contractors. One good reason is that treating your workers as independent contractors is a recognized practice of a significant segment of the industry in which the worker is engaged.
- The person you hire has organized his business as a corporation.

Sometimes it's easier to work with an agency. Generally, household workers obtained through an agency or maintenance company are not your employees—they are the employees of their agencies. For example, a babysitter hired through a placement agency or a cleaning person hired through a maintenance company is the employee of the company you deal with as long as the company sets and collects the fee, pays the employee and controls the terms of work.

If your child or elder care worker or housecleaner *is* your employee, you have enhanced legal obligations to her. You also become responsible for a certain amount of paperwork and record-keeping.

Social Security and Income Taxes. If you pay a care worker or housecleaner $1,000 or more in a calendar year, you must make quarterly Social Security (FICA) payments on those wages and withhold the employee's share of FICA. You must prepay the amounts—that is, make the deposits with the IRS before withholding the money from your employee. You do not have to deduct income taxes from wages paid to a household employee for working in your home unless she requests it and you agree to do so.

Unemployment Compensation. If you pay a household employee $1,000 or more in a three-month period, you must pay quarterly taxes under the Federal Unemployment Tax Act (FUTA), using IRS Form 940 or 940-EZ. As with FICA, these amounts must be prepaid.

Workers' Compensation. Your state may require you to provide workers' compensation insurance against job-related injuries or illnesses suffered by your employees. Check with your state department of labor or employment.

Minimum Wage. The federal minimum hourly wage was $5.15 in 1998, but it may go up. Your care and other household workers may be entitled to minimum wage, depending upon their particular hours and earnings. Contact your state department of labor or employment for specific information.

Overtime. Under federal law, most domestic workers (other than live-in workers) qualify for overtime pay. Workers must be paid overtime at a rate of one-and-a-half times the regular rate for all hours worked beyond a 40-hour workweek.

New Hire Reporting Form. Within a short time after you hire someone—20 days or less, depending on your state's rules—you must file a New Hire Reporting Form with a designated state agency. The information on the form becomes part of the National Directory of New Hires, used primarily to locate parents in order to collect child support. Contact your state department of labor or employment to get the forms and information on where to return them.

Federal ID Number. If you hire a household employee, you must obtain a federal employer identification number (EIN), required by the IRS of all employers for tax filing and reporting purposes. Call 800-424-FORM to request IRS Form SS-4, Application for Employer Identification Number.

For information on hiring independent contractors, see *Hiring Independent Contractors: The Employer's Legal Guide*, by Stephen Fishman. For information on hiring and legally managing and firing employees, see the *Legal Guide for Starting and Running a Small Business*, by Fred Steingold. Both are published by Nolo Press.

The IRS has a number of publications that might help you. Call the IRS at 800-424-FORM or visit its Website at http://www.ustreas.irs.gov. Specifically, you may want to look at:

- Form SS-8, which contains IRS definitions of independent contractor and employee
- Form 942, *Employer's Quarterly Tax Return for Household Employees*, for use in reporting Social Security taxes and any federal income tax withheld
- Publication 926, *Employment Taxes for Household Employers*, which describes the major tax responsibilities of employers, and
- Circular E, *Employer's Tax Guide*, for federal income tax withholding tables.

Reality Check

Many families don't follow the law by paying either required taxes or Social Security for household workers, some of whom are undocumented aliens. This chapter is not intended to preach about the law, but to alert you to the laws that affect your relationships with child care and domestic workers. No question, if you don't pay Social Security and meet your other legal obligations as an employer, there may be several negative consequences:

- You may be assessed substantial financial penalties. For example, if your full-time babysitter files for Social Security five years from now and can prove prior earnings, but no Social Security has been paid, the IRS could back-bill you at high interest rates.
- If you don't meet a state requirement to provide workers' compensation insurance, and your housekeeper is injured while on the job and can't work for a few months, you may be in hot water if she files for workers' compensation. You will probably be held liable for the worker's medical costs and a portion of her lost wages, as well as be fined for not having the insurance in the first place.
- If you are a parent paying for a child care worker, you will not be able to take a child care tax credit on your federal income taxes. The credit is based on your work-related expenses and income.

Form 77: Child Care Agreement

A child care provider who takes care of your children in your house, either part-time or full-time, may live out (often called a care giver or babysitter) or live in (an au pair or nanny). The responsibilities of the position may vary widely, from performing a wide range of housekeeping services to only taking care of the children.

If your child care worker will be your employee, make sure your written agreement clearly specifies her responsibilities, hours, benefits, form and schedule of payment and termination policy. The best approach is to be as detailed as possible, even though it means spending a few additional minutes completing this form. Also, ignore the clause confirming independent contractor status.

If your elder care worker is an independent contractor, check off the clause confirming that status and *do not* specify responsibilities, hours or benefits. If you do, you may inadvertently override the independent contractor clause.

Shared In-Home Care

Some families pool their resources and share an in-home child care provider. These arrangements are ideal for neighbors or co-workers with children who are close in age. Just as a written agreement between a family and a child care worker can clarify expectations and prevent conflicts, written understanding between the two families who are sharing a child care provider can accomplish the same objectives. If you share in-home care with another family, be sure you both agree on the key issues before drafting your contract with the child care worker, including location of the care, performance standards, splitting expenses, termination procedures and supervision.

Form 78: Elder Care Agreement

An elder care provider who takes care of your parent or other older relative in your house, either part-time or full-time, may live out or live in. The responsibilities of this position may vary widely, from performing a wide range of housekeeping

services to attending to the personal needs of the older adult.

If your elder care worker will be your employee, make sure your written agreement clearly specifies his responsibilities, hours, benefits, form and schedule of payment and termination policy. The best approach is to be as detailed as possible, even though it means spending a few additional minutes completing this form. Also, ignore the clause confirming independent contractor status.

If your elder care worker is an independent contractor, check off the clause confirming that status and *do not* specify responsibilities, hours or benefits. If you do, you may inadvertently override the independent contractor clause.

Form 79: Housekeeping Services Agreement

If you hire the same person every week to clean your house, a written contract can be a valuable way to clearly define the worker's responsibilities and benefits. If your housecleaner will be your employee, make sure your written agreement clearly specifies the housecleaner's hours, benefits, amount and schedule of payment and termination policy. It should cover regular weekly tasks—for example, cleaning the bathrooms—while special projects such as washing blinds and ironing curtains may require a separate agreement or a special addendum to the contract if you want them completed regularly. Also, ignore the clause confirming independent contractor status.

A regular housecleaner who has his own business or works for a large firm will probably come complete with a contract; in this case, our agreement will be useful as a checklist of key issues. If your housecleaner is an independent contractor but does not provide his or her own contract, use ours, check off the clause confirming that status and *do not* specify responsibilities, hours or benefits. If you do, you may inadvertently override the independent contractor clause. ∎

Living Together

A contract is simply an agreement where one party (person, business or governmental agency) promises to do something in exchange for the other party's reciprocal promise—for example, I'll paint your house if you pay me $6,000. Although usually contracts are formed by the parties themselves, occasionally the law imposes them. Such is the case when people marry. Saying "I do" commits each member of a couple to a well-established set of state laws and rules governing, among other things, the couple's property rights. Although this state-sanctioned "marriage contract" is rarely explained to people before they reach the altar, it is commonly relied on if the couple divorces or if one spouse dies without a will.

Prenuptial contracts are a way people who plan to marry can modify the contract imposed by state law. There is no need to passively accept most of the rules contained in your state's legal code. By signing a prenuptial agreement—or even an agreement drafted during the marriage—a couple can substitute many of their own rules. For example, if instead of adhering to joint ownership rules you want to keep all of your property separate (a common desire of older couples), or you want to agree in advance as to how much support one spouse will pay the other in case of divorce, you can accomplish this in most states by signing a prenuptial contract.

Unmarried couples—gay and straight—become subject to no similar state-imposed legal contract rights when they begin living together. This means that unless they make their own contract as to who owns what, they will conduct their relationship in a legal vacuum. Fortunately, when it comes to financial and property concerns, unmarried couples do have the right to create whatever kind of living-together contracts they want. Sometimes these contracts are made in anticipation of ending a relationship. But more often they are entered into to define rights and enhance one or both partners' peace of mind at either the start of the relationship or when the couple makes a major purchase. Creating a well-drafted agreement not only helps you figure how you really want to own your property, but can also serve as a useful reminder of your agreement if misunderstandings develop later.

Nolo's *Living Together Kit*, by Ralph Warner and Toni Ihara, and *A Legal Guide for Lesbian and Gay Couples*, by Hayden Curry, Denis Clifford and Robin Leonard, contain information and forms designed for unmarried couples to define who owns what property. In addition to half a dozen contracts to deal with different joint house-purchase situations, these books include numerous other sample contracts, including:

- Joint Personal Property Purchase Contract
- Contract to Jointly Own an Item Purchased on Credit in One Partner's Name
- Comprehensive Contract for Long-Term Couples
- Contract to Share Household Expenses
- Joint Project Agreement
- Agreement to Give Each Partner Time Off From Work
- Reciprocal Educational Support Contract
- Homemaker Compensation Contract.

Form 80: Agreement to Keep Property Separate

Especially in the first year or two after they get together, most unmarried couples decide to keep all or most of their property separate. We don't mean that you'll ban your partner from sitting on your couch or that your lover won't let you use her electric mixer. The point is—with the occasional exception, such as a joint account to pay household bills or an agreement to jointly purchase one or more items—that members of the couple agree to keep separate their money, credit and any items of property either purchase.

You may at first think a decision to keep your property ownership separate is so simple there is no need for a written agreement. Think again. Because most states recognize oral contracts between unmarried couples, the lack of a written agreement can be an invitation for one partner to later claim the existence of an oral property sharing agreement. This is just what commonly occurs in the so-called "palimony cases" that regularly hit the headlines.

To avoid the possibility of future misunderstandings concerning property ownership, use Form 80 to confirm that each of you plans to keep his or her property separate.

Form 81: Agreement for a Joint Purchase

When people live together for any extended period of time, it is common for them to jointly purchase one or more pieces of property. This could be a backpack tent, a small boat, a sound system, a new bed or any one of a dozen other things. Whatever type of property is purchased, it is important that your joint ownership agreement be written down. And this is especially true if you have previously signed an agreement to keep the bulk of your property separate (Form 80). Form 81 allows you to record your joint ownership of a particular item quickly and easily.

Form 82: Agreement to Share Property

Especially if you've been together several years or more and have begun to jointly purchase property, you may want to do what a fair number of unmarried couples do—abandon your agreement to keep property separate, and instead treat all property either of you purchases as jointly owned. If this is your understanding, write it down. Use Form 82 to establish that all newly acquired property—except that given to or inherited by one partner—is to be jointly owned by both.

Form 83: Declaration of Legal Name Change

Unmarried partners occasionally prefer to use the same last name, or a hyphenated version of both last names. But doing this means that one or both partners must change their existing name. There are two ways adults can do this; by going to court and obtaining a judge's order or by simply using the new name consistently, in all aspects of your business, personal and social life. Parents wishing to change a minor's name must use the court petition method.

You cannot change your name for a fraudulent purpose. It is illegal to change your name with the intent of avoiding your creditors or to steal the identity of another person. For example, you could become John Clinton or even Billy Bob Clinton, but not William Jefferson Clinton.

Letting official agencies such as the Department of Motor Vehicles and Social Security Administration know about your name change is particularly important to getting it accepted. Once you follow those agencies' procedures—it is usually easiest to start with the DMV—and actually get official documents in your new name, it will be easy to switch over other accounts and documents.

Form 82, the Declaration of Legal Name Change, officially states that you have changed to a new name.

Notary seal. This form contains a notary seal notice. Because you will be using this Declaration to change your name with government agencies, be sure to have the form notarized. Doing this will give the form a great degree of legitimacy.

CHAPTER

13

Preparing for Divorce or Separation

Nearly one-half of all marriages end in divorce. It's no secret that getting a divorce is often a painful, wrenching and expensive process. This chapter can't mend a broken heart—or even tame your spouse's maniacal divorce lawyer—but it can provide you several common-sense and cost-saving tools to use to help you prepare for the end of your marriage or other long-term relationship.

Form 84: Property Division Worksheet

If you've accumulated any property or debts during your marriage (we use marriage as shorthand for any long-term relationship), you'll probably spend considerable time trying to divide them equitably. Some couples do this with remarkable efficiency; others fight for months or even years. Most fall somewhere in between. The process of dividing things up—lawyers often call it "negotiating a divorce settlement"—usually consists of a series of offers and counteroffers. Realize that your decisions become crucial in this phase of the divorce process, because once your property settlement is final, it is costly, time-consuming and often almost impossible to modify. Far better to take the time to negotiate a satisfactory agreement in the first place, rather than trying to alter it later.

Form 84 is for people who have made the decision to separate or divorce and have begun the process of dividing property and debts. Begin by listing your property and debts; you can use the rest of the form for a couple of purposes:

- to arrive at your own property division proposal using the columns labeled Ideal Settlement and Worst Deal I'll Accept; if you are on decent terms with your spouse, have your spouse do the same exercise, and
- to record your joint decisions in the Final Settlement column to use as a draft for preparing your court papers.

Dividing Property at Divorce: Who Owns What?

Divorcing couples who are able to work together (not everyone, to be sure) have the legal right to divide their jointly owned property however they want. But as part of doing this, many couples want to know how a court would separate their property following state law. Here are the basics.

Community Property States. In California, Nevada, Arizona, New Mexico, Idaho, Texas, Louisiana, Washington and Wisconsin, absent a written marital agreement to the contrary, all property acquired by either spouse during the marriage (for example, from the earnings of either) except by gift or inheritance, is community property and belongs to both. At divorce, if the parties don't otherwise agree, a court will divide community property 50-50, although it's common for a family residence to be ordered sold and the profits divided only when the youngest child reaches 18. All property acquired by either spouse before marriage, after permanent separation or during the marriage with assets acquired before the marriage is the separate property of that spouse.

Common Law Property States. In all other states, courts use the legal concept of equitable distribution to divide property no matter whose name it is in. This means that a court must divide property equitably, or fairly. While some courts divide property 50-50, in most situations the split is more like 60-40 or 70-30, with the higher wage earner often receiving more of the property.

More information on dividing property at divorce—including tricky items such as family businesses, pension plans and the value of a professional degree—can be found in *Divorce and Money: How to Make the Best Financial Decisions During Divorce*, by Violet Woodhouse and Victoria F. Collins, with M.C. Blakeman, which also discusses the need for spouses to consider the tax value (basis) of all property—for example, property now worth $100,000 that has tripled in value is not worth the same as property just purchased for $100,000, because the property that has gone up in value is subject to capital gains tax when sold. Contracts for dividing property in the course of a separation of a long-term couple are in *The Living Together Kit*, by Ralph Warner and Toni Ihara, and *A Legal Guide for Lesbian and Gay Couples*, by Hayden Curry, Denis Clifford and Robin Leonard. All books are published by Nolo Press.

Form 85: Custody and Visitation Worksheet

A key aspect of a separation or divorce involving children involves wrestling with custody and visitation. Use Form 85 to identify the key issues involved in raising your kids and, hopefully, to jointly work toward agreeing on a custody and visitation agreement. Some of the more common problems you'll want to be prepared to deal with include the following:

- your children's schooling and religious training
- when a parent with physical custody wants to move to a new area
- when a parent begins living with someone else
- who will provide medical and dental coverage
- who will pay for after-school and other extra-curricular activities, such as summer camp, and
- what to do when one parent believes the other is an inadequate parent.

In the top part of the form, write down the issues you think must be discussed in your negotiations. In the bottom part of the form, specify your hopes and fears, and the final settlement.

It's more important to avoid a fight than it is to be right. No question, agreeing on custody and visitation arrangements is commonly gut-wrenching. But it will be tougher if you insist on an agreement that is completely fair to everyone involved. Instead, focus on the true needs of your kids—one of which is almost certainly to be free from a long and bitter court battle, even if that

means that you accept a custody and visitation plan that is less than fair.

Information and forms key to developing a comprehensive parenting plan to deal with custody and visitation issues can be found in *Child Custody: Building Agreements That Work*, by Mimi Lyster (Nolo Press). This valuable book presents a range of solutions to virtually all child custody problems.

Form 86: Divorce or Separation Agreement

Every state provides some form of "no fault" divorce, meaning that to legally end a marriage neither spouse has to prove that the other was guilty of cruelty, adultery, abandonment or any other nasty behavior. In many states, a spouse wanting a divorce can simply allege incompatibility, irreconcilable differences or something similar. In other states, a couple can get a divorce without alleging fault by living apart for a specified period of time.

Whether you work with a lawyer or do your own divorce using a detailed self-help divorce manual, you'll need to develop an agreement which contains most or all of the information on Form 86. This form can also be extremely useful if yours is a trial separation and you are not yet sure whether you'll divorce. But if you go ahead and initiate the divorce process, you'll need to enter the information you collect here on your state's court-approved forms. Sorry, because state paperwork rules vary too much, we can't give you the final court form. Your lawyer or self-help law book should have one.

State's pre-set child support rules. While you have a lot of flexibility in dividing your property and debts any way you see fit, and a judge usually won't question your decision about child custody or alimony, you don't have the right to exercise that kind of discretion when it comes to child support. Every state has a set of guidelines used to establish the basic minimum, and a judge will not approve a child support amount for less.

Unmarried couples have a special need to work together to divide property. Even if you aren't legally married, you can use Form 86 to record your final agreement. Indeed, to avoid the possibility of a nosy lawsuit over who owns what, you have a big incentive to do so.

Form 87: Consent to Change Child's Name

It is not uncommon for a parent who has remarried and has custody of her child from a previous relationship to want to change the child's last name to conform to the one the parent is now using. Normally the parent—even if she has sole legal custody

of the child—cannot change the child's name without a court order, because the change would affect the rights of the other legal parent. In most states, however, a court order is relatively easy to obtain—even without going through an adoption—if the other legal parent consents or, in some instances, if that parent has legally abandoned the child by failing to visit and support for an extended period.

As a first step to filing a court petition to change your child's name, you can use Form 87 to obtain the non-custodial parent's consent.

Notary seal. This form contains a notary seal notice. Because you will be using this Consent Form in support of a court petition, be sure to have the form notarized. ■

CHAPTER

14

Settling Legal Disputes

Becoming involved in any legal dispute can be harrowing. Many people lose sleep, time and money trying to right their wrongs, even informally. Then, take it to the next step—the prospect of going to court and facing an unpredictable court trial can scare even the bravest person. That's why it's so easy to appreciate the traditional Mexican curse that says, "May you have a lawsuit in which you know you are right."

Fortunately, most legal disputes are resolved long before anyone sees the inside of a courtroom—one person demands a settlement, the other person counters and the negotiations continue from there. If settlement still proves illusive, it's common to turn for help to a mediator who will attempt to help the parties come to an agreement. Whether the parties arrive at their own compromise settlement or do so with the help of a neutral third party, this chapter presents useful tools you can use to try and settle your dispute. And if you do settle, it also provides several releases you or the other party should sign so neither of you risks being hauled into court after you write or receive the check you believe settles the matter.

Additional information and sample forms for settling disputes can be found in *Everybody's Guide to Small Claims Court*, by Ralph Warner, and *Mediate Your Dispute*, by Peter Lovenheim. For a detailed discussion of representing yourself in court, see *Represent Yourself in Court,* by Paul Bergman and Sarah Berman-Barrett. All titles are published by Nolo Press.

answer seems to be that a written document often acts like a slap in the face to convince the other party you really are serious about going to court if you can't settle the matter. Also, your demand letter gives you a chance to carefully organize the facts of your case. This means if you wind up in mediation, arbitration or court (such as small claims court), you will have already done much of your preparation.

When writing your demand letter, here are some suggestions:

- Use a typewriter or computer.
- Be polite. Avoid personally attacking your adversary.
- Concisely review the main facts of the dispute—even though your adversary knows them, a judge, mediator or other third party may eventually see your letter.
- Ask for exactly what you want—the return of property, $1,000 or whatever.
- If you are willing to try mediation, make that clear. (Mediation is usually a great way for disputing people to resolve their differences.)
- Conclude by stating that if the problem isn't resolved within a set period of time (seven to ten days is often good), you will take further action, such as filing a court case, if necessary.
- Keep a copy of your letter in your files.

Sample demand letters can be found in *Everybody's Guide to Small Claims Court*, by Ralph Warner, and *Represent Yourself in Court,* by Paul Bergman and Sarah Berman-Barrett. Both are published by Nolo Press.

Form 88: Demand Letter

Assuming your dispute has escalated to the point where you and the other party can no longer civilly discuss a compromise, your next step in trying to resolve it is to send a demand letter clearly stating what you want. Studies show that in as many as one-third of all disputes, your letter will serve as a catalyst to arriving at a settlement. It is fair to ask why demand letters work so frequently to resolve disputes that couldn't simply be talked out. The

Form 89: Request for Warranty Coverage

Some legal disputes come with built-in solutions, or at least built-in first steps that might lead to the problem going away. For example, most new and even some used products you buy come with a warranty that in theory, at least, offers protection if the product fails during the warranty period. Unfortunately, if the manufacturer or seller resists meeting its obligations, understanding how to take advantage of your rights under warranty law can often be extremely confusing, even to lawyers. But here are the basic rules:

- If a new or used product comes with a written warranty from either the seller or the manufacturer, you have the right to rely on it.
- If instead of or in addition to a written warranty a seller makes a statement describing a product's feature—for example, "this sleeping bag will keep you warm at 25 degrees below zero"—and you rely on the statement to buy the product, the statement is an express warranty that you have a right to rely on.
- In addition to all other warranties, for most purchases you automatically have an implied warranty of general fitness for the intended use or "merchantability"—for example, that a lawnmower will cut grass. If it doesn't, you should be able to return it for a full refund.

If a warranty is breached—for example, a TV set with a six-month written warranty on parts and labor breaks after two weeks' time—call or stop by the store and ask for redress. Many reputable sellers will replace or repair the item immediately, no questions asked.

If the seller won't help, use Form 89 to formally notify the seller and manufacturer in writing of your demand for them to make good under the warranty. Give them a reasonable chance—such as 30 days— to make necessary repairs or replace the defective product. If they fail to do so, consider further action. Often this will involve filing your case in small claims court or, if the dollar amount is too high, formal court.

Form 90: Accident Claim Worksheet

Many types of legal disputes involve claims against a person, business or insurance company arising out of an accident where you and your property were injured. Use Form 90 to keep track of the information you will need to process this type of claim. It is for your personal reference and is not intended to become part of your claim.

Get witness statements in writing as soon as possible. Don't count on an eyewitness remembering what she saw, especially given the fact that the witness is likely to be contacted by the other party. Ask the person to make and sign a note as to what she saw as soon after the accident as possible.

Additional information and sample forms for settling a claim with an insurance company can be found in *How to Win Your Personal Injury Claim*, by Joseph Matthews (Nolo Press).

Releases

A common means of settling minor disputes (anything from an argument about an unpaid loan or minor fender bender to a golf ball crashing through a window) is for one party to pay the other a sum of money in exchange for giving up his legal claim. Another way to settle a claim is for the person in the wrong to do something of benefit for the other. For example, if your neighbor's dog destroys your garden, you might agree to take no further action if your neighbor agrees to replace your most valuable plants and build a fence.

In either situation, you'll want to write out your agreement in the form of a contract commonly called a release. Essentially, a release usually consists of no more than one party saying, "I'll pay a certain amount or do a certain thing," and the other party saying that, "in exchange, I'll forever give up my legal claim." For a court to be willing to enforce a release, however, it must satisfy two contract law requirements:

- **Voluntary.** Each side must enter into the agreement voluntarily. For example, if a party was coerced into signing an agreement because of the other's threats or intimidation, a court may consider it involuntary and therefore unenforceable. Courts are quite leery about tossing out a release for this reason, however. For example, one party telling the other "I'll sue for $100,000 tomorrow if you don't agree to this release" is not the kind of threat that will make a release unenforceable.

• **Arrived at fairly.** Certain basic rights are often deemed too important to contract away. This is especially true if a party is tricked into signing a release (signed two hours after an accident while still groggy) or doesn't understand the meaning of the document or the rights he is waiving (can't speak English). If fraud, misrepresentation or excessive pressure has been used to arrive at a settlement, a court may refuse to enforce a release.

Releases are powerful documents. If you sign one forever giving up a legal claim in exchange for $500 and six months later learn that the extent of your damage is much greater than you realized when you signed the release, you are out of luck unless a court declares the release unenforceable for one of the above reasons.

Practically, in most situations where both sides understand the dispute and the consequences of various settlement options, a release can be safely signed with the knowledge that the dispute will be finally laid to rest. But it is always wise to ask the following questions before you sign on the dotted line:

• Do both parties understand the issues that underlie the dispute?
• Do both parties fully understand what the release accomplishes?

If the answer to these questions is yes, it's wise to ask another two questions, but this time just of yourself:

• Do I understand the legal result I am likely to obtain and the time and dollars I am likely to expend to obtain it if I choose to go to court rather than accept the release and settle?
• Have I discussed my decision to sign the release with someone with good business sense or, if a lot of money is involved, an attorney with practical experience in this field?

Especially if big bucks are at stake and the answer to either of the second two questions is "no," or even a waffling "maybe," do the necessary homework before agreeing to release the other party from liability.

If you were injured. As a general rule, do not sign a release based on a personal injury until a doctor has examined you, clearly established the scope of your injury and unequivocally stated you have fully recovered.

This chapter contains several release forms:
• General Release—to settle a dispute over a contract, debt or minor personal injury when only one party is alleged to have been injured or suffered damage.
• General Mutual Release—to settle a dispute over a contract, debt or minor personal injury where both parties claim the other is at fault and that each has suffered damage or injury as a result.
• Release for Damage to Real Estate—to settle a dispute between landowners where one owner's property is damaged by another owner's action or inaction.
• Release for Property Damage in Auto Accident—to settle a dispute over minor property damage from an auto accident. Do not use it if personal injuries are involved.
• Release for Personal Injury—to settle a dispute when one party has suffered a relatively minor personal injury because of another's actions.
• Mutual Release of Contract Claims—to settle a disagreement that arises from the breach of a written or oral contract.

One note of terminology: A person with the claim who releases the other is called the releasor. The person accused of the wrongdoing who agrees to pay money or do something in exchange for the release is the releasee.

Form 91: General Release

The first release, Form 91, is appropriate for settling personal disputes over a contract, debt or minor personal injury when only one party is alleged to have been injured or suffered damage.

You want the release to be binding on others. If the releasor dies, you want the release to be binding on her heirs, and so our release forms contain such a clause (the one that contains the jargon about successors, assigns and heirs). In addition, in all community property states and some others, one spouse is generally liable for the debts of the other, even if the first spouse had nothing to do with the event leading up to the liability. For that reason, our release forms are binding on spouses and require the spouse's signature. If the releasor is not married, type or write "N/A" on the spouse line.

Form 92: General Mutual Release

Form 92 is appropriate for settling disputes over a contract, debt or minor personal injury where both parties claim the other is at fault and that each has suffered damage or injury as a result. Here the main point is often to trade legal releases, although it is not unusual for the person who suffered the more serious loss (or who was less at fault) to also receive a cash payment.

This release uses the legal term "consideration," which simply means something of value promised or given in exchange for something else of value either handed over when the release is signed or promised. To be binding, all contracts—including releases—require an exchange of things of value (consideration). This can be money or property or a promise to do or not to do something. Here are several examples of situations where things of value ("consideration") are exchanged:

- In exchange for agreeing not to file a lawsuit, Party 1 will receive from Party 2 the sum of $500, to be paid by *[date]*.
- In exchange for agreeing not to file a lawsuit, Party 2 will receive from Party 1 six months, free use of the spa facility owned and operated by Party 1.
- In exchange for Party 1 agreeing not to sue Party 2, Party 2 agrees not to sue Party 1.

Form 93: Release for Damage to Real Estate

Form 93 is appropriate for settling disputes between landowners that arise when one owner's property is damaged by another owner's action or inaction—common examples include one neighbor's tree overhanging another's yard or pool, or an uphill neighbor digging a ditch to divert rain runoff onto a downhill neighbor's property. And, of course, walls, fences, view-blocking trees and noise can all lead to serious disagreements between neighbors.

 Before you settle a neighbor dispute, it will help for you to understand the legal issues—for example, if a tree grows on the border, which neighbor owns it? For answers to that and similar questions, see *Neighbor Law*, by Cora Jordan (Nolo Press). You might also consider getting help in settling a neighbor dispute from a community mediation project. Additional information is contained in *Mediate Your Dispute*, by Peter Lovenheim (Nolo Press).

Form 94: Release for Property Damage in Auto Accident

Use Form 94 to settle claims over minor property damage from an auto accident. Do not use it if personal injuries are involved. In that case, use Form 95.

Form 95: Release for Personal Injury

Use Form 95 when one party has suffered a relatively minor personal injury because of another's actions. We stressed in the introduction to this chapter that releases involving personal injuries should only be signed when the parties are sure that the scope of the injury is fully known—for example, an injury has completely healed and your doctor is convinced there will be no further problem. It is almost never wise to sign soon after an injury—you never know what problems might develop later.

Here are a few examples of language describing an injury for use in Clause 2:

- Dog bite wounds sustained on both arms after she was attacked by releasee's dog, Roscoe.
- A sprained left ankle he sustained after tripping on a loose step at releasee's home.
- Cuts he sustained from a shattered window when a baseball hit by releasee's son broke a window in releasor's home.

Form 96: Mutual Release of Contract Claims

This final release can be used to settle a disagreement that arises from the breach of a written or oral contract. Unlike the general release (Form 91) or the general mutual release (Form 92), this release is only useful to deal with contract disputes. ■

Dealing With Direct Marketers and Telemarketers

The telephone is—depending on one's mood—a boon or a scourge of modern life. One of its undeniably bad aspects is its wide use by telemarketers. Fortunately, a federal law called the Telephone Consumer Protection Act, 47 U.S.C. § 227, puts some limits on how telemarketers must act. Some provisions are part of an effort to curb telemarketing fraud; others are aimed at reducing annoyance to consumers.

For example, before you pay (usually by credit card) for something purchased from a telemarketer, the seller must accurately state the total cost, quantity of goods or services and all other important conditions and restrictions. A seller must also explain its refund policy or state that it doesn't allow a refund, exchange or cancellation.

Luckily, few of us are the subject of telemarketing fraud. More likely, our biggest beef is that we receive annoying telephone calls just around dinner time. At least telemarketers can't legally call before 8 a.m. or after 9 p.m. unless they have your permission. They also must put you on a "do not call list" if you so request. And that's where this chapter comes in—we show you how to tell a company to stop calling you and what to do if it doesn't.

Sometimes, your mailbox can become just as irritating as your telephone. For most of us, catalogues, credit card offers and all kinds of other junk mail take up more space than our first-class mail. Again, fortunately some federal laws (recent amendments to the Fair Credit Reporting Act restrict credit bureaus' use of your name for marketing purposes) can help you get off various mailing lists. In this chapter, we provide you with the easy-to-use forms to accomplish this.

Form 97: Notice to Remove Name From List

It's quite possible that you want to receive some catalogues, promotional mailings or telemarketing phone calls, but not others. To get yourself onto only the lists you want to be on requires a two step-approach. First, send Form 97 to all companies that collect names in order to sell them to direct

marketers and telemarketers, telling them to remove your name. Then, send Form 98 to only those businesses whose materials or phone calls you want to receive.

Dozens of companies gather names and addresses to sell to direct marketers and telemarketers. While some lists are larger than others, you will get yourself off of most lists if you send Form 97 to:

- Experian Opt Out, P.O. Box 919, Allen, TX 75013
- Equifax Opt Out, P.O. Box 740123, Atlanta, GA 30374
- Trans Union Opt Out Requests, TransMark, Inc., 555 West Adams Street, Chicago, IL 60661
- Mail Preference Service, Direct Marketing Association, P.O. Box 9008, Farmingdale, NY 11735
- Polk Opt Out Program, List Order Services, 1621 18th Street, Denver, CO 80202
- Donnelley Marketing, Inc., Database Operations, 1235 N. Avenue, Nevada, IA 50201.

We can't list here every company that maintains a marketing mailing list. But someone else has. An excellent resource for getting off of direct marketing and telemarketing lists is *Stop Junk Mail (Telemarketing and Spamming, Too) Forever*, by Marc Eisenson, Nancy Castleman, Marcy Ross and the "Stop Junk Mail-Man" ($3.95, Good Advice Press, Box 78, Elizaville, NY 12523).

If your junk mail arrives in more than one name. More than one adult in the house might be getting junk mail, or you may be receiving junk mail in more than one name. Form 97 allows you to list up to three names to have removed from the marketing lists.

Form 98: Notice to Add or Retain Name but Not Sell or Trade It

After sending Form 97 to all businesses that sell lists of names to direct marketers and telemarketers to get your name off lists, use Form 98 to get onto or keep yourself on the lists maintained by businesses whose mailings and/or phone calls you do want to receive.

Form 99: Telemarketing Phone Call Log

A federal law, the Telephone Consumer Protection Act, requires every telemarketer to keep a list of consumers who say that they do not want to be called again. The law has some real teeth: If you tell a telemarketer not to call you, but you get another call within 12 months, you can sue for up to $500. If the court finds that the telemarketer willfully or knowingly violated the law, the court can award you up to $1,500. Most states' small claims courts allow claims of at least $2,000, so you can sue on your own, without hiring a lawyer.

Use Form 99 to keep a log of telemarketing phone calls. You will need to note the date, the time of the call, the company, the telemarketer's name (probably a fake, but write it down anyway), the product being sold and the fact that you stated "put me on a 'do not call' list." You will need this evidence to prove that you received more than one call from the same telemarketing company.

Form 100: Notice to Put Name on "Do Not Call" List

Proving that a telemarketer willfully violated the law by calling you more than once may be difficult. One way you can generate evidence of a company's willful act is to *always* follow up your phone call by

stating "Put me on your 'do not call' list," with a letter stating the same. You can use Form 100 for this purpose. You will need to find out the mailing address of the company in order to send your letter. Here are a few suggestions:

- Ask one of the telemarketers who calls you for the address. (The caller may not have it, because telemarketers often work for independent companies that make telemarketing calls for businesses, not the businesses themselves.)
- If it's a local company, or you know the city in which a nonlocal company is located, get the phone number from directory assistance or your phone book; call and ask for the mailing address.
- Consult *Hoover's Handbook of American Business: Profiles of Major U.S. Companies.* Your local library should have a copy, or you can visit the website at http://www.hoovers.com. The site contains a lot of self-promotional ads and other companies' banners, but you can get the information you need if you keep trying.

Form 101: Demand for Damages for Excessive Calls

You can use Form 101 after you receive a second (or third or fourth) telemarketing call from the same business. You will need to find out the mailing address of the company in order to send your letter. See the discussion that precedes Form 100 for some suggestions on obtaining the address. ■

APPENDIX

A

Using the Forms Disk

The sample forms provided in the Appendix B are also included on a 3½" floppy disk in the back of the book.

This forms disk is formatted for the PC (MS-DOS), and can be used by any PC running Windows or DOS. If you use a Mac, you must have a Super Disk drive and PC Exchange, or a similar utility, to use this disk. These files can be opened, filled in and printed out with your word processing program or text editor.

⚠️ **The disk does not contain software and you do not need to install any files.** The forms disk contains only files that can be opened and edited using a word processor. This is not a software program. See below and the README.TXT file included on the disk for additional instructions on how to use these files.

How to View the README File

If you do not know how to view the file README.TXT, insert the forms disk into your computer's floppy disk drive and follow these instructions:

- Windows 95: (1) On your PC's desktop, double-click the My Computer icon; (2) double-click the icon for the floppy disk drive into which the forms disk was inserted; (3) double-click the file README.TXT.
- Windows 3.1: (1) Open File Manager; (2) double-click the icon for the floppy disk drive into which the forms disk was inserted; (3) double-click the file README.TXT.
- Macintosh: (1) On your Mac desktop, double-click the icon for the floppy disk that you inserted; (2) double-click on the file README.TXT.
- DOS: At the DOS prompt, type EDIT A:README.TXT and press the Enter key.

While the README file is open, print it out by using the Print command in the File menu.

A. Copying the Disk Files Onto Your Computer

Before you do anything else, copy the files from the forms disk onto your hard disk. Then work on these copies only. This way the original files and instructions will be untouched and can be used again. Instructions on how to copy files are provided below.

In accordance with U.S. copyright laws, remember that copies of the disk and its files are for your personal use only.

Insert the forms disk and do the following:

1. Windows 95 Users

(These instructions assume that the A: drive is the source you want to copy from and that the C: drive is the location you want to copy the files to.)

Step 1. Double-click the My Computer icon to open the My Computer window.

Step 2. Double-click the A: drive icon in the My Computer window to open the drive window.

Step 3. First, choose Select All from the Edit menu (Ctrl+A). Then choose Copy from the Edit menu (Ctrl+C). Then close the drive window.

Step 4. Double-click the My Computer icon to open the My Computer window.

Step 5. Double-click the C: drive icon in the My Computer window to open the drive window.

Step 6. Choose New... from the File menu, then choose Folder to create a new, untitled folder on the C drive.

Step 7. Type "101 Law Forms" to rename the untitled folder.

Step 8. Double-click on the "101 Law Forms" folder icon to open that folder.

Step 9. Choose Paste from the Edit menu (Ctrl+V).

2. Windows 3.1 Users

(These instructions assume that the A: drive is the source you want to copy from and that the C: drive is the location you want to copy the files to.)

Step 1. Open File Manager.

Step 2. Double-click the A drive icon at the top of the File Manager window.

Step 3. Choose Select Files... from the File menu to open the Select Files dialog box.

Step 4. First, click the Select button to select all the files on the floppy disk. Then click the Close button to close the Select Files dialog box.

Step 5. Choose Copy... from the File menu to open the Copy dialog box.

Step 6. In the TO box, type C:\101FORMS and click OK. Click OK again when you're asked if you want to copy the selected files to the C:\101FORMS directory.

3. Macintosh Users

Step 1. If the 101FORMS folder is open, close it.

Step 2. Click on the 101FORMS disk icon and drag it onto the icon of your hard disk.

Step 3. Read the message to make sure you want to go ahead, then click OK.

4. DOS Users

(These instructions assume that the A: drive is the source you want to copy from and that the C: drive is the location you want to copy the files to.)

Step 1. To create a directory named "101FORMS" on your C: hard disk drive, type the following at the DOS prompt:

C: <ENTER>

CD\ <ENTER>

MD 101FORMS <ENTER>

Step 2. To change to the 101FORMS directory you just created, type:

CD 101FORMS <ENTER>

Step 3. To copy all the files from the floppy disk (in your A: drive) to the current directory, at the C:\101FORMS> prompt, type:

XCOPY A:*.* /s <ENTER>

All of the files in all directories on the floppy disk will be copied to the 101FORMS directory on your C: drive.

B. Creating Your Documents With the Forms Disk Files

This disk contains all forms in two file types (or formats):

- the standard ASCII text format (TXT), and
- rich text format (RTF).

For example, Form 13, Codicil for a Simple Will, discussed in Chapter 2 is on the files FORM13.RTF and FORM13.TXT, located in the folder (or directory) CHAPT02.

ASCII text files can be read by every word processor or text editor including DOS Edit, all flavors of MS Word and WordPerfect (including Macintosh), Windows Notepad, Write and WordPad, and Macintosh SimpleText and TeachText.

RTF files have the same text as the ASCII files, but have additional formatting. They can be read by most recent word processing programs including all versions of MS Word for Windows and Macintosh, WordPad for Windows 95, and recent versions of WordPerfect for Windows and Macintosh.

To use a form on the disk to create your documents you must: (1) open a file in your word processor or text editor; (2) edit the form by filling in the required information; (3) print it out; (4) save your revised file.

The following are general instructions on how to do this. Each word processor, however, uses different commands to open, format, save and print documents. Please read your word processor's manual for specific instructions on performing these tasks.

Do not call nolo's technical support if you have questions on how to use your word processor.

Step 1: Opening a File

To open a file in your word processor, you need to start your word processing program and open the file from within the program. This process usually entails going to the File menu and choosing the Open command. This opens a dialog box where you will tell the program (1) the type of file you want to open (either *.TXT or *.RTF) and (2) the location and name of the file (you will need to navigate through the directory tree to get to the folder/directory on your hard disk that you created and copied the disk's files to). If these directions are unclear you will need to look through the manual for your word processing program—Nolo's technical support department will NOT be able to help you with the use of your word processing program.

Which File Format Should You Use?

If you are not sure which file format to use with your word processor, try opening the RTF files first. Rich text files (RTF) contain most of the formatting included in the sample forms found in this book and in Appendix B. Most current Windows and Macintosh word processing programs, such as Microsoft Word or WordPerfect, can read RTF files.

If you are unable to open the RTF file in your word processor, or a bunch of "garbage" characters appear on screen when you do, then use the TXT files instead. All word processors and text editors can read TXT files, which contain only text, tabs and carriage returns; all other formatting and special characters have been stripped.

Windows and Mac users can also open a file more directly by double-clicking on it. Use File Manager (Windows 3.1), My Computer or Windows Explorer (Windows 95) or the Finder (Macintosh) to go to the folder/directory you created and copied the disk's files to. Then, double-click on the specific file you want to open. If you click on an RTF file and you have a program installed that "understands" RTF, your word processor should launch and load the file that you double-clicked on. If the file isn't loaded, or if it contains a bunch of garbage characters, use your word processor's Open command, as described above, to open the TXT file instead. If you directly double-click on a TXT file, it will load into a basic text editor like Notepad or SimpleText rather than your word processor.

Step 2: Editing Your Document

Fill in the appropriate information according to the instructions and sample agreements in the book. Underlines are used to indicate where you need to enter your information, frequently followed by instructions in brackets. Be sure to delete the underlines and instructions from your edited document. If you do not know how to use your word processor to edit a document, you will need to look through the manual for your word processing program—Nolo's technical support department will NOT be able to help you with the use of your word processing program.

Editing Forms That Have Checkboxes

Some of the forms have checkboxes before text. The checkboxes indicate:

- optional text, which you choose whether to include or exclude
- alternative text, where you select one alternative to include and exclude the other alternatives.

If you are using the tear-out forms in Appendix B, you simply mark the appropriate box to make your choice.

If you are using the forms disk, however, we recommend that instead of marking the checkboxes, you do the following:

Optional text

If you **don't want** to include optional text, just delete it from your document.

If you **do want** to include optional text, just leave it in your document.

In either case, delete the checkbox itself as well as the italicized instructions that the text is optional.

Alternative text

First delete all the alternatives that you do not want to include.

Then delete the remaining checkbox as well as the italicized instructions that you need to select one of the alternatives provided.

Step 3: Printing Out the Document

Use your word processor's or text editor's Print command to print out your document. If you do not know how to use your word processor to print a document, you will need to look through the manual for your word processing program—Nolo's technical support department will NOT be able to help you with the use of your word processing program.

Step 4: Saving Your Document

After filling in the form, do a "save as" and give the file a new name. *If you do not rename the file, the underlines that indicate where you need to enter your information will be lost and you will not be able to create a new document with this file without recopying the original file from the floppy disk. Make sure never to edit the original file on your floppy.*

If you do not know how to use your word processor to save a document, you will need to look through the manual for your word processing program—Nolo's technical support department will NOT be able to help you with the use of your word processing program. ■

Tear-Out Forms

Form	Instructions Begin on Page

Form	Instructions Begin on Page

Guardianship Authorization for Care of Minor

Minor

Name: _____

Permanent address: _____

Phone: _____ Birthdate: _____ Age: _____

School: _____

Address: _____

Phone: _____ Grade: _____

Doctor (or HMO): _____

Address: _____

Phone: _____ Medical #: _____

Dentist: _____

Address: _____

Phone: _____ Ins. #: _____

Parent 1

Name: _____

Address: _____

_____

Home phone: _____ Work phone: _____

Fax: _____ E-mail: _____

Parent 2

Name: _____

Address: _____

_____

Home phone: _____ Work phone: _____

Fax: _____ E-mail: _____

Guardian

Name: _____

Address: _____

_____

Home phone: _____ Work phone: _____

Fax: _____ E-mail: _____

Relationship to minor: _____

In case of emergency, if the guardian cannot be reached, please contact: _____

_____

Home phone: _____ Work phone: _____

Fax: _____ E-mail: _____

Authorization and Consent of Parent(s)

1. I affirm that the minor child named above is my child and that I have legal custody of that child.

2. I give my full authorization and consent for my child to live with and travel with the guardian, and for the guardian to establish a place of residence for my child.

3. I give the guardian permission to act in my place and make decisions pertaining to my child's educational, recreational and religious activities.

4. I give the guardian permission to authorize medical and dental care for my child, including but not limited to medical examinations, x-rays, tests, anesthesia, surgical operations, hospital care or other treatments that in the guardian's sole opinion are needed or useful for my child. Such medical treatment shall be provided only upon the advice of and supervision by a physician, surgeon, dentist or other medical practitioner licensed to practice in the United States.

5. This authorization shall cover the period from _____, _____, to

   _____, _____ .

6. While the guardian cares for my child, the costs of my child's upkeep, living expenses, medical and dental expenses shall be paid as follows: _____

   _____

   _____

   _____

I declare under penalty of perjury under the laws of the state of _____
that the foregoing is true and correct.

_____   _____
Parent 1's signature   Date

_____   _____
Parent 2's signature   Date

Consent of Guardian

I solemnly affirm that I will assume full responsibility for the minor who will live with me during the period designated above. I agree to make necessary decisions and to provide consent for the minor as set forth in the above Authorization and Consent of Parent(s). I also agree to the terms of the costs of the minor's upkeep, living expenses, medical and dental expenses as set forth in the above Authorization and Consent of Parent(s).

I declare under penalty of perjury under the laws of the state of _____
that the foregoing is true and correct.

_____   _____
Guardian's signature   Date

[Notary Seal]

Authorization for a Minor's Medical Treatment

Minor

Name: _____

Birthdate: _____ Age: _____ Grade in school: _____

Doctor (or HMO): _____

Address: _____

Phone: _____ Medical #: _____

Allergies (medications): _____

Allergies (other): _____

Conditions for which child is currently receiving treatment: _____

_____

_____

Other important medical information: _____

_____

_____

_____

_____

Dentist: _____

Address: _____

Phone: _____ Ins. #: _____

Parent 1

Name: _____

Address: _____

_____

Home phone: _____ Work phone: _____

Fax: _____ E-mail: _____

Parent 2

Name: _____

Address: _____

_____

Home phone: _____ Work phone: _____

Fax: _____ E-mail: _____

Other Adult to Notify in Case Parent(s) Cannot Be Reached

Name: _____

Address: _____

_____

Home phone: _____ Work phone: _____

Fax: _____ E-mail: _____

Authorization and Consent of Parent(s)

I affirm that the minor child indicated above is my child and that I have legal custody of that child. I give my authorization and consent for _____

[name of supervising adult], who is ☐ employed by ☐ a volunteer for _____

_____ *[name*

of organization], to authorize necessary medical or dental care for my child. Such medical treatment shall be provided upon the advice of and supervision by any physician, surgeon, dentist or other medical practitioner licensed to practice in the United States.

_____   _____

Parent 1's signature   Date

_____   _____

Parent 2's signature   Date

[Notary Seal]

Authorization for Foreign Travel With Minor

To Whom It May Concern:

This letter concerns my child, _____

[name of child], a United States citizen and a minor born on _____ , _____ ,

[child's date of birth], who carries a United States passport with the number _____ .

I affirm that I have legal custody of my child, and that there are no pending divorce or child custody

proceedings that involve my child. I give my full authorization and consent for my child to travel outside

of the United States with _____

[name of adult with whom child will travel], who is the _____ *[state adult's*

relationship with child] of my child. The purpose of the travel is _____

_____

[specify vacation, touring, to visit relatives, to accompany adult on business trip or other reason].

I have approved the following travel plans:

Dates of travel	Destinations/Accommodations
_____	_____
_____	_____
_____	_____
_____	_____
_____	_____
_____	_____

Furthermore, I hereby authorize_____

[name of adult with whom child will travel] to modify the travel plans specified above as he/she deems

necessary.

I declare under penalty of perjury under the laws of the state of _____

that the foregoing is true and correct.

_____   _____

Parent 1's Signature   Date

_____

Print name

_____   _____

Parent 2's Signature   Date

_____

Print name

[Notary Seal]

Pet Care Agreement

Owner

Name: _____

Home address: _____

_____

Home phone: _____ Work phone: _____

Fax: _____ E-mail: _____

Temporary address while pet is in Caregiver's care: _____

[if more than one, attach itinerary]

Phone: _____ Fax: _____ E-mail: _____

Caregiver

Name: _____

Home address: _____

_____

Home phone: _____ Work phone: _____

Fax: _____ E-mail: _____

1. Pets

Caregiver will take care of these pets: _____

_____

_____

[list name, species, breed, age and, if necessary, any distinguishing characteristics]

2. Dates of Care

Caregiver will care for the animals from _____ *[beginning date]*

☐ until_____ *[ending date]*. OR

☐ until Owner notifies Caregiver otherwise.

3. Compensation

Owner will reimburse Caregiver for reasonable out-of-pocket expenses, including veterinary bills, incurred while caring for the animals. Owner will also compensate Caregiver as follows *[select none, one or both]*:

☐ payment of $ _____

☐ other: _____

4. Care Instructions

Caregiver will exercise reasonable care to protect the animals from sickness, injury and theft, and will follow these instructions:

Food

Type of food: _____

Amount: _____ Frequency: _____

Special instructions: _____

_____

Medication

1. Name:_____ Dosage:_____

   Special instructions: _____

2. Name:_____ Dosage:_____

   Special instructions: _____

Exercise

Type: _____

Special instructions: _____

Veterinary Care

Name: _____

Address: _____

Phone: _____ Veterinary insurance policy: _____

Special instructions: _____

Grooming

Frequency and type:_____

Special instructions: _____

5. Emergency Contact

If Caregiver becomes unable to care for the pets, Caregiver will contact _____

_____ to try to make substitute arrangements for their care.

If arrangements cannot be made, Caregiver will turn the pets over to _____

_____ and promptly notify Owner.

6. Disputes

If any dispute arises under this agreement, the parties agree to select a mutually agreeable third party to help them mediate it, and to share equally any costs of mediation.

7. Entire Agreement

This agreement contains the entire agreement between Owner and Caregiver. Any modifications must be in writing.

8. Additional Terms

_____

_____

_____

Signatures

_____

Owner's name

_____   _____

Signature   Date

_____

Caregiver's name

_____   _____

Signature   Date

Authorization to Drive a Motor Vehicle

Vehicle Owner (Owner)

Name: _____

Address: _____

_____

Home phone: _____ Work phone: _____

Fax: _____ E-mail: _____

Make, model and year of vehicle: _____

Vehicle license plate number: _____

State of registration: _____ Vehicle registration number: _____

Insurance company: _____

Insurance policy number: _____

Person Authorized to Drive (Borrower)

Name: _____

Address: _____

_____

Home phone: _____ Work phone: _____

Fax: _____ E-mail: _____

Motor vehicle insurance company (if any): _____

Insurance policy number (if any): _____

Authorization and Consent of Vehicle Owner

I am the lawful owner of the vehicle indicated above. I give my authorization and consent for Borrower to use this vehicle as follows:

Dates of use: _____

Area in which vehicle may be used: _____

Any restrictions or conditions on use: _____

I declare under penalty of perjury under the laws of the state _____
of that the foregoing is true and correct.

_____   _____
Owner's signature   Date

Power of Attorney for Finances (Full Power)

WARNING TO PERSON EXECUTING THIS DOCUMENT

THIS IS AN IMPORTANT LEGAL DOCUMENT. IT CREATES A POWER OF ATTORNEY FOR FINANCES. BEFORE EXECUTING THIS DOCUMENT, YOU SHOULD KNOW THESE IMPORTANT FACTS:

THIS DOCUMENT MAY PROVIDE THE PERSON YOU DESIGNATE AS YOUR ATTORNEY-IN-FACT WITH BROAD LEGAL POWERS, INCLUDING THE POWERS TO MANAGE, DISPOSE, SELL AND CONVEY YOUR REAL AND PERSONAL PROPERTY AND TO BORROW MONEY USING YOUR PROPERTY AS SECURITY FOR THE LOAN.

THESE POWERS WILL EXIST UNTIL YOU REVOKE OR TERMINATE THIS POWER OF ATTORNEY. IF YOU SO STATE, THESE POWERS WILL CONTINUE TO EXIST EVEN IF YOU BECOME DISABLED OR INCAPACITATED. YOU HAVE THE RIGHT TO REVOKE OR TERMINATE THIS POWER OF ATTORNEY AT ANY TIME.

THIS DOCUMENT DOES NOT AUTHORIZE ANYONE TO MAKE MEDICAL OR OTHER HEALTHCARE DECISIONS FOR YOU.

IF THERE IS ANYTHING ABOUT THIS FORM THAT YOU DO NOT UNDERSTAND, YOU SHOULD ASK A LAWYER TO EXPLAIN IT TO YOU.

1. Principal and Attorney-in-Fact

I, _____ [your name],

of _____ [your city and state],

appoint _____

[name of your attorney-in-fact] as my attorney-in-fact to act for me in any lawful way with respect to the powers delegated in Part 5 below. If that person (or all of those persons, if I name more than one) is unable or unwilling to serve as attorney-in-fact, I appoint the following alternates, to serve alone in the order named:

First Alternate

Name: _____

Address: _____

_____

Second Alternate

Name: _____

Address: _____

_____

2. Authorization of Attorneys-in-Fact

If I have named more than one attorney-in-fact, they are authorized to act:

☐ jointly.

☐ independently.

3. Delegation of Authority

☐ My attorney-in-fact may delegate, in writing, any authority granted under this power of attorney to a person he or she selects. Any such delegation shall state the period during which it is valid and specify the extent of the delegation.

☐ My attorney-in-fact may not delegate any authority granted under this power of attorney.

4. Effective Dates

This power of attorney is not durable. It shall begin on _____ , _____ , and shall continue until terminated in writing, or until _____ , whichever comes first.

5. Powers of the Attorney-in-Fact

I grant my attorney-in-fact power to act on my behalf in the following matters, as indicated by my initials next to each granted power or on line (14), granting all the listed powers. Powers that are struck through are not granted.

INITIALS

_____ (1) Real estate transactions.

_____ (2) Tangible personal property transactions.

_____ (3) Stock and bond, commodity and option transactions.

_____ (4) Banking and other financial institution transactions.

_____ (5) Business operating transactions.

_____ (6) Insurance and annuity transactions.

_____ (7) Estate, trust and other beneficiary transactions.

_____ (8) Living trust transactions.

_____ (9) Legal actions.

_____ (10) Personal and family care.

_____ (11) Government benefits.

_____ (12) Retirement plan transactions.

_____ (13) Tax matters.

_____ (14) ALL POWERS (1 THROUGH 13) LISTED ABOVE.

These powers are defined in Part 13, below.

6. Special Instructions to the Attorney-in-Fact

_____

_____

_____

_____

_____

_____

_____

_____

_____

_____

7. Compensation and Reimbursement of the Attorney-in-Fact

☐ My attorney-in-fact shall not be compensated for services, but shall be entitled to reimbursement, from my assets, for reasonable expenses. Reasonable expenses include but are not limited to reasonable fees for information or advice from accountants, lawyers or investment experts relating to my attorney-in-fact's responsibilities under this power of attorney.

☐ My attorney-in-fact shall be entitled to reimbursement for reasonable expenses and reasonable compensation for services. What constitutes reasonable compensation shall be determined exclusively by my attorney-in-fact. If more than one attorney-in-fact is named in this document, each shall have the exclusive right to determine what constitutes reasonable compensation for his or her own duties.

☐ My attorney-in-fact shall be entitled to reimbursement for reasonable expenses and compensation for services in the amount of $ _____ . If more than one attorney-in-fact is named in this document, each shall be entitled to receive this amount.

8. Personal Benefit to the Attorney-in-Fact

☐ My attorney-in-fact may buy any assets of mine or engage in any transaction he or she deems in good faith to be in my interest, no matter what the interest or benefit to my attorney-in-fact.

☐ My attorney-in-fact may not benefit personally from any transaction engaged in on my behalf.

9. Commingling by the Attorney-in-Fact

☐ My attorney-in-fact may commingle any of my funds with any funds of his or hers.

☐ My attorney-in-fact may not commingle any of my funds with any funds of his or hers.

10. Liability of the Attorney-in-Fact

My attorney-in-fact shall not incur any liability to me, my estate, my heirs, successors or assigns for acting or refraining from acting under this document, except for willful misconduct or gross negligence. My attorney-in-fact is not required to make my assets produce income, increase the value of my estate, diversify my investments or enter into transactions authorized by this document, as long as my attorney-in-fact believes his or her actions are in my best interests or in the interests of my estate and of those interested in my estate. A successor attorney-in-fact shall not be liable for acts of a prior attorney-in-fact.

11. Reliance on This Power of Attorney

Any third party who receives a copy of this document may rely on and act under it. Revocation of the power of attorney is not effective as to a third party until the third party has actual knowledge of the revocation. I agree to indemnify the third party for any claims that arise against the third party because of reliance on this power of attorney.

12. Severability

If any provision of this document is ruled unenforceable, the remaining provisions shall stay in effect.

13. Definition of Powers Granted to the Attorney-in-Fact

The powers granted in Part 5 of this document authorize my attorney-in-fact to do the following:

(1) Real estate transactions

Act for me in any manner to deal with all or any part of any interest in real property that I own at the time of execution of this document or later acquire, under such terms, conditions and covenants as my attorney-in-fact deems proper. My attorney-in-fact's powers include but are not limited to the power to:

(a) Accept as a gift, or as security for a loan, reject, demand, buy, lease, receive or otherwise acquire ownership or possession of any estate or interest in real property.

(b) Sell, exchange, convey with or without covenants, quitclaim, release, surrender, mortgage, encumber, partition or consent to the partitioning of, grant options concerning, lease, sublet or otherwise dispose of any interest in real property.

(c) Maintain, repair, improve, insure, rent, lease, and pay or contest taxes or assessments on any estate or interest in real property I own or claim to own.

(d) Prosecute, defend, intervene in, submit to arbitration, settle and propose or accept a compromise with respect to any claim in favor of or against me based on or involving any real estate transaction.

(2) Tangible personal property transactions

Act for me in any manner to deal with all or any part of any interest in personal property that I own at the time of execution of this document or later acquire, under such terms as my attorney-in-fact deems proper. My attorney-in-fact's powers include but are not limited to the power to lease, buy, exchange, accept as a gift or as security for a loan, acquire, possess, maintain, repair, improve, insure, rent, convey, mortgage, pledge and pay or contest taxes and assessments on any tangible personal property.

(3) Stock and bond, commodity, option and other securities transactions

Do any act which I can do through an agent, with respect to any interest in a bond, share, other instrument of similar character or commodity. My attorney-in-fact's powers include but are not limited to the power to:

(a) Accept as a gift or as security for a loan, reject, demand, buy, receive or otherwise acquire ownership or possession of any bond, share, instrument of similar character, commodity interest or any investment with respect thereto, together with the interest, dividends, proceeds or other distributions connected with it.

(b) Sell (including short sales), exchange, transfer, release, surrender, pledge, trade in or otherwise dispose of any bond, share, instrument of similar character or commodity interest.

(c) Demand, receive and obtain any money or other thing of value to which I am or may become or may claim to be entitled as the proceeds of any interest in a bond, share, other instrument of similar character or commodity interest.

(d) Agree and contract, in any manner, with any broker or other person and on any terms, for the accomplishment of any purpose listed in this section.

(e) Execute, acknowledge, seal and deliver any instrument my attorney-in-fact thinks useful to accomplish a purpose listed in this section, or any report or certificate required by law or regulation.

(4) Banking and other financial institution transactions

Do any act that I can do through an agent in connection with any banking transaction that might affect my financial or other interests. My attorney-in-fact's powers include but are not limited to the power to:

(a) Continue, modify and terminate any deposit account or other banking arrangement, or open either in the name of the agent alone or my name alone or in both our names jointly, a deposit account of any type in any financial institution, rent a safe deposit box or vault space, have access to a safe deposit box or vault to which I would have access and make other contracts with the institution.

(b) Make, sign and deliver checks or drafts, and withdraw my funds or property from any financial institution by check, order or otherwise.

(c) Prepare financial statements concerning my assets and liabilities or income and expenses and deliver them to any financial institution, and receive statements, notices or other documents from any financial institution.

(d) Borrow money from a financial institution on terms my attorney-in-fact deems acceptable, give security out of my assets, and pay, renew or extend the time of payment of any note given by or on my behalf.

(5) Business operating transactions

Do any act that I can do through an agent in connection with any business operated by me that my attorney-in-fact deems desirable. My attorney-in-fact's powers include but are not limited to the power to:

(a) Perform any duty and exercise any right, privilege or option which I have or claim to have under any contract of partnership, enforce the terms of any partnership agreement, and defend, submit to arbitration or settle any legal proceeding to which I am a party because of membership in a partnership.

(b) Exercise in person or by proxy and enforce any right, privilege or option which I have as the holder of any bond, share or instrument of similar character and defend, submit to arbitration or settle a legal proceeding to which I am a party because of any such bond, share or instrument of similar character.

(c) With respect to a business owned solely by me, continue, modify, extend or terminate any contract on my behalf; demand and receive all money that is due or claimed by me and use such funds in the operation of the business; engage in banking transactions my attorney-in-fact deems desirable; determine the location of the operation, the nature of the business it undertakes, its name, methods of manufacturing, selling, marketing, financing and accounting, form of organization and insurance and method of hiring and paying employees and independent contractors.

(d) Execute, acknowledge, seal and deliver any instrument of any kind that my attorney-in-fact thinks useful to accomplish any purpose listed in this section.

(e) Pay, compromise or contest business taxes or assessments.

(f) Demand and receive money or other things of value to which I am or claim to be entitled as the proceeds of any business operation, and conserve, invest, disburse or use anything so received for purposes listed in this section.

(6) Insurance and annuity transactions

Do any act that I can do through an agent, in connection with any insurance or annuity policy, that my attorney-in-fact deems desirable. My attorney-in-fact's powers include but are not limited to the power to:

(a) Continue, pay the premium on, modify, rescind or terminate any annuity or policy of life, accident, health, disability or liability insurance procured by me or on my behalf before the execution of this power of attorney. My attorney-in-fact cannot name himself or herself as beneficiary of a renewal, extension or substitute for such a policy unless he or she was already the beneficiary before I signed the power of attorney.

(b) Procure new, different or additional contracts of health, disability, accident or liability insurance on my life; modify, rescind or terminate any such contract and designate the beneficiary of any such contract.

(c) Sell, assign, borrow on, pledge or surrender and receive the cash surrender value of any policy.

(7) Estate, trust and other beneficiary transactions

Act for me in all matters that affect a trust, probate estate, guardianship, conservatorship, escrow, custodianship or other fund from which I am, may become or claim to be entitled, as a beneficiary, to a share or payment. My attorney-in-fact's authority includes the power to disclaim any assets from which I am, may become or claim to be entitled, as a beneficiary, to a share or payment.

(8) Living trust transactions

Transfer any of my interests in real property, stocks, bonds, accounts with financial institutions, insurance or other property to the trustee of a revocable trust I have created as settlor.

(9) Legal actions

Act for me in all matters that affect claims in favor of or against me and proceedings in any court or administrative body. My attorney-in-fact's powers include but are not limited to the power to:

(a) Hire an attorney to assert any claim or defense before any court, administrative board or other tribunal.

(b) Submit to arbitration or mediation or settle any claim in favor of or against me or any litigation to which I am a party, pay any judgment or settlement and receive any money or other things of value paid in settlement.

(10) Personal and family maintenance

Do all acts necessary to maintain my customary standard of living, and that of my spouse and children and other persons customarily supported by or legally entitled to be supported by me. My attorney-in-fact's powers include but are not limited to the power to:

(a) Pay for medical, dental and surgical care, living quarters, usual vacations and travel expenses, shelter, clothing, food, appropriate education and other living costs.

(b) Continue arrangements with respect to automobiles or other means of transportation; charge accounts; discharge of any services or duties assumed by me to any parent, relative or friend; and contributions or payments incidental to membership or affiliation in any church, club, society or other organization.

(11) Government benefits

Act for me in all matters that affect my right to government benefits, including Social Security, Medicare, Medicaid or other governmental programs or civil or military service. My attorney-in-fact's powers include but are not limited to the power to:

(a) Prepare, execute, file, prosecute, defend, submit to arbitration or settle a claim on my behalf to benefits or assistance, financial or otherwise.

(b) Receive the proceeds of such a claim and conserve, invest, disburse or use them on my behalf.

(12) Retirement plan transactions

Act for me in all matters that affect my retirement plans. My attorney-in-fact's powers include but are not limited to the power to select payment options under any retirement plan in which I participate, make contributions to those plans, exercise investment options, receive payment from a plan, roll over plan benefits into other retirement plans, designate beneficiaries under those plans and change existing beneficiary designations.

(13) Tax matters

Act for me in all matters that affect my local, state and federal taxes. My attorney-in-fact's powers include but are not limited to the power to:

(a) Prepare, sign and file federal, state, local and foreign income, gift, payroll, Federal Insurance Contributions Act returns and other tax returns; claims for refunds; requests for extension of time; petitions; any power of attorney required by the Internal Revenue Service or other taxing authority and other documents.

(b) Pay taxes due, collect refunds, post bonds, receive confidential information, exercise any election available to me and contest deficiencies determined by a taxing authority.

I understand the importance of the powers I delegate to my attorney-in-fact in this document. I recognize that the document gives my attorney-in-fact broad powers over my assets.

Signed: This _____ day of _____ ,

State of: _____ County of: _____

Signature: _____ SSN: _____

Witnesses

On the date written above, the principal declared to me that this instrument is his or her financial power of attorney, and that he or she willingly executed it as a free and voluntary act. The principal signed this instrument in my presence.

Witness 1

_____

Signature

_____

Name

_____

Address

_____

Witness 2

_____
Signature

_____
Name

_____
Address

_____

[Notary Seal]

Preparation Statement

This document was prepared by:

_____
Name

_____
Address

Power of Attorney for Finances (Limited Power)

I, _____ *[your name]*,

of_____ *[your city and state]*,

appoint _____

[name of your attorney-in-fact] to act in my place for the purposes of:

_____

_____

_____

_____

_____

_____

_____

_____

_____

This power of attorney takes effect on _____ ,

and shall continue until terminated in writing, or until _____ ,

whichever comes first.

I grant my attorney-in-fact full authority to act in any manner both proper and necessary to the exercise of the foregoing powers, and I ratify every act that my attorney-in-fact may lawfully perform in exercising those powers.

I agree that any third party who receives a copy of this document may act under it. Revocation of the power of attorney is not effective as to a third party until the third party has actual knowledge of the revocation. I agree to indemnify the third party for any claims that arise against the third party because of reliance on this power of attorney.

Signed: This _____ day of _____ ,

State of: _____ County of: _____

Signature:_____ SSN: _____

Witnesses

On the date written above, the principal declared to me that this instrument is his or her financial power of attorney, and that he or she willingly executed it as a free and voluntary act. The principal signed this instrument in my presence.

Witness 1

_____

Signature

_____

Name

_____

Address

_____

Witness 2

_____

Signature

_____

Name

_____

Address

[Notary Seal]

Preparation Statement

This document was prepared by:

Name: _____

Address: _____

_____

Notice of Revocation of Power of Attorney

I, _____ *[your name]*,

of _____ *[your city and state]*,

revoke the power of attorney dated _____ , empowering

_____ *[name of your*

attorney-in-fact] to act as my attorney-in-fact. I revoke and withdraw all power and authority granted

under that power of attorney.

[if applicable]: That power of attorney was recorded on _____,

in Book _____ , at Page _____ , of the Official Records, County of _____,

State of _____ .

Signed: This _____ day of _____,

State of: _____ County of: _____

Signature: _____ SSN: _____

[Notary Seal]

Property Worksheet

[Describe each asset. If an asset is jointly owned, specify the percentage you own. If you've already named someone to take an asset after your death, such as in a retirement account, insurance policy or pay-on-death bank account, write down the beneficiary's name.]

Property   **Name of Any Existing Beneficiary**

Real Estate *(list each piece of real estate by address)*

_____   _____
_____   _____
_____   _____
_____   _____

Cash and Other Liquid Assets

cash

_____   _____
_____   _____
_____   _____

checking accounts

_____   _____
_____   _____
_____   _____

savings and money market accounts

_____   _____
_____   _____
_____   _____

certificates of deposit

_____   _____
_____   _____
_____   _____

precious metals

_____   _____
_____   _____
_____   _____

Securities (not in retirement accounts)

mutual funds

_____   _____
_____   _____
_____   _____

listed and unlisted stocks

_____   _____
_____   _____
_____   _____

Property

Name of Any Existing Beneficiary

Securities (continued)
government, corporate and municipal bonds

_____   _____
_____   _____
_____   _____

annuities

_____   _____
_____   _____
_____   _____

Retirement Plan Assets (IRAs, Keoghs, Roth IRAs, 401(k) and 403(b) plans)

_____   _____
_____   _____
_____   _____

Vehicles
automobiles, trucks and recreational vehicles

_____   _____
_____   _____
_____   _____

planes, boats and other vehicles

_____   _____
_____   _____

Other Personal Property
household goods

_____   _____
_____   _____

valuable clothing, jewelry and furs

_____   _____
_____   _____
_____   _____

collectibles, including artworks and antiques

_____   _____
_____   _____
_____   _____

tools and equipment

_____   _____
_____   _____
_____   _____

Property	**Name of Any Existing Beneficiary**

Other Personal Property (continued)

livestock or other valuable animals

_____   _____

_____   _____

money owed you (personal loans, etc.)

_____   _____

_____   _____

_____   _____

death benefits

_____   _____

_____   _____

_____   _____

_____   _____

life insurance (other than term insurance)

_____   _____

_____   _____

miscellaneous (any personal property not listed above)

_____   _____

_____   _____

_____   _____

_____   _____

Business Personal Property

business ownerships (partnerships, sole proprietorships, limited partnerships, limited liability
companies, corporations)

_____   _____

_____   _____

_____   _____

_____   _____

patents, copyrights, trademarks (including the right to receive royalties)

_____   _____

_____   _____

miscellaneous receivables (mortgages, deeds of trust or promissory notes held by you; any
rents due from income property owned by you; and payments due for professional or
personal services or property sold by you that have not been fully paid by the purchaser)

_____   _____

_____   _____

_____   _____

_____   _____

Beneficiary Worksheet

Beneficiaries of Specific Gifts

Beneficiary already named

☐ **Item:** _____

Beneficiary(ies): _____

Address(es): _____

Alternate Beneficiary(ies): _____

Address(es): _____

☐ **Item:** _____

Beneficiary(ies): _____

Address(es): _____

Alternate Beneficiary(ies): _____

Address(es): _____

☐ **Item:** _____

Beneficiary(ies): _____

Address(es): _____

Alternate Beneficiary(ies): _____

Address(es): _____

☐ **Item:** _____

Beneficiary(ies): _____

Address(es): _____

Alternate Beneficiary(ies): _____

Address(es): _____

☐ **Item:** _____

Beneficiary(ies): _____

Address(es): _____

Alternate Beneficiary(ies): _____

Address(es): _____

☐ **Item:** _____

Beneficiary(ies): _____

Address(es): _____

Alternate Beneficiary(ies): _____

Address(es): _____

☐ **Item:** _____

Beneficiary(ies): _____

Address(es): _____

Alternate Beneficiary(ies): _____

Address(es): _____

☐ **Item:** _____

Beneficiary(ies): _____

Address(es): _____

Alternate Beneficiary(ies): _____

Address(es): _____

☐ **Item:** _____

Beneficiary(ies): _____

Address(es): _____

Alternate Beneficiary(ies): _____

Address(es): _____

☐ **Item:** _____

Beneficiary(ies): _____

Address(es): _____

Alternate Beneficiary(ies): _____

Address(es): _____

Debts Forgiven

Amount Forgiven: _____ Date of loan: _____

Debtor: _____

Amount Forgiven: _____ Date of loan: _____

Debtor: _____

Amount Forgiven: _____ Date of loan: _____

Debtor: _____

Amount Forgiven: _____ Date of loan: _____

Debtor: _____

Residuary Beneficiary or Beneficiaries

Residuary beneficiary(ies) and percentage each one receives:

_____

_____

_____

_____

_____

_____

First Alternate Residuary Beneficiary or Beneficiaries

Residuary beneficiary(ies) and percentage each one receives:

_____

_____

_____

_____

_____

⚠️ ***Do not just fill in and sign this form.*** *As mentioned in Chapter 2, to be legally valid, your will must be printed out (using the disk that comes with this book) or typed, eliminating all items that don't apply to you. Do not just fill in the blanks of this form and try to use the completed form as your will.*

Will for Adult With No Children

Will of _____

I, _____,
a resident of_____ [county], State of _____,
declare that this is my will.

1. **Revocation.** I revoke all wills that I have previously made.
2. **Marital Status.** I am ☐ married ☐ single.
3. **Specific Gifts.** I make the following specific gifts:

I leave _____
_____
_____
to _____
or, if ☐ he ☐ she ☐ they ☐ do ☐ does not survive me, to _____
_____.

I leave _____
_____
_____
to _____
or, if ☐ he ☐ she ☐ they ☐ do ☐ does not survive me, to _____
_____.

I leave _____
_____
_____
to _____
or, if ☐ he ☐ she ☐ they ☐ do ☐ does not survive me, to _____
_____.

I leave _____
_____
_____
to _____
or, if ☐ he ☐ she ☐ they ☐ do ☐ does not survive me, to _____
_____.

[repeat as needed]

4. **Residuary Estate.** I leave my residuary estate, that is, the rest of my property not otherwise specifically and validly disposed of by this will or in any other manner, to _____

_____

or, if ☐ he ☐ she ☐ they ☐ do ☐ does not survive me, to _____

_____.

5. **Beneficiary Provisions.** The following terms and conditions apply to the beneficiary clauses of this will.

   A. **45-Day Survivorship Period.** As used in this will, the phrase "survive me" means to be alive or in existence as an organization on the 45th day after my death. Any beneficiary, except any alternate residuary beneficiary, must survive me to take property under this will.

   B. **Shared Gifts.** If I leave property to be shared by two or more beneficiaries, it shall be shared equally between them unless this will provides otherwise.

      If any beneficiary of a shared specific gift left in a single paragraph of the Specific Gifts clause, above, does not survive me, that deceased beneficiary's portion of the gift shall be given to the surviving beneficiaries in equal shares.

      If any residuary beneficiary of a shared residuary gift does not survive me, that deceased beneficiary's portion of the residue shall be given to the surviving residuary beneficiaries in equal shares.

   C. **Encumbrances.** All property that I leave by this will shall pass subject to any encumbrances or liens on the property.

6. **Executor.** I name _____

as executor, to serve without bond. If he/she does not qualify, or ceases to serve, I name

_____

as executor, also to serve without bond.

   I direct that my executor take all actions legally permissible to probate this will, including filing a petition in the appropriate court for the independent administration of my estate.

   I grant to my executor the following powers, to be exercised as the executor deems to be in the best interests of my estate:

   A. To retain property, without liability for loss or depreciation resulting from such retention.

   B. To sell, lease or exchange property and to receive or administer the proceeds as a part of my estate.

   C. To vote stock, convert bonds, notes, stocks or other securities belonging to my estate into other securities, and to exercise all other rights and privileges of a person owning similar property.

   D. To deal with and settle claims in favor of or against my estate.

   E. To continue, maintain, operate or participate in any business which is a part of my estate, and to incorporate, dissolve or otherwise change the form of organization of the business.

   F. To pay all debts and taxes that may be assessed against my estate, as provided under state law.

   G. To do all other acts, which in the executor's judgment may be necessary or appropriate for the proper and advantageous management, investment and distribution of my estate.

These powers, authority and discretion are in addition to the powers, authority and discretion vested in an executor by operation of law, and may be exercised as often as deemed necessary, without approval by any court in any jurisdiction.

Signature

I subscribe my name to this will this _____ day of _____ , _____ , at

_____ [county], State of _____ .

I declare that it is my will, that I sign it willingly, that I execute it as my free and voluntary act for the

purposes expressed and that I am of the age of majority or otherwise legally empowered to make a will

and under no constraint or undue influence.

Signature: _____

Witnesses

On this _____ day of _____ , _____ , the testator,

_____ ,

declared to us, the undersigned, that this instrument was ☐ his ☐ her will and requested us to act as

witnesses to it. The testator signed this will in our presence, all of us being present at the same time. We

now, at the testator's request, in the testator's presence and in the presence of each other, subscribe our

names as witnesses and each declare that we are of sound mind and of proper age to witness a will. We

further declare that we understand this to be the testator's will, and that to the best of our knowledge the

testator is of the age of majority, or is otherwise legally empowered to make a will and appears to be of

sound mind and under no constraint or undue influence.

We declare under penalty of perjury that the foregoing is true and correct, this _____ day of

_____ , _____ , at _____ [county],

State of _____ .

Witness 1

Signature: _____

Typed or printed name: _____

Residing at: _____

City, state, zip: _____

Witness 2

Signature: _____

Typed or printed name: _____

Residing at: _____

City, state, zip: _____

Witness 3

Signature: _____

Typed or printed name: _____

Residing at: _____

City, state, zip: _____

⚠️ **Do not just fill in and sign this form.** As mentioned in Chapter 2, to be legally valid, your will must be printed out (using the disk that comes with this book) or typed, eliminating all items that don't apply to you. Do not just fill in the blanks of this form and try to use the completed form as your will.

Will for Adult With Child(ren)

Will of _____

I, _____ ,

a resident of _____ *[county]*, State of _____ ,

declare that this is my will.

1. **Revocation.** I revoke all wills that I have previously made.

2. **Marital Status.** I am ☐ married ☐ single.

3. **Children.** I have the following natural and legally adopted child(ren):

Name   Date of Birth

_____   _____

_____   _____

_____   _____

_____   _____

_____   _____

_____   _____

_____   _____

[repeat as needed]

If I do not leave property to one or more of the children whom I have identified above, my failure to do so is intentional.

4. **Specific Gifts.** I make the following specific gifts:

I leave _____

_____

_____

to _____

or, if ☐ he ☐ she ☐ they ☐ do ☐ does not survive me, to _____

_____ .

I leave _____

_____

_____

to _____

or, if ☐ he ☐ she ☐ they ☐ do ☐ does not survive me, to _____

_____ .

I leave _____

_____

_____

to _____

or, if ☐ he ☐ she ☐ they ☐ do ☐ does not survive me, to _____

_____.

I leave _____

_____

_____

to _____

or, if ☐ he ☐ she ☐ they ☐ do ☐ does not survive me, to _____

_____.

[repeat as needed]

5. **Residuary Estate.** I leave my residuary estate, that is, the rest of my property not otherwise specifically and validly disposed of by this will or in any other manner, to _____

_____

or, if ☐ he ☐ she ☐ they ☐ do ☐ does not survive me, to _____

_____.

6. **Beneficiary Provisions.** The following terms and conditions apply to the beneficiary clauses of this will.

   A. **45-Day Survivorship Period.** As used in this will, the phrase "survive me" means to be alive or in existence as an organization on the 45th day after my death. Any beneficiary, except any alternate residuary beneficiary, must survive me to take property under this will.

   B. **Shared Gifts.** If I leave property to be shared by two or more beneficiaries, it shall be shared equally between them unless this will provides otherwise.

   If any beneficiary of a shared specific gift left in a single paragraph of the Specific Gifts clause, above, does not survive me, that deceased beneficiary's portion of the gift shall be given to the surviving beneficiaries in equal shares.

   If any residuary beneficiary of a shared residuary gift does not survive me, that deceased beneficiary's portion of the residue shall be given to the surviving residuary beneficiaries in equal shares.

   C. **Encumbrances.** All property that I leave by this will shall pass subject to any encumbrances or liens on the property.

7. **Executor.** I name _____

as executor, to serve without bond. If he/she does not qualify, or ceases to serve, I name

_____

as executor, also to serve without bond.

I direct that my executor take all actions legally permissible to probate this will, including filing a petition in the appropriate court for the independent administration of my estate.

I grant to my executor the following powers, to be exercised as the executor deems to be in the best interests of my estate:

   1. To retain property, without liability for loss or depreciation resulting from such retention.

   2. To sell, lease or exchange property and to receive or administer the proceeds as a part of my estate.

3. To vote stock, convert bonds, notes, stocks or other securities belonging to my estate into other securities, and to exercise all other rights and privileges of a person owning similar property.

4. To deal with and settle claims in favor of or against my estate.

5. To continue, maintain, operate or participate in any business which is a part of my estate, and to incorporate, dissolve or otherwise change the form of organization of the business.

6. To pay all debts and taxes that may be assessed against my estate, as provided under state law.

7. To do all other acts, which in the executor's judgment may be necessary or appropriate for the proper and advantageous management, investment and distribution of my estate.

8. **Personal Guardian.** If at my death any of my children are minors, and a personal guardian is needed, I nominate _____

to be appointed personal guardian of my minor children. If ☐ he ☐ she cannot serve as personal guardian, I nominate _____

to be appointed personal guardian.

   I direct that no bond be required of any personal guardian.

9. **Property Guardian.** If at my death any of my children are minors, and a property guardian is needed, I appoint _____

as the property guardian of my minor children. If ☐ he ☐ she cannot serve as property guardian, I appoint _____

as property guardian.

   I direct that no bond be required of any property guardian.

10. **Gifts Under the Uniform Transfers to Minors Act.** All property left by this will to _____

_____ [name of minor]

shall be given to _____ [name of custodian]

as custodian for _____ [name of minor]

under the Uniform Transfers to Minors Act of _____ [your state].

   If _____ [name of custodian]

cannot serve as custodian, _____

[name of successor custodian] shall serve as custodian. If _____

[your state] allows testators to choose the age at which the custodianship ends, I choose the oldest age allowed by my state's Uniform Transfers to Minors Act.

[repeat as needed]

Signature

I subscribe my name to this will this _____ day of _____ , _____ , at

_____ [county], State of _____ .

I declare that it is my will, that I sign it willingly, that I execute it as my free and voluntary act for the purposes expressed and that I am of the age of majority or otherwise legally empowered to make a will and under no constraint or undue influence.

Signature:_____

Witnesses

On this _____ day of _____ , _____ , the testator,

_____ ,

declared to us, the undersigned, that this instrument was ☐ his ☐ her will and requested us to act as witnesses to it. The testator signed this will in our presence, all of us being present at the same time. We now, at the testator's request, in the testator's presence and in the presence of each other, subscribe our names as witnesses and each declare that we are of sound mind and of proper age to witness a will. We further declare that we understand this to be the testator's will, and that to the best of our knowledge the testator is of the age of majority, or is otherwise legally empowered to make a will and appears to be of sound mind and under no constraint or undue influence.

We declare under penalty of perjury that the foregoing is true and correct, this _____ day of _____ , _____ , at _____[county], State of _____ .

Witness 1

Signature: _____

Typed or printed name: _____

Residing at: _____

City, state, zip: _____

Witness 2

Signature: _____

Typed or printed name: _____

Residing at: _____

City, state, zip: _____

Witness 3

Signature: _____

Typed or printed name: _____

Residing at: _____

City, state, zip: _____

Will Codicil

First Codicil to the Will of _____

I, _____ ,

a resident of_____ *[county]*, State of _____ ,

declare this to be the first codicil to my will dated _____ , _____ .

FIRST: I revoke the provision of Clause _____ of my will that provided:

[include the exact will language you wish to revoke]

_____

_____

_____

_____

_____

SECOND: I add the following provision to Clause _____ of my will:

[add whatever is desired]

_____

_____

_____

_____

_____

THIRD: In all other respects I confirm and republish my will dated _____ , _____ .

Dated _____ , _____ .

Signature

I subscribe my name to this codicil this _____ day of _____ , _____ .

_____ *[county]*, State of _____ .

I declare under penalty of perjury that I sign and execute this codicil willingly, that I execute it as my free and voluntary act for the purposes expressed and that I am of the age of majority or otherwise legally empowered to make a codicil and under no constraint or undue influence.

Signature: _____

Witnesses

On this _____ day of _____ , _____ ,

_____ *[codicil maker's name]*,

declared to us, the undersigned, that this instrument was the codicil to ☐ his ☐ her will and requested us to act as witnesses to it. The testator signed this codicil in our presence, all of us being present at the same time. We now, at the testator's request, in the testator's presence and in the presence of each other, subscribe our names as witnesses and declare we understand this to be the testator's codicil and that to the best of our knowledge the testator is of the age of majority, or is otherwise legally empowered to make a codicil and is under no constraint or undue influence.

We declare under penalty of perjury that the foregoing is true and correct, this _____ day of
_____, _____, at _____[county],
State of _____ .

Witness 1

Signature: _____

Typed or printed name: _____

Residing at: _____

City, state, zip: _____

Witness 2

Signature: _____

Typed or printed name: _____

Residing at: _____

City, state, zip: _____

Witness 3

Signature: _____

Typed or printed name: _____

Residing at: _____

City, state, zip: _____

Request for Death Certificate

Bureau of Vital Statistics

_____

_____

_____

[insert bureau's address]

Name of deceased: _____

Place of birth: _____ Social Security number: _____

Date of death: _____ Place of death: _____

Cause of death: _____

Please send me _____ certified copies of the death certificate of the above-named person. I have enclosed a check in the amount of $ _____ and a stamped, self-addressed envelope.

Thank you for your assistance.

Signature: _____

Printed or typed name: _____

Relationship to deceased: _____

Address: _____

_____

Home phone: _____ Work phone: _____

Notice to Creditor of Death

_____

_____
                          .
_____

_____

[insert name and address of creditor]

Name of deceased:_____

Account number: _____ Date of death: _____

This letter is to notify you of the deceased's death. Please cancel this account at once.

Please also acknowledge that you received this notice by signing the duplicate of this letter and returning it to me in the enclosed stamped, self-addressed envelope.

If there is any outstanding balance on this account, please promptly forward it to me at the address set out below.

Thank you for your assistance.

Signature:_____

Printed or typed name: _____

Relationship to deceased: _____

Address: _____

_____

Home phone: _____ Work phone: _____

Receipt acknowledged by:

Signature:_____

Printed or typed name: _____

Title: _____

Notice to Social Security Administration of Death

Social Security Administration

_____

_____

_____

[insert address where Social Security checks originate]

Name of deceased:_____

Social Security number:_____

Date of death: _____

This letter is to notify you of the deceased's death. Please cease sending checks or depositing them directly into his/her account. *[if applicable: Enclosed is the deceased's most recent check, which is being returned as required.]*

Please acknowledge receipt of this notice by signing the duplicate of this letter and returning it to me in the enclosed stamped, self-addressed envelope.

Thank you for your assistance.

Signature:_____

Printed or typed name: _____

Relationship to deceased: _____

Address: _____

_____

Home phone: _____ Work phone: _____

Receipt acknowledged by:

Signature:_____

Printed or typed name: _____

Title: _____

General Notice of Death

_____

_____

_____

_____

[insert name and address of organization]

This letter is to notify you that _____

died on _____ .

Signature: _____

Printed or typed name: _____

Relationship to deceased: _____

Apartment-Finding Service Checklist

Name of company:_____

Address: _____

Phone number: _____ Hours: _____

Date this form is completed:_____

1. Description of listings

Geographical areas covered: _____

Type of rentals: _____

Total number of listings: _____ Number of new listings per day: _____

Frequency of listing updates (as available or once a day): _____

% of listings exclusive to this service: _____

Type of information available for each listing:

_____

_____

2. Type of access to listings, cost and duration of service

☐ phone:_____ ☐ fax: _____

☐ e-mail:_____ ☐ pager: _____

☐ listing books available in office: _____

3. Free phone available in office for members' use? ☐ yes ☐ no

4. Other services and costs

☐ roommate referrals:_____

☐ credit screening: _____

☐ other:_____

5. Percentage of members who find a rental unit through service: _____

6. Refund if rental unit not found through company:_____

7. Length of time in business: _____

8. Other comments: _____

_____

_____

_____

_____

_____

Rental Application

Separate application required from each applicant age 18 or older.

THIS SECTION TO BE COMPLETED BY LANDLORD

Address of property to be rented: _____

_____

Rental Term: ☐ month-to-month ☐ lease from _____ to _____

Amounts Due Prior to Occupancy

First month's rent .... $_____

Security deposit.. $_____

Credit check fee .... $_____

Other (specify): _____ $_____

TOTAL .... $_____

Applicant

Full name—include all names you use(d): _____

Home phone: (   ) _____   Work phone: (   ) _____

Social Security number: _____   Driver's license number/state: _____

Vehicle make: _____   Model: _____   Color: _____   Year: _____

License plate number/state: _____

Additional Occupants

List everyone, including children, who will live with you:

Full name _____   Relationship to applicant _____

_____

_____

_____

_____

Rental History

Current address: _____

Dates lived at address: _____   Reason for leaving: _____

Landlord/manager: _____   Landlord/manager's phone: (   ) _____

Previous address: _____

Dates lived at address: _____   Reason for leaving: _____

Landlord/manager: _____   Landlord/manager's phone: (   ) _____

Previous address: _____

Dates lived at address: _____ Reason for leaving: _____

Landlord/manager: _____ Landlord/manager's phone: ( )

Employment History

Name and address of current employer: _____

_____ Phone: ( )

Name of supervisor: _____ Supervisor's phone: ( )

Dates employed at this job: _____ Position or title: _____

Name and address of previous employer: _____

_____ Phone: ( )

Name of supervisor: _____ Supervisor's phone: ( )

Dates employed at this job: _____ Position or title: _____

Income

1. Your gross monthly employment income (before deductions): $ _____

2. Average monthly amounts of other income (specify sources): $ _____

_____

_____

TOTAL: $ _____

Credit and Financial Information

Bank/financial accounts	Account number	Bank/institution	Branch
Savings account:			
Checking account:			
Money market or similar account:			

Credit accounts & loans	Type of account (Auto loan, Visa, etc.)	Account Number	Name of Creditor	Amount Owed	Monthly Payment
Major credit card:					
Major credit card:					
Loan (mortgage, car, student loan, etc.):					
Other major obligation:					

Miscellaneous

Describe the number and type of pets you want to have in the rental property: _____

_____

Describe water-filled furniture you want to have in the rental property: _____

_____

Do you smoke? ☐ yes ☐ no

Have you ever: Filed for bankruptcy? ☐ yes ☐ no   Been sued? ☐ yes ☐ no

Been evicted? ☐ yes ☐ no   Been convicted of a crime? ☐ yes ☐ no

Explain any "yes" listed above: _____

_____

References and Emergency Contact

Personal reference: _____ Relationship: _____

Address: _____

Phone: (_____) _____

Personal reference: _____ Relationship: _____

Address: _____

Phone: (_____) _____

Contact in emergency: _____ Relationship: _____

Address: _____

Phone: (_____) _____

I certify that all the information given above is true and correct and understand that my lease or rental agreement may be terminated if I have made any false or incomplete statement in this application. I authorize verification of the information provided in this application from my credit sources, credit bureaus, current and previous landlords and employers, and personal references.

_____   _____

Applicant   Date

Notes (landlord/manager): _____

_____

_____

_____

_____

_____

Fixed-Term Residential Lease

Clause 1. Identification of Landlord and Tenant

This Agreement is entered into between _____ ("Tenant")

and _____ ("Landlord").

Each Tenant is jointly and severally liable for the payment of rent and performance of all other terms of this Agreement.

Clause 2. Identification of Premises

Subject to the terms and conditions in this Agreement, Landlord rents to Tenant, and Tenant rents from Landlord, for residential purposes only, the premises located at _____

_____ ("the premises"),

together with the following furnishings and appliances:_____

_____ .

Rental of the premises also includes: _____

_____ .

Clause 3. Limits on Use and Occupancy

The premises are to be used only as a private residence for Tenant(s) listed in Clause 1 of this Agreement and the following minor children: _____

_____ .

Occupancy by guests for more than _____ is prohibited without Landlord's written consent and will be considered a material breach of this Agreement.

Clause 4. Term of the Tenancy

The term of the rental will begin on _____ , _____ , and end

on _____ .

Clause 5. Payment of Rent

Regular monthly rent.

Tenant will pay to Landlord a monthly rent of $ _____ , payable in advance on the first day of each month, except when that day falls on a weekend or a legal holiday, in which case rent is due on the next business day. Rent will be paid in the following manner unless Landlord designates otherwise:

Delivery of payment.

Rent will be paid:

☐ by mail, to _____ .

☐ in person, at _____ .

Form of payment.

Landlord will accept payment in these forms:

☐ personal check made payable to _____ .

☐ cashier's check made payable to _____ .

☐ credit card.

☐ money order.

☐ cash.

☐ other (specify) _____ .

Prorated first month's rent.

For the period from Tenant's move-in date, _____ , _____ , through

the end of the month, Tenant will pay to Landlord a prorated monthly rent of $ _____ . This

amount will be paid on or before the date the Tenant moves in.

Clause 6. Late Charges

If Tenant fails to pay the rent in full before the end of the _____ day after it's due, Tenant will pay

Landlord a late charge of $ _____ , plus $ _____ for each additional day that

the rent remains unpaid. The total late charge for any one month will not exceed $ _____ .

Landlord does not waive the right to insist on payment of the rent in full on the date it is due.

Clause 7. Returned Check and Other Bank Charges

If any check offered by Tenant to Landlord in payment of rent or any other amount due under this

Agreement is returned for lack of sufficient funds, a "stop payment" or any other reason, Tenant will

pay Landlord a returned check charge of $ _____ .

Clause 8. Security Deposit

On signing this Agreement, Tenant will pay to Landlord the sum of $ _____ as a security

deposit. Tenant may not, without Landlord's prior written consent, apply this security deposit to the

last month's rent or to any other sum due under this Agreement. Within _____

after Tenant has vacated the premises, returned keys and provided Landlord with a forwarding address,

Landlord will return the deposit in full or give Tenant an itemized written statement of the reasons for,

and the dollar amount of, any of the security deposit retained by Landlord, along with a check for any

deposit balance.

Other details on security deposit: _____

_____

_____

Clause 9. Utilities

Tenant will pay all utility charges, except for the following, which will be paid by Landlord:_____

_____ .

Clause 10. Assignment and Subletting

Tenant will not sublet any part of the premises or assign this Agreement without the prior written

consent of Landlord.

Clause 11. Tenant's Maintenance Responsibilities

Tenant will:

a. keep the premises clean, sanitary and in good condition and, upon termination of the tenancy,

   return the premises to Landlord in a condition identical to that which existed when Tenant took

   occupancy, except for ordinary wear and tear and any additions or alterations authorized by

   Landlord

b. immediately notify Landlord of any defects or dangerous conditions in and about the premises of which Tenant becomes aware, and

c. reimburse Landlord, on demand by Landlord, for the cost of any repairs to the premises damaged by Tenant or Tenant's guests or business invitees through misuse, accident or neglect.

Tenant has examined the premises, including appliances, fixtures, carpets, drapes and paint, and has found them to be in good, safe and clean condition and repair, except as noted in the Landlord-Tenant Checklist.

Clause 12. Repairs and Alterations by Tenant

a. Except as provided by law or as authorized by the prior written consent of Landlord, Tenant will not make any repairs or alterations to the premises, including nailing holes in the walls or painting the rental unit.

b. Unless authorized by law, Tenant will not, without Landlord's prior written consent, alter, re-key or install any locks to the premises or install or alter any burglar alarm system. Tenant will provide Landlord with a key or keys capable of unlocking all such re-keyed or new locks as well as instructions on how to disarm any altered or new burglar alarm system.

Clause 13. Violating Laws and Causing Disturbances

Tenant and guests or invitees will not use the premises or adjacent areas in such a way as to:

a. violate any law or ordinance, including laws prohibiting the use, possession or sale of illegal drugs

b. commit waste (severe property damage), or

c. create a nuisance by annoying, disturbing, inconveniencing or interfering with the quiet enjoyment and peace and quiet of any other tenant or nearby resident.

Clause 14. Pets

No animal, bird or other pet will be kept on the premises, even temporarily, except properly trained dogs needed by blind, deaf or disabled persons and _____

under the following conditions: _____

_____ .

Clause 15. Landlord's Right to Access

Landlord or Landlord's agents may enter the premises in the event of an emergency, to make repairs or improvements or to show the premises to prospective buyers or tenants. Landlord may also enter the premises to conduct an annual inspection to check for safety or maintenance problems. Except in cases of emergency, Tenant's abandonment of the premises, court order or where it is impractical to do so, Landlord shall give Tenant _____ notice before entering.

Clause 16. Extended Absences by Tenant

Tenant will notify Landlord in advance if Tenant will be away from the premises for _____ or more consecutive days. During such absence, Landlord may enter the premises at times reasonably necessary to maintain the property and inspect for needed repairs.

Clause 17. Possession of the Premises

a. Tenant's failure to take possession.

If, after signing this Agreement, Tenant fails to take possession of the premises, Tenant will still be responsible for paying rent and complying with all other terms of this Agreement.

b. Landlord's failure to deliver possession.

If Landlord is unable to deliver possession of the premises to Tenant for any reason not within Landlord's control, including but not limited to partial or complete destruction of the premises, Tenant will have the right to terminate this Agreement upon proper notice as required by law. In such event, Landlord's liability to Tenant will be limited to the return of all sums previously paid by Tenant to Landlord.

Clause 18. Tenant Rules and Regulations

Tenant acknowledges receipt of, and has read a copy of, tenant rules and regulations, which are attached to and incorporated into this Agreement by this reference.

Clause 19. Payment of Court Costs and Attorney Fees in a Lawsuit

In any action or legal proceeding to enforce any part of this Agreement, the prevailing party
☐ shall not ☐ shall   recover reasonable attorney fees and court costs.

Clause 20. Disclosures

Tenant acknowledges that Landlord has made the following disclosures regarding the premises:

☐ disclosure of information on lead-based paint and/or lead-based paint hazards

☐ other disclosures: _____

_____

Clause 21. Authority to Receive Legal Papers

The Landlord, any person managing the premises and anyone designated by the Landlord are authorized to accept service of process and receive other notices and demands, which may be delivered to:

☐ the Landlord, at the following address: _____

_____.

☐ the Manager, at the following address: _____

_____.

☐ the following person, at the following address: _____

_____.

Clause 22. Additional Provisions

Additional provisions are as follows: _____

_____

_____

_____

_____

_____

_____

_____

Clause 23. Validity of Each Part

If any portion of this Agreement is held to be invalid, its invalidity will not affect the validity or enforceability of any other provision of this Agreement.

Clause 24. Grounds for Termination of Tenancy

The failure of Tenant or their guests or invitees to comply with any term of this Agreement is grounds for termination of the tenancy, with appropriate notice to Tenant and procedures as required by law.

Clause 25. Entire Agreement

This document and any Attachments constitutes the entire Agreement between the parties, and no promises or representations, other than those contained here and those implied by law, have been made by Landlord or Tenant. Any modifications to this Agreement must be in writing signed by Landlord and Tenant.

_____   _____
Landlord/Agent's signature   Date

_____
Title

_____
Address

_____   _____
                                                          Phone

_____   _____
Tenant 1's signature   Date

_____
Print name

_____   _____
Tenant 2's signature   Date

_____
Print name

_____   _____
Tenant 3's signature   Date

_____
Print name

Month-to-Month Residential Rental Agreement

Clause 1. Identification of Landlord and Tenant

This Agreement is entered into between _____ ("Tenant")

and _____ ("Landlord").

Each Tenant is jointly and severally liable for the payment of rent and performance of all other terms of this Agreement.

Clause 2. Identification of Premises

Subject to the terms and conditions in this Agreement, Landlord rents to Tenant, and Tenant rents from Landlord, for residential purposes only, the premises located at _____

_____ ("the premises"),

together with the following furnishings and appliances:_____

_____.

Rental of the premises also includes: _____

_____.

Clause 3. Limits on Use and Occupancy

The premises are to be used only as a private residence for Tenant(s) listed in Clause 1 of this

Agreement and the following minor children: _____

_____.

Occupancy by guests for more than _____ is prohibited without Landlord's written consent and will be considered a material breach of this Agreement.

Clause 4. Term of the Tenancy

The term of the rental will begin on_____, _____ , and continue on

a month-to-month basis. Landlord may terminate the tenancy or modify the terms of this Agreement by

giving the Tenant _____ days written notice. Tenant may terminate the tenancy by

giving the Landlord_____ days written notice.

Clause 5. Payment of Rent

Regular monthly rent.

Tenant will pay to Landlord a monthly rent of $ _____ , payable in advance on the first

day of each month, except when that day falls on a weekend or a legal holiday, in which case rent is

due on the next business day. Rent will be paid in the following manner unless Landlord designates

otherwise:

Delivery of payment.

Rent will be paid:

☐ by mail, to _____.

☐ in person, at _____.

Form of payment.

Landlord will accept payment in these forms:

☐ personal check made payable to _____.

☐ cashier's check made payable to _____.

☐ credit card.

☐ money order.

☐ cash.

☐ other (specify) _____ .

Prorated first month's rent.

For the period from Tenant's move-in date, _____ , _____ , through

the end of the month, Tenant will pay to Landlord a prorated monthly rent of $ _____ .

This amount will be paid on or before the date the Tenant moves in.

Clause 6. Late Charges

If Tenant fails to pay the rent in full before the end of the _____ day after it's due, Tenant will pay

Landlord a late charge of $ _____ , plus $ _____ for each additional day that

the rent remains unpaid. The total late charge for any one month will not exceed $ _____ .

Landlord does not waive the right to insist on payment of the rent in full on the date it is due.

Clause 7. Returned Check and Other Bank Charges

If any check offered by Tenant to Landlord in payment of rent or any other amount due under this

Agreement is returned for lack of sufficient funds, a "stop payment" or any other reason, Tenant will

pay Landlord a returned check charge of $ _____ .

Clause 8. Security Deposit

On signing this Agreement, Tenant will pay to Landlord the sum of $ _____ as a security

deposit. Tenant may not, without Landlord's prior written consent, apply this security deposit to the

last month's rent or to any other sum due under this Agreement. Within _____

after Tenant has vacated the premises, returned keys and provided Landlord with a forwarding address,

Landlord will return the deposit in full or give Tenant an itemized written statement of the reasons for,

and the dollar amount of, any of the security deposit retained by Landlord, along with a check for any

deposit balance.

Other details on security deposit: _____

_____

_____ .

Clause 9. Utilities

Tenant will pay all utility charges, except for the following, which will be paid by Landlord:_____

_____ .

Clause 10. Assignment and Subletting

Tenant will not sublet any part of the premises or assign this Agreement without the prior written

consent of Landlord.

Clause 11. Tenant's Maintenance Responsibilities

Tenant will:

a. keep the premises clean, sanitary and in good condition and, upon termination of the tenancy,

return the premises to Landlord in a condition identical to that which existed when Tenant took

occupancy, except for ordinary wear and tear and any additions or alterations authorized by
Landlord

b. immediately notify Landlord of any defects or dangerous conditions in and about the premises of
which Tenant becomes aware, and

c. reimburse Landlord, on demand by Landlord, for the cost of any repairs to the premises damaged
by Tenant or Tenant's guests or business invitees through misuse, accident or neglect.

Tenant has examined the premises, including appliances, fixtures, carpets, drapes and paint, and has
found them to be in good, safe and clean condition and repair, except as noted in the Landlord-Tenant
Checklist.

Clause 12. Repairs and Alterations by Tenant

a. Except as provided by law or as authorized by the prior written consent of Landlord, Tenant will not
make any repairs or alterations to the premises, including nailing holes in the walls or painting the
rental unit.

b. Unless authorized by law, Tenant will not, without Landlord's prior written consent, alter, re-key or
install any locks to the premises or install or alter any burglar alarm system. Tenant will provide
Landlord with a key or keys capable of unlocking all such re-keyed or new locks as well as
instructions on how to disarm any altered or new burglar alarm system.

Clause 13. Violating Laws and Causing Disturbances

Tenant and guests or invitees will not use the premises or adjacent areas in such a way as to:

a. violate any law or ordinance, including laws prohibiting the use, possession or sale of illegal drugs

b. commit waste (severe property damage), or

c. create a nuisance by annoying, disturbing, inconveniencing or interfering with the quiet enjoyment
and peace and quiet of any other tenant or nearby resident.

Clause 14. Pets

No animal, bird or other pet will be kept on the premises, even temporarily, except properly trained
dogs needed by blind, deaf or disabled persons and _____
under the following conditions: _____
_____ .

Clause 15. Landlord's Right to Access

Landlord or Landlord's agents may enter the premises in the event of an emergency, to make repairs or
improvements or to show the premises to prospective buyers or tenants. Landlord may also enter the
premises to conduct an annual inspection to check for safety or maintenance problems. Except in cases
of emergency, Tenant's abandonment of the premises, court order or where it is impractical to do so,
Landlord shall give Tenant _____ notice before entering.

Clause 16. Extended Absences by Tenant

Tenant will notify Landlord in advance if Tenant will be away from the premises for _____
or more consecutive days. During such absence, Landlord may enter the premises at times reasonably
necessary to maintain the property and inspect for needed repairs.

Clause 17. Possession of the Premises

a. Tenant's failure to take possession.

If, after signing this Agreement, Tenant fails to take possession of the premises, Tenant will still be responsible for paying rent and complying with all other terms of this Agreement.

b. Landlord's failure to deliver possession.

If Landlord is unable to deliver possession of the premises to Tenant for any reason not within Landlord's control, including but not limited to partial or complete destruction of the premises, Tenant will have the right to terminate this Agreement upon proper notice as required by law. In such event, Landlord's liability to Tenant will be limited to the return of all sums previously paid by Tenant to Landlord.

Clause 18. Tenant Rules and Regulations

Tenant acknowledges receipt of, and has read a copy of, tenant rules and regulations, which are attached to and incorporated into this Agreement by this reference.

Clause 19. Payment of Court Costs and Attorney Fees in a Lawsuit

In any action or legal proceeding to enforce any part of this Agreement, the prevailing party ☐ shall not ☐ shall   recover reasonable attorney fees and court costs.

Clause 20. Disclosures

Tenant acknowledges that Landlord has made the following disclosures regarding the premises:

☐ disclosure of information on lead-based paint and/or lead-based paint hazards

☐ other disclosures: _____

_____

Clause 21. Authority to Receive Legal Papers

The Landlord, any person managing the premises and anyone designated by the Landlord are authorized to accept service of process and receive other notices and demands, which may be delivered to:

☐ the Landlord, at the following address: _____

_____.

☐ the Manager, at the following address:_____

_____.

☐ the following person, at the following address:_____

_____.

Clause 22. Additional Provisions

Additional provisions are as follows: _____

_____

_____

_____

_____

_____

_____

_____

Clause 23. Validity of Each Part

If any portion of this Agreement is held to be invalid, its invalidity will not affect the validity or enforceability of any other provision of this Agreement.

Clause 24. Grounds for Termination of Tenancy

The failure of Tenant or their guests or invitees to comply with any term of this Agreement is grounds for termination of the tenancy, with appropriate notice to Tenant and procedures as required by law.

Clause 25. Entire Agreement

This document and any Attachments constitutes the entire Agreement between the parties, and no promises or representations, other than those contained here and those implied by law, have been made by Landlord or Tenant. Any modifications to this Agreement must be in writing signed by Landlord and Tenant.

_____   _____
Landlord/Agent's signature   Date

_____
Title

_____
Address

_____   _____
                                                        Phone

_____   _____
Tenant 1's signature   Date

_____
Print name

_____   _____
Tenant 2's signature   Date

_____
Print name

_____   _____
Tenant 3's signature   Date

_____
Print name

Cancellation of Lease

Landlord: _____ and

Tenant: _____

agree that the lease they entered into for the time period of _____ , _____ ,

to _____ , _____ , for premises at _____

_____

will terminate on _____ .

Additional conditions for cancellation of lease: _____

_____

_____ .

_____   _____
Landlord's signature   Date

_____
Print name

_____   _____
Tenant's signature   Date

_____
Print name

Consent to Assignment of Lease

Landlord: _____

Tenant: _____

Assignee: _____

Landlord, Tenant and Assignee agree as follows:

1. Location of Premises

Tenant has leased the premises located at _____
from Landlord.

2. Lease Beginning and Ending Dates

The lease was signed on _____ , _____ .

It will expire on _____ , _____ .

3. Assignment

Tenant is assigning the balance of Tenant's lease to Assignee, beginning on _____ ,
_____ . It will end on _____ , _____ .

4. Tenant's Future Liability

Tenant's financial responsibilities under the terms of the lease are ended by this assignment.
Specifically, Tenant's responsibilities for future rent and future damage are ended.

5. Tenant's Right to Occupy

As of the effective date of the assignment, Tenant permanently gives up the right to occupy the
premises.

6. Binding Nature of Agreement

Assignee is bound by every term and condition in the lease that is the subject of this assignment.

_____   _____
Landlord's signature   Date

_____
Print name

_____   _____
Tenant's signature   Date

_____
Print name

_____   _____
Assignee's signature   Date

_____
Print name

Landlord-Tenant Checklist

GENERAL CONDITION OF RENTAL UNIT AND PREMISES

Street Address   Unit Number City

	Condition on Arrival	Condition on Departure	Estimated Cost of Repair/Replacement
LIVING ROOM			
Floors & floor coverings			
Drapes & window coverings			
Walls & ceilings			
Light fixtures			
Windows, screens & doors			
Front door & locks			
Fireplace			
Other			
Other			
KITCHEN			
Floors & floor coverings			
Walls & ceilings			
Light fixtures			
Windows, screens & doors			
Cabinets			
Counters			
Stove/oven			
Refrigerator			
Dishwasher			
Garbage disposal			
Sink & plumbing			
Other			
Other			
DINING ROOM			
Floors & floor covering			
Walls & ceilings			
Light fixtures			
Windows, screens & doors			
Other			
Other			

	Condition on Arrival	Condition on Departure	Estimated Cost of Repair/Replacement
BATHROOM 1			
Floors & floor coverings			
Walls & ceilings			
Windows, screens & doors			
Light fixtures			
Bathtub/shower			
Sink & counters			
Toilet			
Other			
Other			
BATHROOM 2			
Floors & floor coverings			
Walls & ceilings			
Windows, screens & doors			
Light fixtures			
Bathtub/shower			
Sink & counters			
Toilet			
Other			
Other			
BEDROOM 1			
Floors & floor coverings			
Windows, screens & doors			
Walls & ceilings			
Light fixtures			
Other			
Other			
Other			
BEDROOM 2			
Floors & floor coverings			
Windows, screens & doors			
Walls & ceilings			
Light fixtures			
Other			
Other			
Other			

	Condition on Arrival	Condition on Departure	Estimated Cost of Repair/Replacement
BEDROOM 3			
Floors & floor coverings			
Windows, screens & doors			
Walls & ceilings			
Light fixtures			
Other			
Other			
Other			
Other			
OTHER AREAS			
Furnace/heater			
Air conditioning			
Lawn/ground covering			
Garden			
Patio, terrace, deck, etc.			
Other			
Other			
Other			
Other			
Other			
Other			
Other			

☐ Tenants acknowledge that all smoke detectors and fire extinguishers were tested in their presence and found to be in working order, and that the testing procedure was explained to them. Tenants agree to test all detectors at least once a month and to report any problems to Landlord/Manager in writing. Tenants agree to replace all smoke detector batteries as necessary.

FURNISHED PROPERTY

	Condition on Arrival	Condition on Departure	Estimated Cost of Repair/Replacement
LIVING ROOM			
Coffee table			
End tables			
Lamps			
Chairs			
Sofa			
Other			
Other			
KITCHEN			
Broiler pan			
Ice trays			
Other			
Other			
DINING AREA			
Chairs			
Stools			
Table			
Other			
Other			
BATHROOM 1			
Dresser tables			
Mirrors			
Shower curtain			
Hamper			
Other			
BATHROOM 2			
Dresser tables			
Mirrors			
Shower curtain			
Hamper			
Other			
BEDROOM 1			
Beds (single)			
Beds (double)			
Chairs			

	Condition on Arrival	Condition on Departure	Estimated Cost of Repair/Replacement
Chests			
Dressing tables			
Lamps			
Mirrors			
Night tables			
Other			
Other			
BEDROOM 2			
Beds (single)			
Beds (double)			
Chairs			
Chests			
Dressing tables			
Lamps			
Mirrors			
Night tables			
Other			
Other			
BEDROOM 3			
Beds (single)			
Beds (double)			
Chairs			
Chests			
Dressing tables			
Lamps			
Mirrors			
Night tables			
Other			
Other			
OTHER AREAS			
Bookcases			
Desks			
Pictures			
Other			
Other			

Use this space to provide any additional explanation:

_____

_____

_____

_____

_____

_____

_____

_____

_____

_____

_____

_____

Landlord-Tenant Checklist completed on moving in on _____ *[date]* and approved by:

_____ and _____
Landlord/Manager   Tenant

                                                          _____
                                                          Tenant

                                                          _____
                                                          Tenant

Landlord-Tenant Checklist completed on moving out on _____ *[date]* and approved by:

_____ and _____
Landlord/Manager   Tenant

                                                          _____
                                                          Tenant

                                                          _____
                                                          Tenant

Notice of Needed Repairs

To: _____ *[name of landlord or manager]*

At: _____

From: _____ *[tenant]*

At: _____
    [address]

I am writing to inform you of the following problem(s) in my rental unit:

_____

_____

_____

_____

_____

_____

_____ .

I would very much appreciate it if you would promptly look into the problem(s). Please call me so that I'll know when to expect you or a repair person. You can reach me as follows:

Work (daytime): _____ Home (evenings): _____

Thank you very much for your attention to this problem.

_____   _____
Signature   Date

Tenant's Notice of Intent to Move Out

Date:_____

Landlord/Manager: _____

Street address: _____

City and state: _____

Regarding:

Rental unit address: _____

Dear _____ :

This is to notify you that the undersigned tenant(s) will be moving from the above noted rental unit on _____, _____, or _____ days from today.

This notice provides you with at least _____ days' written notice, as required in our rental agreement.

_____
Tenant 1's signature

_____
Print name

_____
Tenant 2's signature

_____
Print name

_____
Tenant 3's signature

_____
Print name

Loan Comparison Worksheet

Purpose of loan: _____

Amount looking to borrow:_____

	Loan 1	Loan 2	Loan 3
General Information			
Lender:	_____	_____	_____
Contact:	_____	_____	_____
Address:	_____	_____	_____
	_____	_____	_____
	_____	_____	_____
Phone:	_____	_____	_____
Loan Terms			
APR:	_____	_____	_____
Interest rate:	_____	_____	_____
Adjustable?	_____	_____	_____
Cap:	_____	_____	_____
Number of months:	_____	_____	_____
Monthly payment:	_____	_____	_____
Total payments (# of mos.			
X monthly payment):	_____	_____	_____
Other Costs			
Loan application fee:	_____	_____	_____
Credit check:	_____	_____	_____
Credit insurance:	_____	_____	_____
Other:	_____	_____	_____
Other Features			
Collateral required?	_____	_____	_____
If yes, specify:	_____	_____	_____
Balloon payment?	_____	_____	_____
Prepayment penalty?	_____	_____	_____
If yes, amount:	_____	_____	_____
Cosigner required?	_____	_____	_____
Payment due date:	_____	_____	_____
Grace period?	_____	_____	_____
Late fee?	_____	_____	_____
Possible loan discounts:	_____	_____	_____
Account with lender:	_____	_____	_____
Automatic deduction:	_____	_____	_____
On-time payments:	_____	_____	_____

Authorization to Conduct Credit Check

Borrower

Full name—include generations (Jr., Sr., III): _____

Other names used: _____

Street address: _____

City, state and zip code: _____

Date moved into current address: _____

Previous address: _____

City, state and zip code: _____

Dates there: _____

Home phone: _____ Social Security number: _____

Date of birth: _____

Employment History

Name and address of current employer: _____

_____

Name of supervisor: _____ Supervisor's phone: _____

Annual income: _____

Credit and Financial Information

Bank/Financial Accounts	Account Number	Bank/Institution	Branch
Bank savings account:			
Bank checking account:			
Bank certificate of deposit:			
Mutual fund account:			
Brokerage account:			
Other:			
Other:			
Other:			

Credit accounts & loans	Type of account (auto loan, Visa, etc.)	Account Number	Name of Creditor	Amount Owed	Monthly Payment
Credit card:					
Credit card:					
Loan (specify type):					
Loan (specify type):					
Loan (specify type):					
Other (specify type):					

I certify that all the information given above is true and correct. I authorize verification of the information provided from my credit sources and employer.

_____   _____

Signature   Date

Monthly Payment Record

Name of lender: _____

Original amount borrowed: _____ Date loan made: _____

Month	(A) Beginning balance (or prior month ending balance)	(B) Annual interest rate divided by 12	(C) Interest due (A) x (B)	(D) Amount of payment made	(E) Principal reduction (D)–(C)	(F) New balance (A)–(E)
1						
2						
3						
4						
5						
6						
7						
8						
9						
10						
11						
12						
13						
14						
15						
16						
17						
18						
19						
20						
21						
22						
23						
24						
25						
26						
27						
28						
29						
30						

Promissory Note

Loan repayable in installments with interest

Name of Borrower 1: _____

Name of Borrower 2: _____

Name of Lender: _____

1. For value received, Borrower promises to pay to Lender the amount of $ _____

   at _____

   [address where payments are to be sent] at the rate of _____% per year from the date this note

   was signed until the date it is *[choose one]:*

   ☐ paid in full *[Borrower will receive credits for prepayments, reducing the total amount of interest to

   be repaid].*

   ☐ due or is paid in full, whichever date occurs last *[Borrower will not receive credits for prepayments].*

2. Borrower agrees that this note shall be paid in installments, which include principal and interest, of not

   less than $ _____ per month, due on the first day of each month, until such time as the

   principal and interest are paid in full.

3. If any installment payment due under this note is not received by Lender within _____days of its due

   date, the entire amount of unpaid principal shall become immediately due and payable at the option

   of Lender without prior notice to Borrower.

4. In the event Lender prevails in a lawsuit to collect on it, Borrower agrees to pay Lender's attorney fees

   in an amount the court finds to be just and reasonable.

*The term Borrower refers to one or more borrowers. If there is more than one borrower, they agree to be jointly and
severally liable. The term Lender refers to any person who legally holds this note, including a buyer in due course.*

_____   _____

Borrower 1's signature   Date

_____

Print name

_____

Location *[city or county where signed]*

_____

Address

_____   _____

Borrower 2's signature   Date

_____

Print name

_____

Location *[city or county where signed]*

_____

Address

Promissory Note

Loan repayable in installments with interest and balloon payment

Name of Borrower 1: _____

Name of Borrower 2: _____

Name of Lender: _____

1. For value received, Borrower promises to pay to Lender the amount of $ _____
    at _____
    [address where payments are to be sent] at the rate of _____% per year from the date this note
    was signed until the date it is *[choose one]:*
    ☐ paid in full *[Borrower will receive credits for prepayments, reducing the total amount of interest to
       be repaid].*
    ☐ due or is paid in full, whichever date occurs last *[Borrower will not receive credits for prepayments].*

2. Borrower agrees that this note shall be paid in installments, which include principal and interest, of not
    less than $ _____ per month, due on the first day of each month, until such time as the
    principal and interest are paid in full.

3. Borrower agrees to make one final payment for the entire balance owed on or before_____
    [date balloon payment is due].

4. If any installment payment due under this note is not received by Lender within _____ days of its due
    date, the entire amount of unpaid principal shall become immediately due and payable at the option
    of Lender without prior notice to Borrower.

5. In the event Lender prevails in a lawsuit to collect on it, Borrower agrees to pay Lender's attorney fees
    in an amount the court finds to be just and reasonable.

*The term Borrower refers to one or more borrowers. If there is more than one borrower, they agree to be jointly and
severally liable. The term Lender refers to any person who legally holds this note, including a buyer in due course.*

_____   _____
Borrower 1's signature   Date

_____
Print name

_____
Location *[city or county where signed]*

_____
Address

_____   _____
Borrower 2's signature   Date

_____
Print name

_____
Location *[city or county where signed]*

_____
Address

Promissory Note

Loan repayable in installments without interest

Name of Borrower 1: _____

Name of Borrower 2: _____

Name of Lender: _____

1. For value received, Borrower promises to pay to Lender the amount of $ _____

    at _____

    [address where payments are to be sent].

2. Borrower also agrees that this note shall be paid in equal installments of $ _____ per

    month, due on the first day of each month, until the principal is paid in full.

3. If any installment payment due under this note is not received by Lender within _____ days of

    its due date, the entire amount of unpaid principal shall become immediately due and payable at the

    option of Lender without prior notice to Borrower.

4. In the event Lender prevails in a lawsuit to collect on it, Borrower agrees to pay Lender's attorney fees

    in an amount the court finds to be just and reasonable.

*The term Borrower refers to one or more borrowers. If there is more than one borrower, they agree to be jointly and
severally liable. The term Lender refers to any person who legally holds this note, including a buyer in due course.*

_____   _____

Borrower 1's signature   Date

_____

Print name

_____

Location *[city or county where signed]*

_____

Address

_____   _____

Borrower 2's signature   Date

_____

Print name

_____

Location *[city or county where signed]*

_____

Address

Promissory Note

Loan repayable in lump sum with interest

Name of Borrower 1: _____

Name of Borrower 2: _____

Name of Lender: _____

1. For value received, Borrower promises to pay to Lender the amount of $ _____

   at _____

   [address where payments are to be sent].

2. Simple interest shall be charged on the sum specified in Clause 1 at the rate of _____ % per year

   from the date this note was signed until the date it is *[choose one]:*

   ☐ paid in full (Borrower will receive credits for prepayments, reducing the total amount of interest to

   be repaid).

   ☐ due or is paid in full, whichever date occurs last (Borrower will not receive credits for making

   prepayments).

3. In the event Lender prevails in a lawsuit to collect on it, Borrower agrees to pay Lender's attorney fees

   in an amount the court finds to be just and reasonable.

The term Borrower refers to one or more borrowers. If there is more than one borrower, they agree to be jointly and severally liable. The term Lender refers to any person who legally holds this note, including a buyer in due course.

_____   _____

Borrower 1's signature   Date

_____

Print name

_____

Location *[city or county where signed]*

_____

Address

_____   _____

Borrower 2's signature   Date

_____

Print name

_____

Location *[city or county where signed]*

_____

Address

Promissory Note

Loan repayable in lump sum without interest

Name of Borrower 1: _____

Name of Borrower 2: _____

Name of Lender: _____

1. For value received, Borrower promises to pay to Lender the amount of $ _____
   at _____
   [address where payments are to be sent].

2. In the event Lender prevails in a lawsuit to collect on it, Borrower agrees to pay Lender's attorney fees in an amount the court finds to be just and reasonable.

The term Borrower refers to one or more borrowers. If there is more than one borrower, they agree to be jointly and severally liable. The term Lender refers to any person who legally holds this note, including a buyer in due course.

_____   _____
Borrower 1's signature   Date

_____
Print name

_____
Location *[city or county where signed]*

_____
Address

_____   _____
Borrower 2's signature   Date

_____
Print name

_____
Location *[city or county where signed]*

_____
Address

Cosigner Provision

Name of Cosigner 1: _____

Name of Cosigner 2: _____

Name of Borrower 1: _____

Name of Borrower 2: _____

Name of Lender: _____

1. Borrower has agreed to pay to Lender the amount indicated in the attached Promissory Note under the terms specified in that Note.

2. Cosigner agrees to guarantee this debt; Cosigner wants to accept this responsibility and understands this obligation means the following:

   • If Borrower doesn't pay the debt on time, that fact may become a part of Cosigner's credit record.

   • If Borrower doesn't pay the debt at all, Cosigner will be legally obligated to do so.

   • Cosigner may have to pay late fees or collection costs, which will increase this amount.

   • Lender can collect this debt from Cosigner without first trying to collect from Borrower.

   • Lender can use the same collection methods against Cosigner that can be used against Borrower, including filing a lawsuit against Cosigner, and if the lawsuit is successful, garnishing Cosigner's wages, seizing other personal property of Cosigner and putting a lien against Cosigner's house.

The term Cosigner refers to one or more cosigner. If there is more than one cosigner, they agree to be jointly and severally liable.

_____   _____
Cosigner 1's signature   Date

_____
Print name

_____
Location *[city or county where signed]*

_____
Address

_____   _____
Cosigner 2's signature   Date

_____
Print name

_____
Location *[city or county where signed]*

_____
Address

Security Agreement Provision for Promissory Note

Borrower agrees that until such time as the principal and interest owed under this note are paid in full, the note shall be secured by the following described mortgage, deed of trust or security agreement:

_____

_____

_____

Here are some examples of the kind of language to include in the security agreement provision.

House as Security:

Borrower agrees that until such time as the principal and interest owed under this note are paid in full, the note shall be secured by the following mortgage or deed of trust:

Deed of trust to real property commonly known as: _____

_____ *[address or other description]*

owned by: _____ *[name of owner]*

executed on: _____ *[date signed]* at: _____

_____ *[place signed]*

and recorded at: _____ *[place recorded]*

in the records of:_____ *[county and state where recorded]*

Vehicle as Security:

Borrower agrees that until such time as the principal and interest owed under this note are paid in full, the note shall be secured by the following security agreement:

Security agreement signed by: _____ *[name of owner]*

on: _____ *[date signed]* which gives title to: _____

_____ *[date, make, model and VIN of vehicle]*

Valuable Personal Property as Security:

Borrower agrees that until such time as the principal and interest owed under this note are paid in full, the note shall be secured by the following security agreement:

Security agreement signed by: _____ *[name of owner]*

on: _____ *[date signed]* which gives a security interest in: _____

_____ *[description of the collateral]*

U.C.C. Financing Statement

This Financing Statement is presented for filing under the Uniform Commercial Code as adopted in

_____ *[name of your state].*

Name of Borrower:_____

Address of Borrower: _____

_____

Name of Lender/Secured party: _____

Address of Lender/Secured party:_____

_____

The term Borrower refers to one or more borrowers. If there is more than one borrower, they agree to be jointly and severally liable. The term Lender refers to any person who legally holds this note, including a buyer in due course.

The property listed as collateral in the security agreement is as follows *[identify or describe]:*

_____

_____

This Financing Statement secures the following debt:

Promissory note dated: _____

Amount of debt: _____

Pay back due date: _____

All other terms and conditions are stated in the promissory note, which is attached.

Borrower's signature: _____

Print name: _____

Date:_____

(For Use of the Filing Officer)

Date of filing: _____ Time of filing: _____

File number and address of filing office:_____

_____

Release of U.C.C. Financing Statement

This Release of Financing Statement is presented for filing under the Uniform Commercial Code as adopted in _____ *[name of your state]*.

Name of Borrower:_____

Address of Borrower: _____

_____

Name of Lender/Secured party: _____

Address of Lender/Secured party:_____

_____

The term Borrower refers to one or more borrowers. The term Lender refers to any person who legally holds this note, including a buyer in due course.

The property listed as collateral in the security agreement is as follows *[identify or describe]*:

_____

_____

File number of Financing Statement: _____

Date filed: _____

Address of filing office: _____

Borrower's signature: _____

Print name: _____

Date:_____

(For Use of the Filing Officer)

Date of filing: _____ Time of filing:_____

File number and address of filing office:_____

_____

Release of Security Interest

Name of Borrower: _____

Address of Borrower: _____

_____

Name of Lender/Secured party: _____

Address of Lender/Secured party: _____

_____

For valuable consideration, Lender releases Borrower from the following specific security agreement *[identify the security agreement, including the date signed, amount borrowed, collateral named and pay back date]*:

_____

_____

_____

The term Borrower refers to one or more borrowers. The term Lender refers to any person who legally holds this note, including a buyer in due course.

Any claims and obligations not specifically mentioned here are not covered by this Release.

Lender has not assigned any claims or obligations covered by this Release to any other party.

Lender will sign a Release of U.C.C. Financing Statement if such a statement was filed with a public agency.

_____   _____

Lender's signature   Date

_____

Print name

Agreement to Modify Promissory Note

Name of Borrower 1: _____

Name of Borrower 2: _____

Name of Lender: _____

1. This Agreement modifies an original promissory note dated _____ , _____ ,
   under which Borrower promises to pay to Lender the amount of $ _____ at the rate of
   _____% per year from the date this note was signed until _____ , _____ .

2. Lender and Borrower agree to the following modifications *[choose all that apply]*:

   ☐ Borrower has until _____ to pay the note in full.

   ☐ Borrower will make interest-only payments beginning on _____ , _____ ,
      until _____ , _____ , at which time the remaining principal balance
      will be reamortized over the remaining months of the note.

   ☐ Beginning on _____ , _____ , the interest rate will change
      to _____ %. The new monthly payments will be in the amount of $ _____ .

   ☐ Other: _____ .

The term Borrower refers to one or more borrowers. If there is more than one borrower, they agree to be jointly and severally liable. The term Lender refers to any person who legally holds this note, including a buyer in due course.

_____   _____
Borrower 1's signature   Date

_____
Print name

_____
Location *[city or county where signed]*

_____
Address

_____   _____
Borrower 2's signature   Date

_____
Print name

_____
Location *[city or county where signed]*

_____
Address

Overdue Payment Demand

Date: _____

To:

_____

_____

_____

[insert name and address of check writer]

Re: Promissory Note dated _____

Dear _____ :

This is to notify you that I have not received the following payment(s) under our Promissory Note.

Amount:	$ _____	Due date:	_____
Amount:	$ _____	Due date:	_____
Total:	$ _____		

Please let me know at once if there is a problem. If I do not hear from you within 15 days, I will have no choice but to assume that you do not intend to repay me what is due under this Note. I will proceed to enforce my rights under the Promissory Note, including possibly filing a lawsuit, to collect the entire balance.

Sincerely,

_____

Signature

_____

Print name

Demand to Make Good on Bad Check

Date: _____

To:

_____

_____

_____

[insert name and address of check writer]

Re: Check # _____ Dated _____ , _____

Issuing institution: _____

Dear _____ :

Your check was returned to my bank and refused payment for the following reason *[choose one]*:

☐ insufficient funds in the account on which the check was drawn to cover the amount of the check.

☐ the account on which the check was drawn has been closed.

Please let me know at once if there is a problem. If I do not hear from you within 30 days, I will have no choice but to assume that you do not intend to make good on this check. I will proceed to enforce my rights, which may include filing a lawsuit. I will request that the court award me the following monetary damages:

☐ the amount of the check

☐ bad check processing fee charged by my bank

☐ expenses incurred in attempting to collect on the check

☐ other: damages permitted under the law of the state of _____ as follows:

_____

_____

Sincerely,

_____

Signature

_____

Print name

Ideal House Profile

	Must Have	Hope to Have
Upper price limit:	_____	_____
Maximum down payment:	_____	_____
Special financing needs:	_____	_____
_____	_____	_____
Type of street:	_____	_____
_____	_____	_____
Type of neighborhood or location:	_____	_____
_____	_____	_____
_____	_____	_____
Quality of school district:	_____	_____
_____	_____	_____
Desired neighborhood features:	_____	_____
_____	_____	_____
_____	_____	_____
_____	_____	_____
Length of commute:	_____	_____
_____	_____	_____
Access to public transportation:	_____	_____
_____	_____	_____
Size of house:	_____	_____
_____	_____	_____
Number and type of rooms:	_____	_____
_____	_____	_____
_____	_____	_____
Condition, age and type of house:	_____	_____
_____	_____	_____
Type of yard and grounds:	_____	_____
_____	_____	_____
Other desired features:	_____	_____
_____	_____	_____
_____	_____	_____
_____	_____	_____
Features that are "no-nos":	_____	_____
_____	_____	_____
_____	_____	_____

House Priorities Worksheet

Date visited: _____

Address: _____

Price: $ _____

Contact: _____ Phone #: _____

Must have:

☐ _____

☐ _____

☐ _____

☐ _____

☐ _____

☐ _____

☐ _____

☐ _____

Hope to have:

☐ _____

☐ _____

☐ _____

☐ _____

☐ _____

☐ _____

☐ _____

☐ _____

Absolute no way:

☐ _____

☐ _____

☐ _____

☐ _____

Comments about the particular house:

_____

_____

_____

_____

House Comparison Worksheet

	Address	Address	Address	Address
	_____	_____	_____	_____
	_____	_____	_____	_____
	_____	_____	_____	_____
	_____	_____	_____	_____

Must have:

_____	_____	_____	_____	_____
_____	_____	_____	_____	_____
_____	_____	_____	_____	_____
_____	_____	_____	_____	_____
_____	_____	_____	_____	_____
_____	_____	_____	_____	_____
_____	_____	_____	_____	_____
_____	_____	_____	_____	_____
_____	_____	_____	_____	_____

Hope to have:

_____	_____	_____	_____	_____
_____	_____	_____	_____	_____
_____	_____	_____	_____	_____
_____	_____	_____	_____	_____
_____	_____	_____	_____	_____
_____	_____	_____	_____	_____
_____	_____	_____	_____	_____
_____	_____	_____	_____	_____
_____	_____	_____	_____	_____
_____	_____	_____	_____	_____
_____	_____	_____	_____	_____

No ways:

_____	_____	_____	_____	_____
_____	_____	_____	_____	_____
_____	_____	_____	_____	_____
_____	_____	_____	_____	_____

Family Financial Statement

	Borrower	Co-Borrower
Name:		
Address:		
Home phone:		
Employer:		
Employer's address:		
Work phone:		

Worksheet 1: Income and Expenses

I. INCOME	Borrower ($)	Co-Borrower ($)	Total ($)
A. Monthly gross income			
1. Employment			
2. Dividends			
3. Royalties			
4. Interest/investments			
5. Retirement pay			
6. Public benefits			
7. Other (specify):_____			
B. Total			

II. MONTHLY EXPENSES	Borrower ($)	Co-Borrower ($)	Total ($)
A. Non-housing			
1. Child care			
2. Clothing			
3. Food			
4. Insurance			
a. Auto			
b. Life			
c. Medical			
5. Other medical			
6. Personal			
7. Education			
8. Taxes (non-housing)			
9. Transportation			
10. Other (specify):_____			
B. Housing			
1. Mortgage			
2. Taxes			
3. Insurance			
4. Utilities			
5. Rent			
6. Other (specify):_____			
C. Total			

Worksheet 2: Assets and Liabilities

	Borrower ($)	Co-Borrower ($)	Total ($)
I. ASSETS (Cash or Market Value)			
A. Cash and cash equivalents			
1. Cash			
2. Deposits (list):			
_____			
_____			
B. Marketable securities			
1. Stocks/bonds (bid price)			
2. Other securities			
3. Mutual funds			
4. Life insurance			
5. Other (specify):			
_____			
_____			
C. Total			
D. Non-liquid assets			
1. Real estate			
2. Retirement funds			
3. Business			
4. Motor vehicles			
5. Other (specify):			
_____			
_____			
E. Total non-liquid assets			
F. Total all assets			
II. LIABILITIES			
A. Debts			
1. Real estate loans			
2. Student loans			
3. Motor vehicle loans			
4. Child or spousal support			
5. Personal loans			
6. Credit cards (specify):			
_____			
_____			
_____			
7. Other (specify):			
_____			
_____			
B. Total liabilities			
III. NET WORTH			
(Total assets minus total liabilities)			

Monthly Carrying Costs Worksheet

1. Estimated purchase price $ _____

2. Down payment $ _____

3. Loan amount (line 1 minus line 2) $ _____

4. Interest rate   _____ %

5. Mortgage payment factor   _____

6. Monthly mortgage payment
   (multiply line 3 by line 5) $ _____

7. Homeowner's insurance (monthly) $ _____

8. Property taxes (monthly) $ _____

9. Total monthly carrying costs
   (add lines 6-8) $ _____

10. Long-term debts (monthly payments)

    _____ $ _____

    _____ $ _____

    _____ $ _____

    _____ $ _____

    Total long-term debts (monthly payments) $ _____

11. Private mortgage insurance $ _____

12. Homeowners' association fee $ _____

13. Total monthly carrying costs and
    long-term debts (add lines 9-12) $ _____

14. Lender qualification (between .28 and .38)   _____%

15. Monthly income to qualify (divide line 13 by line 14) $ _____

16. Yearly income to qualify (multiply line 15 by 12 (months)) $ _____

Mortgage Rates and Terms Worksheet

Lender: _____ _____ _____

Loan agent: _____ _____ _____

Phone number: _____ _____ _____

Date: _____ _____ _____

1. General Information

Fixed or adjustable	☐ F ☐ A	☐ F ☐ A	☐ F ☐ A
Fixed interest rate	_____ %	_____ %	_____ %
Government financing	☐ Y ☐ N	☐ Y ☐ N	☐ Y ☐ N
Minimum down payment	_____ %	_____ %	_____ %
PMI required	☐ Y ☐ N	☐ Y ☐ N	☐ Y ☐ N
Impound account	☐ Y ☐ N	☐ Y ☐ N	☐ Y ☐ N
Term of mortgage	_____ Years	_____ Years	_____ Years
Assumable	☐ Y ☐ N	☐ Y ☐ N	☐ Y ☐ N
Prepayment penalty	☐ Y ☐ N	☐ Y ☐ N	☐ Y ☐ N
Negative amortization	☐ Y ☐ N	☐ Y ☐ N	☐ Y ☐ N
Rate lock-in available	☐ Y ☐ N	☐ Y ☐ N	☐ Y ☐ N
Cost to lock-in	21 Days $ _____	21 Days $ _____	21 Days $ _____
	30 Days $ _____	30 Days $ _____	30 Days $ _____
	45 Days $ _____	45 Days $ _____	45 Days $ _____

2. Debt-to-Income Ratios Information

Allowable monthly carrying costs as % of income	_____ %	_____ %	_____ %
Allowable monthly carrying costs plus long-term debts as % of monthly income	_____ %	_____ %	_____ %
Maximum loan you qualify for based on debt-to-income ratios	$ _____	$ _____	$ _____

3. Loan Costs

Number of points	$ _____	$ _____	$ _____
Cost of points	$ _____	$ _____	$ _____
PMI	$ _____	$ _____	$ _____
Additional loan fee	$ _____	$ _____	$ _____
Credit report	$ _____	$ _____	$ _____
Application fee	$ _____	$ _____	$ _____

Appraisal fee $ _____ $ _____ $ _____

Miscellaneous fees $ _____ $ _____ $ _____

Estimated total loan costs $ _____ $ _____ $ _____

4. Time Limits

Credit/employment check _____ Days _____ Days _____ Days

Lender appraisal _____ Days _____ Days _____ Days

Loan approval _____ Days _____ Days _____ Days

Loan funding _____ Days _____ Days _____ Days

Loan due date each month _____ _____ _____

Grace period _____ Days _____ Days _____ Days

Late fee _____ % _____ % _____ %

5. Other Features

[such as a discount for having an account
with a certain bank, or a lender discount
of interest rate on initial payments]

_____ _____ _____ _____

_____ _____ _____ _____

6. Fixed Rate Two-Step Loans

Initial annual interest rate _____ % _____ % _____ %

Over how many years _____ Years _____ Years _____ Years

7. Fixed Rate Balloon Payment Loans

Interest rate _____ % _____ % _____ %

Monthly payment $ _____ $ _____ $ _____

Term of loan _____ Years _____ Years _____ Years

Amount of balloon payment $ _____ $ _____ $ _____

8. Convertible Loans

Earliest conversion period _____ Months _____ Months _____ Months

Conversion window _____ Weeks _____ Weeks _____ Weeks

Index: 11th District COFI ☐ _____ % ☐ _____ % ☐ _____ %

6 Mo. T-Bills ☐ _____ % ☐ _____ % ☐ _____ %

1 Yr. T-Bills ☐ _____ % ☐ _____ % ☐ _____ %

Other _____ ☐ _____ % ☐ _____ % ☐ _____ %

Margin _____ % _____ % _____ %

Conversion fee $ _____ $ _____ $ _____

9. Adjustable Rate Mortgages (ARMs)

Index: 11th District COFI	☐ _____ %	☐ _____ %	☐ _____ %
6 Mo. T-Bills	☐ _____ %	☐ _____ %	☐ _____ %
1 Yr. T-Bills	☐ _____ %	☐ _____ %	☐ _____ %
Other _____	☐ _____ %	☐ _____ %	☐ _____ %
Margin	_____ %	_____ %	_____ %
Convertible	☐ Y ☐ N	☐ Y ☐ N	☐ Y ☐ N
When	Year _____	Year _____	Year _____
Initial interest rate			
How long	___ Mos. ___ Yrs.	___ Mos. ___ Yrs.	___ Mos. ___ Yrs.
Interest rate cap (with negative amortization) or	_____ %	_____ %	_____ %
Interest rate cap (without negative amortization)	_____ %	_____ %	_____ %
Adjustment period	_____ Months	_____ Months	_____ Months
Life-of-loan (overall) cap	_____ %	_____ %	_____ %
Initial payment	_____ Months	_____ Months	_____ Months
Payment cap	_____ %	_____ %	_____ %
Payment cap period	_____ Months	_____ Months	_____ Months

Highest payment or interest rate in:

6 months	___% $ _____	___% $ _____	___% $ _____
12 months	___% $ _____	___% $ _____	___% $ _____
18 months	___% $ _____	___% $ _____	___% $ _____
24 months	___% $ _____	___% $ _____	___% $ _____
30 months	___% $ _____	___% $ _____	___% $ _____
36 months	___% $ _____	___% $ _____	___% $ _____

10. Hybrid Loans

Initial interest rate	_____ %	_____ %	_____ %
Term as a fixed rate loan	_____ Years	_____ Years	_____ Years
Interest rate at first adjustment period	_____ %	_____ %	_____ %

Moving Checklist

[Not all items on this list will apply to you. If you're moving within the same town, you probably won't have to transfer your kids to a new school, get references for a new job or have your car serviced for travel. So just focus on the applicable items.]

I. Two Weeks Before Moving

- ☐ Transfer school records and transcripts; Register your children at new school.
- ☐ Close bank and safe deposit box accounts.
- ☐ Cancel deliveries—newspaper, diapers, laundry.
- ☐ Cancel utilities—gas, electric, cable, phone, water, garbage; transfer services (if possible) or arrange new services; request deposit refunds.
- ☐ Get recommendations or find in advance (especially if a medical condition needs regular attention) new doctors, dentist and veterinarian. If possible, photocopy key medical records to have with you.
- ☐ Get reference letters, if you'll need to find a job.
- ☐ Cancel membership (or transfer membership, if relevant) in religious, civic and athletic organizations.
- ☐ Have car serviced for travel.
- ☐ Arrange for moving pets.
- ☐ Finalize arrangements with moving company. (You should have gotten bids and made preliminary arrangements weeks earlier.)
- ☐ Tell close friends and relatives your schedule.

II. Things to Remember While Packing

- ☐ Before you pack, take the time to do a good inventory and sort through things. This way you can move less and won't end up throwing things away at your new home or taking up storage space.
- ☐ Label boxes on top and side—your name, new city, room of house, contents.
- ☐ Pack phone books.
- ☐ Assemble moving kit—hammer, screwdriver, pliers, tape, nails, tape measure, scissors, flashlight, cleansers, cleaning cloths, rubber gloves, garbage bags, light bulbs, extension cords. If you're driving to your new home, pack a broom and pail in your car. Larger items that are handy when moving in, such as a step stool or vacuum cleaner, should go in the moving van, unless your new house is nearby and you're moving lots of things by car.
- ☐ Keep the basics handy—comfortable clothes, toiletries, towels, alarm clock, disposable plates, cups and utensils, can opener, one pot, one pan, sponge, paper towels, toilet paper, plastic containers and toys for kids.
- ☐ Consider carrying jewelry, extremely fragile items, currency and important documents.
- ☐ Make other arrangements if moving company won't move antiques, art collections, crystal, other valuables or plants.

III. Whom to Send Change of Addresses

☐ Subscriptions.

☐ Government agencies you regularly deal with—Veterans' Administration, Social Security Administration, etc.

☐ Charge and credit accounts.

☐ Installment debt—such as student loan or car loan.

☐ Frequent flyer programs.

☐ Brokers and mutual funds.

☐ Insurance agent/companies.

☐ Medical providers—if you'll be able to use them after moving.

☐ Catalogues you want to keep receiving.

☐ Charities you wish to continue donating to.

☐ Post office. (If you're trying to get off of catalogue and other direct mailing lists, only have first-class mail forwarded. Give your new address to those catalogue companies on whose lists you want to remain, and don't forget to tell them not to trade or sell your name.)

IV. Things to Do After Moving In

☐ Open bank accounts.

☐ Open safe deposit box account.

☐ Begin deliveries—oil, newspaper, diapers, laundry.

☐ Register to vote.

☐ Change (or get new) driver's license.

☐ Change auto registration.

☐ Install new batteries in existing smoke detectors (and install any additionally needed smoke detectors); buy fire extinguisher.

☐ Hold party for the people who helped you find your house and your moving helpers, and take yourself out for a congratulatory dinner!

Lease-Option Contract

Clause 1. Identification of Owner and Tenant

Owner (Lessor/Optionor): _____

Tenant (Lessee/Optionee): _____

This Agreement to create a Lease with Option to Purchase is entered into between Owner and Tenant. Each Tenant is jointly and severally liable for the payment of rent and performance of all other terms of this Agreement.

Clause 2. Identification of the Premises

Subject to the terms and conditions in this Agreement, Owner rents to Tenant, and Tenant rents from Owner, for residential purposes only, the premises located at _____

_____ ("the premises").

Clause 3. Limits on Use and Occupancy

The premises are to be used only as a private residence for Tenant(s) listed in Clause 1 of this Agreement and their minor children.

Occupancy by guests for more than _____ is prohibited without Owner's written consent and will be considered a material breach of this Agreement.

Clause 4. Term of the Tenancy

The rental will begin on _____ , _____ , and will continue for a period of

_____ months, expiring on _____ , _____ .

Clause 5. Amount and Schedule for the Payment of Rent

On signing this Agreement, Tenant will pay to Owner the sum of $ _____ as rent, payable in advance, for the period of _____ , _____ , through _____

_____. Thereafter, Tenant will pay to Owner a monthly rent of $ _____ , payable in advance on the first day of each month, except when the first falls on a weekend or legal holiday, in which case rent is due on the next business day. Rent will be paid to _____

_____. The following forms of payment will be

accepted: _____ .

Clause 6. Late Charges

If Tenant fails to pay the rent in full within _____ days after it is due, Tenant will pay Owner a late charge of $ _____ plus $ _____ for each additional day that the rent continues to be unpaid. The total late charge for any one month will not exceed $ _____ . By this provision, Owner does not waive the right to insist on payment of the rent in full on the day it is due.

Clause 7. Returned Check Charges

If any check offered by Tenant to Owner in payment of rent or any other amount due under this Agreement is returned for lack of sufficient funds, Tenant will pay Owner a returned check charge of

$ _____ .

Clause 8. Security Deposit

On signing this Agreement, Tenant will pay to Owner the sum of $ _____ as a security deposit. Tenant may not, without Owner's prior written consent, apply this security deposit to rent or to any other sum due under this Agreement. Within _____ weeks after Tenant has vacated the premises, Owner will return the deposit in full or give Tenant an itemized written statement of the reasons for, and the dollar amount of, any of the security deposit retained by the Owner, along with a check for any deposit balance.

Other details on security deposit:

_____

_____

Clause 9. Utilities

Tenant will pay all utility charges, except for the following, which will be paid by Owner: _____

_____.

Clause 10. Prohibition of Assignment and Subletting

Tenant will not sublet any part of the premises or assign this lease without the prior written consent of Owner.

Clause 11. Condition of the Premises

Tenant has examined the premises, including appliances, fixtures, carpets, drapes and paint, and has found them to be in good, safe and clean condition and repair, except as otherwise noted on the written inventory of furniture and furnishings on the premises which Tenant has completed and given Owner, a copy of which Owner acknowledges receipt of, and which is incorporated into this Agreement by this reference.

Tenant agrees to:

- keep the premises in good order and repair and, upon termination of tenancy, to return the premises to Owner in a condition identical to that which existed when Tenant took occupancy, except for ordinary wear and tear and any additions or alterations authorized by Owner;
- immediately notify Owner of any defects or dangerous conditions in and about the premises of which Tenant becomes aware; and
- reimburse Owner, on demand by Owner or his or her agent, for the cost of any repairs to the premises damaged by Tenant or Tenant guests or invitees.

The following appliances and fixtures will be included with the property:

☐ for sale if the option is exercised: _____

_____.

☐ for rent only during the period of the lease: _____

_____.

Clause 12. Possession of Premises

a. Tenant's failure to take possession.

If, after signing this Agreement, Tenant fails to take possession of the premises, Tenant will still be responsible for paying rent and complying with all other terms of this Agreement.

b. Owner's failure to deliver possession.

If Owner is unable to deliver possession of the premises to Tenant for any reason not within Owner's control, including but not limited to partial or complete destruction of the premises, Tenant will have the right to terminate this Agreement upon proper notice as required by law. In such event, Owner's liability to Tenant will be limited to the return of all sums previously paid by Tenant to Owner.

Clause 13. Pets

No animal or other pet will be kept on the premises without Owner's prior written consent, except: properly trained dogs needed by blind, deaf or disabled persons, and _____

_____

under the following conditions: _____

_____

_____.

Clause 14. Owner's Right to Access

Owner or Owner's agents may enter the premises in the event of an emergency, to make repairs or improvements or to show the premises to prospective purchasers or tenants. Except in case of emergency, Owner will give Tenant reasonable notice of intent to enter. In order to facilitate Owner's right of access, Tenant will not, without Owner's prior written consent, alter, re-key or install any lock to the premises or install or alter any burglar alarm system. At all times Owner or Owner's agent will be provided with a key or keys capable of unlocking all such locks and gaining entry. Tenant further agrees to provide instructions on how to disarm any burglar alarm system should Owner so request.

Clause 15. Prohibitions Against Violating Laws and Causing Disturbances

Tenant and guests or invitees will not use the premises in such a way as to violate any law or ordinance, including laws prohibiting the use, possession or sale of illegal drugs, commit waste (severe property damage) or create a nuisance by annoying, disturbing, inconveniencing or interfering with the quiet enjoyment of any other tenant or nearby resident.

Clause 16. Repairs and Alterations by Tenant

Except as provided by law or as authorized by the prior written consent of Owner, Tenant will not make any repairs or alterations to the premises.

Clause 17. Option Terms

Tenant will have the option to purchase the property for the sum of $ _____, providing Tenant exercises this option by giving written notice of that exercise to Owner at the address below, not later than _____ , _____ , and completes the purchase not later than one hundred and twenty (120) days from the above notice. The purchase will be completed according to the terms of a purchase contract and escrow instructions mutually executed by the parties within sixty (60) days of Tenant's notice to Owner that Tenant intends to exercise the option.

   For this right, Tenant agrees to:

   ☐ a. pay Owner, with this agreement, the sum of $ _____ ,which is not refundable to Tenant under any circumstance, even if Tenant does not exercise this option.

   ☐ b. pay Owner, in addition to monthly rent stated in Clause 5 above, the sum of $ _____ , each month, beginning on _____ , _____ , and ending on _____ , _____ . This sum is not to be considered as rent but is to be in consideration of the right of option, and is not refundable to the Tenant under any circumstance, even if Tenant does not exercise the option.

   The parties agree that any sums paid by Tenant to Owner under Clause 21 below, will be credited against the purchase price in the event Tenant exercises the option to buy.

Clause 18. Right to Record Option

This option may be recorded in favor of Tenant (Optionee), and for that purpose Owner (Optionor) agrees to sign this Agreement in the presence of a notary.

Clause 19. Right to Assign or Sell Option

This option may be assigned or sold by Tenant to another party during the option period as described in Clause 17.

Clause 20. Costs of Exercising Option

The parties agree that general financing and transaction costs at the time the option is exercised cannot be estimated in advance, and are therefore not contingencies of this contract. However, the parties agree that at the time this option is exercised:

- Expenses of owning the property (real estate taxes, insurance and special assessments) will be prorated or divided between the parties as to the date of close of escrow.

- Tenant will order a title search on the property and pay for title insurance satisfactory to Tenant and any lenders involved in the purchase transaction, and will pay for any necessary escrow, notary and recording fees. Tenant will have ten days from the exercise of the option in which to report in writing any objections to the condition of title, and Owner will make every effort in good faith to remove such exceptions to clear title within ten days thereafter, or else this contract may be canceled at the option of either party.

- Tenant may, at any time prior to the exercise of this option, have the property inspected at his or her own expense by a licensed general contractor, pest control operator or any other professional deemed necessary to advise Tenant concerning the physical condition of the property. If Tenant notifies Owner in writing, on or before the above date for exercise of the option, of objections on the part of Tenant concerning the condition of the property, and the parties cannot reach an agreement concerning these objections, the Tenant need not exercise this option.

Clause 21. Summary of Funds Received by Owner From Tenant

Nonrefundable option fee	$ _____
Refundable security deposit	$ _____
Nonrefundable rent	$ _____
TOTAL	$ _____

Clause 22. Payment of Court Costs and Attorney Fees in a Lawsuit

In any action or legal proceeding to enforce any part of this Agreement, the prevailing party ☐ shall not ☐ shall recover reasonable attorney fees and court costs.

Clause 23. Validity of Each Part

If any portion of this Agreement is held to be invalid, its invalidity will not affect the validity or enforceability of any other provision of this Agreement.

Clause 24. Grounds for Termination of Tenancy

The failure of Tenant or their guests or invitees to comply with any term of this Agreement is grounds for termination of the tenancy, with appropriate notice to Tenant and procedures as required by law.

Clause 25. Additional Provisions

_____

_____

_____

_____

_____

Clause 26. Entire Agreement

This document constitutes the entire Agreement between the parties, and no promises or representations, other than those contained here and those implied by law, have been made by Owner or Tenant. Any modifications to this Agreement must be in writing signed by Owner and Tenant.

_____   _____
Owner 1's signature   Date

_____
Address

_____   _____
Owner 2's signature   Date

_____
Address

_____   _____
Tenant 1's signature   Date

_____
Print name

_____   _____
Tenant 2's signature   Date

_____
Print name

_____   _____
Tenant 3's signature   Date

_____
Print name

Joint Ownership Agreement

1. Identification of Owners

We, _____

and _____ ,

are joint buyers of the property specified in the bill of sale executed on _____ ,

_____ , a copy of which is attached to this Agreement.

2. Form of Ownership

We agree that this property shall be owned by us as *[choose one]*:

☐ tenants in common in equal shares.

☐ tenants in common in the following percentages:

_____

☐ joint tenants with right of survivorship.

☐ tenants by the entirety.

☐ community property.

_____   _____
Signature   Date

_____   _____
Signature   Date

Motor Vehicle Bill of Sale

Seller 1: _____

Address: _____

Seller 2: _____

Address: _____

Buyer 1: _____

Address: _____

Buyer 2: _____

Address: _____

If there is more than one buyer or seller, the use of the singular incorporates the plural.

1. Seller hereby sells the vehicle described here to Buyer: _____

   _____

   Its body type is: _____ .

   It carries the following vehicle identification number (VIN): _____ .

   Vehicle includes the following personal property items: _____

   _____ .

2. The full purchase price for Vehicle is $ _____ . In exchange for Vehicle, Buyer has paid Seller *[choose one]*:

   ☐ the full purchase price.

   ☐ $ _____ as a down payment, balance due in _____ days.

   ☐ $ _____ as a down payment and has executed a promissory note for the balance of the purchase price.

3. Seller warrants that Seller is the legal owner of Vehicle and that Vehicle is free of all legal claims (liens or encumbrances) by others except: _____

   _____ .

   Seller agrees to remove any lien or encumbrance specified in this clause with the proceeds of this sale within _____ days of the date of the bill of sale.

4. Vehicle ☐ has been ☐ has not been   inspected by an independent mechanic at Buyer's request. If an inspection has been made, the inspection report ☐ is attached ☐ is not attached   to and made part of this bill of sale.

5. Seller believes Vehicle to be in good condition except for the following defects: _____

_____

_____ .

6. Other than the warranty of ownership in Clause 3 and the representations in Clause 5, Seller makes no express warranties. **Buyer takes Vehicle as is.** Seller hereby disclaims the implied warranty of merchantability and all other implied warranties which may apply to the extent disclaimers are permitted in the state having jurisdiction over this bill of sale.

7. The odometer reading for Vehicle is:_____ .

8. Additional terms of sale for Vehicle are as follows:_____

_____

_____ .

_____   _____

Seller 1's signature   Date

_____   _____

Seller 2's signature   Date

_____   _____

Buyer 1's signature   Date

_____   _____

Buyer 2's signature   Date

Boat Bill of Sale

Seller 1: _____

Address: _____

Seller 2: _____

Address: _____

Buyer 1: _____

Address: _____

Buyer 2: _____

Address: _____

If there is more than one buyer or seller, the use of the singular incorporates the plural.

1. Seller hereby sells the boat described here to Buyer:

    Year: _____ Make: _____

    Model: _____ Length: _____

    Serial number: _____ Registration number: _____

    General type: _____

2. Boat has ☐ no engine ☐ one engine ☐ two engines ☐ an auxiliary engine.

3. The engine(s) (Engines) are described as follows:

    a. Engine No. 1 is described as follows:

        Year: _____ Make: _____

        Type: _____ Serial number: _____

    b. Engine No. 2 is described as follows:

        Year: _____ Make: _____

        Type: _____ Serial number: _____

    c. The auxiliary engine is described as follows:

        Year: _____ Make: _____

        Type: _____ Serial number: _____

4. Boat contains the following equipment (Equipment) included in this sale *[check and describe all that apply]*:

    ☐ sails: _____

    _____

    ☐ bilge pump: _____

    _____

    ☐ radio: _____

    _____

    ☐ radar: _____

    _____

☐ sonar: _____

_____

☐ transponder: _____

_____

☐ other: _____

_____

5. Seller believes Boat, Engines and Equipment to be in good condition except for the following defects:

_____

_____ .

6. Boat and Engines ☐ have been ☐ have not been independently inspected at Buyer's request. If an inspection has been made, the inspection report ☐ is attached ☐ is not attached to and made part of this bill of sale.

7. The full purchase price for Boat, Engines and Equipment is $ _____ . In exchange for Boat, Engines and Equipment, Buyer has paid Seller *[choose one]*:

☐ the full purchase price.

☐ $ _____ as a down payment, balance due in _____ days.

☐ $ _____ as a down payment and has executed a promissory note for the balance of the purchase price.

8. Seller warrants that Seller is the legal owner of Boat, Engines and Equipment and that Boat, Engines and Equipment are free of all liens and encumbrances except _____

_____ .

Seller agrees to remove any lien or encumbrance specified in this clause with the proceeds of this sale within _____ days of the date of the bill of sale.

9. Other than the warranty of ownership in Clause 8 and the representations in Clause 5, Seller makes no express warranties. **Buyer takes Boat, Engines and Equipment as is.** Seller hereby disclaims the implied warranty of merchantability and all other implied warranties which may apply to the extent that such disclaimers are permitted in the state having jurisdiction over this bill of sale.

10. Additional terms of sale for Boat, Engines and Equipment are as follows: _____

_____

_____

_____   _____
Seller 1's signature   Date

_____   _____
Seller 2's signature   Date

_____   _____
Buyer 1's signature   Date

_____   _____
Buyer 2's signature   Date

Computer System Bill of Sale

Seller 1: _____

Address: _____

Seller 2: _____

Address: _____

Buyer 1: _____

Address: _____

Buyer 2: _____

Address: _____

If there is more than one buyer or seller, the use of the singular incorporates the plural.

1. Seller hereby sells the goods (Goods) described here to Buyer:

   ☐ a computer (boards, cpu, bus, I/O ports) carrying the brand name of: _____
   and the following serial number: _____

   ☐ the following monitors *[specify brand and serial number for each].*

   #1 _____

   #2 _____

   #3 _____

   ☐ one or more external floppy disk drives carrying the brand name of: _____
   and the following serial number: _____

   ☐ one or more external hard disk drives carrying the brand name of: _____
   and the following serial number: _____

   ☐ one or more CD-ROM devices carrying the brand name of: _____
   and the following serial number: _____

   ☐ one or more mass storage devices carrying the brand name of: _____
   and the following serial number: _____

   ☐ the following printers *[specify brand and serial number for each]:*

   #1 _____

   #2 _____

   ☐ a modem carrying the brand name of: _____
   and the following serial number: _____

   ☐ a multimedia system carrying the brand name of: _____
   and the following serial number: _____

   ☐ computer-related furniture or other items as follows: _____
   _____

   ☐ software consisting of the following:

Title _____ **Serial No.** _____

_____ _____

_____ _____

_____ _____

_____ _____

_____ _____

_____ _____

_____ _____

2. The full purchase price for Goods is $ _____ . In exchange for Goods, Buyer has paid Seller _[choose one]:_

   ☐ the full purchase price.

   ☐ $ _____ as a down payment, balance due in _____ days.

   ☐ $ _____ as a down payment and has executed a promissory note for the balance of the purchase price.

3. Seller warrants that Seller is the legal owner of Goods and that Goods are free of all liens and encumbrances except _____

   _____.

   Seller agrees to remove any lien or encumbrance specified in this clause with the proceeds of this sale within _____ days of the date of the bill of sale.

4. Seller believes Goods to be in good condition except for the following defects: _____

   _____.

5. Other than the warranty of ownership in Clause 3 and the representations in Clause 4, Seller makes no express warranties. **Buyer takes Goods as is.** Seller hereby disclaims the implied warranty of merchantability and all other implied warranties which may apply to the extent that such disclaimers are permitted in the state having jurisdiction over this bill of sale.

6. Additional terms of sale for Goods are as follows: _____

   _____

   _____.

_____ _____
Seller 1's signature Date

_____ _____
Seller 2's signature Date

_____ _____
Buyer 1's signature Date

_____ _____
Buyer 2's signature Date

General Bill of Sale

Seller 1: _____

Address: _____

Seller 2: _____

Address: _____

Buyer 1: _____

Address: _____

Buyer 2: _____

Address: _____

If there is more than one buyer or seller, the use of the singular incorporates the plural.

1. Seller hereby sells the goods (Goods) described here to Buyer: _____

   _____

   _____

   _____ .

2. The full purchase price for Goods is $ _____ . In exchange for Goods, Buyer has paid Seller
   [choose one]:

   ☐ the full purchase price.

   ☐ $ _____ as a down payment, balance due in _____ days.

   ☐ $ _____ as a down payment and has executed a promissory note for the balance of the
   purchase price.

3. Seller warrants that Seller is the legal owner of Goods and that Goods are free of all liens and
   encumbrances except _____

   _____ .

   Seller agrees to remove any lien or encumbrance specified in this clause with the proceeds of this
   sale within _____ days of the date of the bill of sale.

4. Seller believes Goods to be in good condition except for the following defects: _____

   _____

   _____ .

5. Other than the warranty of ownership in Clause 3 and the representations in Clause 4, seller makes no
   express warranties. **Buyer takes all goods as is.** Seller hereby disclaims the implied warranty of
   merchantability and all other implied warranties which may apply to the extent that such disclaimers
   are permitted in the state having jurisdiction over this bill of sale.

6. Goods shall be delivered to Buyer in the following manner *[choose one]:*

    ☐ Buyer shall take immediate possession of Goods.

    ☐ Buyer assumes responsibility for picking up goods from _____

       within _____ days.

    ☐ In exchange for an additional delivery charge of $ _____ , receipt of which is hereby

       acknowledged, Seller will deliver Goods within _____ days to the following location:

       _____ .

7. Additional terms of sale for Goods are as follows:_____

      _____

      _____ .

_____   _____
Seller 1's signature   Date

_____   _____
Seller 2's signature   Date

_____   _____
Buyer 1's signature   Date

_____   _____
Buyer 2's signature   Date

Notice to Cancel Contract

To Whom It May Concern:

This letter constitutes written notice to you that I am canceling the following contract:

Name of seller/lender: _____

Name of buyer/borrower: _____

Contract pertains to *[choose one]*:

☐ Goods/services purchased: _____ .

☐ Amount borrowed: _____ .

Date contract signed: _____ , _____

Please acknowledge receipt of this letter by signing below and returning the acknowledgement to me in the enclosed envelope. I understand that under the law, you must refund my money within _____ days. Furthermore, if applicable, I understand that you must either pick up the items purchased, or reimburse me within _____ days for my expense of mailing the goods back to you. If you do not pick up the goods within that time, I am entitled to keep them.

_____   _____
Buyer/borrower's signature   Date

_____   _____
Print name

. . . .

Acknowledgment

_____   _____
Seller/lender's signature   Date

_____   _____
Print name

Personal Property Rental Agreement

Owner's name: _____

Address: _____

Renter's name: _____

Address: _____

If there is more than one owner or renter, the use of the singular incorporates the plural.

1. Property Being Rented

Owner agrees to rent to Renter, and Renter agrees to rent from Owner, the following property: _____

_____

_____ .

2. Duration of Rental Period

This rental will begin at _____ o'clock a.m./p.m. on _____ , _____

and will end at _____ o'clock a.m./p.m. on _____ , _____ .

3. Rental Amount

The rental amount will be $ _____ per *[specify hour, day, week or month]*.

4. Payment

Renter has paid $ _____ to Owner to cover the rental period specified in Clause 2.

☐ **Security deposit** *[optional]*. In addition to the rent, Renter has deposited $ _____ with

Owner. This deposit will be applied toward any additional rent and any amounts owed for damage

to or loss of the property, which Owner and Renter agree has the current value stated in Clause 8.

Owner will return to Renter any unused portion of the deposit.

5. Delivery

☐ Renter will pick up the property from Owner at Owner's place of business on _____ .

☐ Owner will deliver the equipment to Renter ☐ at no charge ☐ for a fee of $ _____

on _____ , _____ at:

☐ Owner's place of business

☐ Renter's residence

☐ Other _____ .

☐ Other delivery arrangements: _____ .

6. Late Return

If Renter returns the property to Owner after the time and date when the rental period ends, Renter will

pay Owner a rental charge of $ _____ per day for each day or partial day beyond the end of the

rental period until the property is returned. Owner may subtract this charge from the security deposit.

7. Condition of Property

Renter acknowledges receiving the property in good condition, except as follows: _____

_____ .

8. Damage or Loss

Renter will return the property to Owner in good condition except as noted in Clause 7. If the property is damaged while in Renter's possession, Renter will be responsible for the cost of repair, up to the current value of the property. If the property is lost while in Renter's possession, Renter will pay Owner its current value. Owner and Renter agree that the current value of the property is $ _____ .

9. Disputes

[choose one]:

☐ **Litigation.** If a dispute arises, either Owner or Renter may take the matter to court.

☐ **Mediation and Possible Litigation.** If a dispute arises, Owner and Renter will try in good faith to settle it through mediation conducted by *[choose one]:*

☐ _____ *[name of mediator].*

☐ a mediator to be mutually selected.

Owner and Renter will share the costs of the mediator equally. If the dispute is not resolved within 30 days after it is referred to the mediator, either Owner or Renter may take the matter to court.

☐ **Mediation and Possible Arbitration**. If a dispute arises, Owner and Renter will try in good faith to settle it through mediation conducted by *[choose one]:*

☐ _____ *[name of mediator].*

☐ a mediator to be mutually selected.

Owner and Renter will share the costs of the mediator equally. If the dispute is not resolved within 30 days after it is referred to the mediator, it will be arbitrated by *[choose one]:*

☐ _____ *[name of arbitrator].*

☐ an arbitrator to be mutually selected.

Judgment on the arbitration award may be entered in any court that has jurisdiction over the matter. Costs of arbitration, including lawyers' fees, will be allocated by the arbitrator.

_____   _____

Owner's signature   Date

_____   _____

Renter's signature   Date

Notice of Termination of Rental Agreement

To *[name of person to whom notice is being sent]*:

1. Notice of Termination

This is a notice that as of _____, _____,

I am terminating the following rental agreement:

Name of Owner: _____

Name of Renter: _____

Property covered by agreement: _____

_____

Date agreement signed: _____, _____

2. Reason for Termination

The reasons for the termination are as follows *[optional, unless a reason to terminate is required by the*

rental agreement]:_____

_____

_____

_____

_____.

3. Return of Property

[choose one]:

☐ I will return the property to Owner on or before _____, _____ *[for renters]*.

☐ Please return the property to Owner on or before _____, _____ *[for owners]*.

4. Return of Security Deposit

☐ Renter has deposited $ _____ with Owner. Owner agrees to inspect the property for damage and refund Renter any unused portion of the security deposit. Within 24 hours of the return of the property, owner will deposit in the U.S. mail a refund check made out to Renter at the following address: _____

_____.

_____   _____
Signature   Date

_____   ☐ Owner ☐ Renter
Print name

Storage Contract

Property Owner: _____

Address: _____

Property Custodian: _____

Address: _____

If there is more than one owner or custodian, the use of the singular incorporates the plural.

1. Property

Owner desires to store with Custodian and Custodian agrees to accept and store for Owner the

following property: _____

_____

_____ .

2. Storage Location

The property shall be stored at the following location: _____

_____ .

Custodian agrees that the property will not be removed from this location without prior written notice

to and written consent of Owner.

3. Storage Term and Payment

[choose one]:

☐ Custodian agrees to store the property on a _____ *[daily, weekly or monthly]* basis

in exchange for payment of $ _____ per _____ , payable on

the first day of each such period.

☐ Custodian agrees to store the property for payment of $ _____ . Payment shall be

made on or before_____ , _____ .

4. Beginning and Ending Dates

[choose one]:

☐ Storage will begin on _____ , _____ , and will continue until Owner claims

the property or Custodian serves Owner with a _____ day written notice terminating this

storage agreement.

☐ Storage will begin on _____, _____ , and will continue until

_____ , _____ , or until Owner claims the property, whichever

occurs first.

5. Failure to Reclaim Property

If Owner fails to reclaim the property on or before the last day of storage indicated in the notice or in

Clause 4, Custodian shall *[choose one]:*

☐ continue to store the property at the rate of $ _____ per _____ until Owner reclaims the property.

☐ send to Owner's last known address by first-class mail a notice to reclaim the property, and wait 30 days; if Owner does not make arrangements to reclaim the property, Custodian may deem the property abandoned, sell it to pay for outstanding storage fees and hold the balance for Owner.

6. Early Reclaiming

If Owner reclaims the property during a period for which payment has been made, no pro rata refund shall be made.

7. Delivery to Someone Other Than Owner

Custodian shall not deliver the property to any person other than Owner without prior written permission from Owner.

8. Value of the Property

Owner and Custodian agree that the approximate ☐ replacement value ☐ fair market value of the property on the date this agreement is signed is $ _____ .

9. Condition of the Property

☐ Property being stored appears to be in good condition except for the following defects or damage:

_____

_____ .

☐ The condition of each item of property being stored is described on Attachment _____ .

10. Care During Storage Period

[choose one]:

☐ Custodian agrees to exercise reasonable care to protect the property from theft or damage. Responsibility for theft or damage to the property that doesn't result from Custodian's negligence shall be borne by Owner.

☐ In exchange for the compensation paid by Owner, Custodian agrees to (a) be fully responsible for returning the property to Owner in the same condition as it was when the storage commenced; and (b) obtain insurance to protect the property against all commonly insurable losses, except _____

_____ .

11. Title to the Property

The title to the property shall remain at all times in Owner.

12. Disputes

[choose one]:

☐ **Litigation.** If a dispute arises, either Owner or Custodian may take the matter to court.

☐ **Mediation and Possible Litigation.** If a dispute arises, Owner and Custodian will try in good faith to settle it through mediation conducted by *[choose one]:*

☐ _____ *[name of mediator].*

☐ a mediator to be mutually selected.

Owner and Custodian will share the costs of the mediator equally. If the dispute is not resolved within 30 days after it is referred to the mediator, either Owner or Custodian may take the matter to court.

☐ **Mediation and Possible Arbitration.** If a dispute arises, Owner and Custodian will try in good faith to settle it through mediation conducted by *[choose one]:*

    ☐ _____ *[name of mediator].*

    ☐ a mediator to be mutually selected.

Owner and Custodian will share the costs of the mediator equally. If the dispute is not resolved within 30 days after it is referred to the mediator, it will be arbitrated by *[choose one]:*

    ☐ _____ *[name of arbitrator].*

    ☐ an arbitrator to be mutually selected.

Judgment on the arbitration award may be entered in any court that has jurisdiction over the matter. Costs of arbitration, including lawyers' fees, will be allocated by the arbitrator.

13. Modification of This Agreement

All agreements between the parties related to storage of the property are incorporated in this contract. Any modification to this contract shall be in writing.

14. Additional Terms

Additional terms for the storage of the property are as follows:_____

_____

_____ .

_____   _____
Owner's signature   Date

_____   _____
Custodian's signature   Date

Home Maintenance Agreement

Homeowner's name: _____

Address: _____

_____ Phone number: _____

Contractor's name: _____

Address: _____

_____ Phone number: _____

Homeowner desires to contract with Contractor to perform certain work on property located at:

_____ .

1. Work to Be Done

The work to be performed under this agreement consists of the following:

_____

_____

_____

_____

_____

_____

_____

_____ .

2. Payment

In exchange for the work specified in Clause 1, Homeowner agrees to pay Contractor as follows
[choose one and check appropriate boxes]:

☐ $ _____ , payable upon completion of the specified work by ☐ cash ☐ check.

☐ $ _____ , payable one half at the beginning of the specified work and one half at the
completion of the specified work by ☐ cash ☐ check.

☐ $ _____ per hour for each hour of work performed, up to a maximum of $ _____ ,
payable at the following times and in the following manner: _____

_____

_____ .

3. Time

The work specified in this contract shall *[check the boxes and provide dates]*:

☐ begin on _____ , _____ .

☐ be completed on _____ , _____ .

4. Independent Contractor Status

Homeowner and Contractor agree that Contractor shall perform the specified work as an independent contractor. Contractor *[check appropriate boxes and provide description, if necessary]:*

☐ maintains his or her own independent business.

☐ shall use his or her own tools and equipment except:

_____

_____.

☐ shall perform the work specified in Clause 1 independent of Homeowner's supervision, being responsible only for satisfactory completion of the work.

5. Additional Terms

Homeowner and Contractor additionally agree that: _____

_____

_____

_____

_____.

All agreements between Homeowner and Contractor related to the specified work are incorporated in this contract. Any modification to the contract shall be in writing.

_____   _____
Homeowner's signature   Date

_____   _____
Contractor's signature   Date

Home Repairs Agreement (Simple)

Homeowner's name: _____

Address: _____

_____ Phone number: _____

Contractor's name: _____

Address: _____

_____ Phone number: _____

Homeowner desires to contract with Contractor to perform certain work on property located at:

_____ .

1. Work to Be Done

The work to be performed under this agreement consists of the following:

_____

_____

_____

_____ .

2. Payment

In exchange for the work specified in Clause 1, Homeowner agrees to pay Contractor as follows
[choose one and check appropriate boxes]:

☐ $ _____ , payable upon completion of the specified work by ☐ cash ☐ check.

☐ $ _____ , payable by ☐ cash ☐ check as follows:

_____ % payable when the following occurs: _____

_____ % payable when the following occurs: _____

_____ % payable when the following occurs: _____ .

☐ $ _____ per hour for each hour of work performed, up to a maximum of $ _____ ,

payable at the following times and in the following manner: _____

_____

_____ .

3. Time

The work specified in Clause 1 shall *[check the boxes and provide dates]*:

☐ begin on _____ , _____ .

☐ be completed on _____ , _____ .

Time is of the essence.

4. Independent Contractor Status

Homeowner and Contractor agree that Contractor shall perform the specified work as an independent contractor. Contractor *[check appropriate boxes and provide description, if necessary]*:

☐ maintains his or her own independent business.

☐ shall use his or her own tools and equipment except:_____

_____

_____.

☐ shall perform the work specified in Clause 1 independent of Homeowner's supervision, being responsible only for satisfactory completion of the work.

5. Licensing and Registration Requirements

Contractor shall comply with all state and local licensing and registration requirements for type of activity involved in the specified work *[check one box and provide description]:*

☐ Contractor's state license or registration is for the following type of work and carries the following number: _____

_____.

☐ Contractor's local license or registration is for the following type of work and carries the following number: _____

_____.

☐ Contractor is not required to have a license or registration for the specified work, for the following reasons:_____

_____.

6. Injury to Contractor

Contractor will carry his or her own insurance. If Contractor is injured in the course of performing the specified work, Homeowner shall be exempt from liability for those injuries to the fullest extent allowed by law.

7. Permits and Approvals

[check all appropriate boxes]:

☐ Contractor ☐ Homeowner shall be responsible for determining which permits are necessary and for obtaining those permits.

☐ Contractor ☐ Homeowner shall pay for all state and local permits necessary for performing the specified work.

☐ Contractor ☐ Homeowner shall be responsible for obtaining approval from the local homeowner's association, if required.

8. Additional Terms

Homeowner and Contractor additionally agree that: _____

_____

_____

_____.

All agreements between Homeowner and Contractor related to the specified work are incorporated in this contract. Any modification to the contract shall be in writing.

_____   _____
Homeowner's signature   Date

_____   _____
Contractor's signature   Date

Home Repairs Agreement (Detailed)

Homeowner's name: _____

Address: _____

_____ Phone number: _____

Contractor's name: _____

Address: _____

_____ Phone number: _____

Homeowner desires to contract with Contractor to perform certain work on property located at:

_____.

1. Work to Be Done

☐ The work to be performed under this agreement consists of the following:

_____

_____

_____

_____

☐ The work to be performed under this agreement is described in a separate document, called
Attachment _____.

2. Payment

In exchange for the work specified in Clause 1, Homeowner agrees to pay Contractor as follows
[choose one and check appropriate boxes]:

☐ $ _____ , payable upon completion of the specified work by ☐ cash ☐ check.

☐ $ _____ , payable for labor upon completion of the specified work by ☐ cash
☐ check. Materials shall be paid for by Homeowner upon their delivery to the work site, or as follows:

_____

_____

☐ $ _____ , payable by for all labor and materials ☐ cash ☐ check as follows:

_____ % payable when the following occurs: _____

_____ % payable when the following occurs: _____

_____ % payable when the following occurs: _____.

☐ $ _____ , payable in installments for labor by ☐ cash ☐ check as follows:

_____

_____.

Materials shall be paid for by Homeowner upon their delivery to the work site, or as follows:

_____

_____.

□ $ _____ per hour for each hour of work performed, up to a maximum of $ _____ ,

payable at the following times and in the following manner: _____

_____

_____ .

3. Time

The work specified in Clause 1 shall *[check the boxes and provide dates]*:

□ begin on _____ , _____ and

□ be completed no later than _____ , _____

OR

□ begin on or about _____ , _____ and

□ be completed on or about _____ , _____

OR

□ begin and be completed as follows: _____

_____ .

In all cases, time is of the essence.

4. Independent Contractor Status

Homeowner and Contractor agree that Contractor shall perform the specified work as an independent contractor. Contractor *[check appropriate boxes and provide description, if necessary]*:

□ maintains his or her own independent business.

□ shall use his or her own tools and equipment except: _____

_____

_____ .

□ shall perform the work specified in Clause 1 independent of Homeowner's supervision, being responsible only for satisfactory completion of the work.

Contractor may use subcontractors, but shall be solely responsible for supervising their work and for the quality of the work they produce.

5. Licensing and Registration Requirements

Contractor shall comply with all state and local licensing and registration requirements for type of activity involved in the specified work *[check one box and provide description]*:

□ Contractor's state license or registration is for the following type of work and carries the following number: _____

_____ .

□ Contractor's local license or registration is for the following type of work and carries the following number: _____

_____ .

□ Contractor is not required to have a license or registration for the specified work, for the following reasons: _____

_____ .

6. Injury to Contractor

Contractor will carry his or her own insurance. If Contractor is injured in the course of performing the specified work, Homeowner shall be exempt from liability for those injuries to the fullest extent allowed by law.

7. Permits and Approvals

[check appropriate boxes]:

☐ Contractor ☐ Homeowner shall be responsible for determining which permits are necessary and for obtaining those permits.

☐ Contractor ☐ Homeowner shall pay for all state and local permits necessary for performing the specified work.

☐ Contractor ☐ Homeowner shall be responsible for obtaining approval from the local homeowner's association, if required.

8. Liens and Waivers of Liens

To protect Homeowner against liens being filed by Contractor, subcontractors and providers of materials, Contractor agrees that *[check all boxes that apply and provide description, if necessary]:*

☐ Final payment to Contractor under Clause 2 shall be withheld by Homeowner until Contractor presents Homeowner with lien waivers, lien releases or acknowledgment of full payment from each subcontractor and materials provider.

☐ All checks to Contractor shall also be made out jointly to all subcontractors and materials suppliers.

☐ Contractor, where legal, shall not:

- use a subcontractor without first obtaining a lien waiver or release and delivering a copy to Homeowner, or

- use any materials without obtaining an "acknowledgment of full payment" from the materials supplier and delivering a copy to Homeowner.

☐ Homeowner and Contractor agree that Homeowner shall be protected against liens in the following manner: _____

_____

_____

_____

_____ .

9. Condition of Materials

All materials shall be new, of good quality, in compliance with all applicable laws and codes, and shall be covered by a manufacturer's warranty if appropriate, except as follows: _____

_____

_____

_____

_____

_____

_____

_____

_____

_____

_____ .

The materials shall consist of *[check one box and provide description, if necessary]*:

☐ the materials described in Clause 1.

☐ the materials described in the Schedule of Materials attached to this contract.

☐ the following items: _____

_____

_____

_____

_____

_____

_____

_____

_____

_____

_____ .

The materials shall be purchased by *[check one box]*:

☐ Contractor, to be reimbursed as provided in Clause 2.

☐ Homeowner

10. Completion

The work specified in Clause 1 shall be considered completed upon approval by Homeowner, provided that Homeowner's approval shall not be unreasonably withheld. Substantial performance of the specified work in a workmanlike manner shall be considered sufficient grounds for Contractor to require final payment by Homeowner, except as provided in Clause 8, Liens and Waivers of Liens.

11. Contractor Warranty

Contractor will complete the specified work in a substantial and workmanlike manner according to standard practices prevalent in Contractor's trade. Contractor warrants that *[check appropriate boxes and provide descriptions, if necessary]*:

☐ the specified work shall comply with all applicable building codes and regulations.

☐ the labor and materials provided as part of the specified work shall be free from defects.

☐ Additional warranties offered by the Contractor are as follows: _____

_____

_____

_____

_____

_____ .

12. Disputes

[choose one]

☐ **Litigation.** If a dispute arises, any party may take the matter to court.

☐ **Mediation and Possible Litigation.** If a dispute arises, the parties will try in good faith to settle it through mediation conducted by *[choose one]:*

    ☐ _____ *[name of mediator].*

    ☐ a mediator to be mutually selected.

    The parties will share the costs of the mediator equally. If the dispute is not resolved within 30 days after it is referred to the mediator, any party may take the matter to court.

☐ **Mediation and Possible Arbitration.** If a dispute arises, the parties will try in good faith to settle it through mediation conducted by *[choose one]:*

    ☐ _____ *[name of mediator].*

    ☐ a mediator to be mutually selected.

    The parties will share the costs of the mediator equally. If the dispute is not resolved within 30 days after it is referred to the mediator, it will be arbitrated by *[choose one]:*

    ☐ _____ *[name of arbitrator].*

    ☐ an arbitrator to be mutually selected.

Judgment on the arbitration award may be entered in any court that has jurisdiction over the matter. Costs of arbitration, including lawyers' fees, will be allocated by the arbitrator.

13. Delay

If performance of the specified work is late, Contractor agrees that *[check one box and provide description, if necessary]:*

☐ Homeowner shall be damaged in the amount of $ _____ per _____ , and that Contractor shall be liable for such sums, which may be credited against any sums owed to Contractor by Homeowner.

☐ A dispute over any damages or loss claimed by Homeowner for the delay in performance of the specified work shall be resolved as provided in Clause 12 of this agreement.

14. Injuries to Subcontractors or Employees

Contractor agrees to *[check appropriate boxes and provide description, if necessary]:*

☐ Obtain adequate business liability insurance that will cover job and any injuries to subcontractors or employees.

☐ Hold harmless and indemnify Homeowner for all damages, costs and attorney fees that arise out of harm caused to Contractor, subcontractors and other third parties, known and unknown, by Contractor's performance of the specified work, except as follows: _____

_____

_____ .

15. Maintenance of Work Site

Contractor agrees to be bound by the following conditions when performing the specified work *[check appropriate boxes and provide descriptions]:*

☐ Contractor shall perform the specified work between the following hours: _____

_____ .

☐ At the end of each day's work, Contractor's equipment shall be stored in the following location:

_____

_____ .

☐ At the end of each day's work, Contractor agrees to clean all debris from the work area and leave all appliances and facilities in good working order except as follows: _____

_____

_____ .

☐ Contractor agrees that disruptively loud activities shall be performed only at the following times:

_____

_____ .

☐ Contractor agrees to confine all work-related activity, materials and products, including dust and debris, to the following areas: _____

_____

_____ .

☐ Contractor agrees that: _____

_____

_____

_____

_____

_____ .

16. Additional Terms

Homeowner and Contractor additionally agree that: _____

_____

_____

_____

_____

_____ .

All agreements between Homeowner and Contractor related to the work specified in Clause 1 are incorporated in this contract. Any modification to the contract shall be in writing.

_____   _____
Homeowner's signature   Date

_____   _____
Contractor's signature   Date

Daily Expenses

Week of _____

Sunday's Expenses	Cost	Monday's Expenses	Cost	Tuesday's Expenses	Cost	Wednesday's Expenses	Cost
_____	_____	_____	_____	_____	_____	_____	_____
_____	_____	_____	_____	_____	_____	_____	_____
_____	_____	_____	_____	_____	_____	_____	_____
_____	_____	_____	_____	_____	_____	_____	_____
_____	_____	_____	_____	_____	_____	_____	_____
_____	_____	_____	_____	_____	_____	_____	_____
_____	_____	_____	_____	_____	_____	_____	_____
_____	_____	_____	_____	_____	_____	_____	_____
_____	_____	_____	_____	_____	_____	_____	_____
_____	_____	_____	_____	_____	_____	_____	_____
_____	_____	_____	_____	_____	_____	_____	_____
_____	_____	_____	_____	_____	_____	_____	_____
Daily Total:	_____	**Daily Total:**	_____	**Daily Total:**	_____	**Daily Total:**	_____

Thursday's Expenses	Cost	Friday's Expenses	Cost	Saturday's Expenses	Cost	Other Expenses	Cost
_____	_____	_____	_____	_____	_____	_____	_____
_____	_____	_____	_____	_____	_____	_____	_____
_____	_____	_____	_____	_____	_____	_____	_____
_____	_____	_____	_____	_____	_____	_____	_____
_____	_____	_____	_____	_____	_____	_____	_____
_____	_____	_____	_____	_____	_____	_____	_____
_____	_____	_____	_____	_____	_____	_____	_____
_____	_____	_____	_____	_____	_____	_____	_____
_____	_____	_____	_____	_____	_____	_____	_____
_____	_____	_____	_____	_____	_____	_____	_____
_____	_____	_____	_____	_____	_____	_____	_____
_____	_____	_____	_____	_____	_____	_____	_____
Daily Total:	_____	**Daily Total:**	_____	**Daily Total:**	_____	**Daily Total:**	_____

Monthly Income

		Amount of each payment	Period covered by each payment	Amount per month

Source of Income

A. Wages or Salary

Job 1: _____   Gross pay, including overtime: $ _____ _____

Subtract:

   Federal taxes   _____

   State taxes   _____

   Social Security (FICA)   _____

   Union dues   _____

   Insurance payments   _____

   Child support withholding   _____

   Other mandatory deductions   _____

   (specify): _____   _____

   Subtotal $ _____ _____ _____

Job 2: _____   Gross pay, including overtime: $ _____ _____

Subtract:

   Federal taxes   _____

   State taxes   _____

   Social Security (FICA)   _____

   Union dues   _____

   Insurance payments   _____

   Child support withholding   _____

   Other mandatory deductions   _____

   (specify): _____   _____

   Subtotal $ _____ _____ _____

Job 3: _____   Gross pay, including overtime: $ _____ _____

Subtract:

   Federal taxes   _____

   State taxes   _____

   Social Security (FICA)   _____

   Union dues   _____

   Insurance payments   _____

   Child support withholding   _____

   Other mandatory deductions   _____

   (specify): _____   _____

   Subtotal $ _____ _____ _____

B. Self-Employment Income

Job 1: _____   Gross pay, including overtime: $ _____ _____
                                            Subtract:

                                                 Federal taxes   _____

                                                   State taxes   _____

                                                   Self-employment taxes   _____

                                                     Other mandatory deductions

                                                     (specify): _____   _____

                                                     Subtotal $ _____ _____ _____

Job 2: _____   Gross pay, including overtime: $ _____ _____
       Subtract:

       Federal taxes   _____

       State taxes   _____

       Self-employment taxes   _____

       Other mandatory deductions

       (specify): _____   _____

       Subtotal $ _____ _____ _____

C. Investment Income

       Dividends   _____

       Interest   _____

       Leases   _____

       Licenses   _____

       Rent   _____

       Royalties   _____

       Other (specify):   _____

       _____   _____

       _____   _____

       Subtotal $ _____ _____ _____

D. Other

       Bonuses   _____

       Note or trust income   _____

       Alimony or child support   _____

       Pension/retirement income   _____

       Social Security   _____

       Other public assistance   _____

       Other (specify):   _____

       _____   _____

       _____   _____

       Subtotal $ _____ _____ _____

       Total Monthly Income $ _____ _____ _____

Monthly Budget

	proj.	Jan.	Feb.	Mar.	April	May	June	July	Aug.	Sept.	Oct.	Nov.	Dec.

Home

rent/mortgage													
property taxes													
renter's ins.													
homeowner's ins.													
homeowner's association dues													
telephone													
gas & electric													
water & sewer													
cable TV													
garbage													
household supplies													
housewares													
furniture & appliances													
cleaning													
yard or pool care													
maintenance & repairs													

Food

groceries													
breakfast out													
lunch out													
dinner out													
coffee/tea													
snacks													

Wearing Apparel

clothing & accessories													
laundry, dry cleaning & mending													

Self Care

toiletries & cosmetics													
haircuts													
massage													
health club membership													
donations													

Health Care

insurance													
medications													
vitamins													
doctors													
dentist													
eyecare													
therapy													

Transportation

insurance													
road service club													
registration													
gasoline													
maintenance & repairs													

	proj.	Jan.	Feb.	Mar.	April	May	June	July	Aug.	Sept.	Oct.	Nov.	Dec.
car wash													
parking & tolls													
public transit & cabs													
parking tickets													

Entertainment

music													
movies & video rentals													
concerts, theater & ballet													
museums													
sporting events													
hobbies & lessons													
club dues or membership													
film development													
books, magazines & newspapers													
software													

Dependent Care

child care													
clothing													
allowance													
school expenses													
toys													
entertainment													

Pet Care

grooming													
vet													
food													
toys & supplies													

Education

tuition or loan payments													
books & supplies													

Travel

Gifts & Cards

holidays													
birthdays & anniversaries													
weddings & showers													

Personal Business

supplies													
photocopying													
postage													
bank & credit card fees													
lawyer													
accountant													
taxes													
savings													

Total Expenses													
Total Income													
Difference													

Statement of Assets and Liabilities

(as of _____)

Assets	Date of Purchase	Account Number	Current Market Value
Cash and Cash Equivalents			
Cash	_____	_____	_____
Checking accounts	_____	_____	_____
Savings accounts	_____	_____	_____
Money market accounts	_____	_____	_____
Other	_____	_____	_____
Subtotal			_____
Real Estate			
House/condo/coop	_____	_____	_____
Vacation home	_____	_____	_____
Income properties	_____	_____	_____
Unimproved lot	_____	_____	_____
Other lot	_____	_____	_____
Subtotal			_____
Personal Property			
Motor vehicles	_____	_____	_____
Furniture	_____	_____	_____
Home furnishings	_____	_____	_____
Electronic equipment	_____	_____	_____
Computer system	_____	_____	_____
Jewelry	_____	_____	_____
Clothing	_____	_____	_____
Collections (coin, stamp)	_____	_____	_____
Animals	_____	_____	_____
Other	_____	_____	_____
Subtotal			_____
Investments			
Life ins. (term cash value)	_____	_____	_____
Life ins. (whole policies)	_____	_____	_____
Stocks	_____	_____	_____
Bonds	_____	_____	_____
Mutual funds	_____	_____	_____
Annuities	_____	_____	_____
IRAs	_____	_____	_____
Keoghs	_____	_____	_____
401k Plans	_____	_____	_____
Other retirement plans	_____	_____	_____
Partnerships	_____	_____	_____
Accounts receivable	_____	_____	_____
Other	_____	_____	_____
Subtotal			_____

Liabilities

Liabilities	Date Incurred	Account Number	Total Balance Due
Secured			
Mortgage			
Mortgage			
Deeds of trust			
Home equity loans			
Liens			
Motor vehicle loans			
Bank loans			
Personal loans			
Other			
Subtotal			_____
Unsecured			
Student loans			
Bank loans			
Personal loans			
Credit card balances			
Judgments			
Taxes			
Support arrears			
Other			
Subtotal			_____

Net Worth Summary

Total Assets

Cash Subtotal _____
Real Estate Subtotal _____
Personal Property Subtotal _____
Investments Subtotal _____
Total Assets _____

Total Liabilities

Secured Subtotal _____
Unsecured Subtotal _____
Total Liabilities _____

Net Worth

(Assets minus liabilities) _____

Estimate of Income Tax Liability

Gross Income
Wages or salary   _____
Pension   _____
Interest and dividends   _____
Capital gains   _____
Self-employment income   _____
Rents or royalties   _____
Alimony   _____
Other   _____
Subtotal Income   _____

Adjustments to Income
IRA deposits   _____
Medical savings   _____
Moving expenses   _____
Alimony paid   _____
Other   _____
Subtotal Adjustments   _____
Difference (adjusted gross income or AGI)   _____

Standard or Itemized Deduction
Standard
Single $4,150
Married/jointly $6,900
Married/separately $3,450
Head of household $6,050

Itemized
Medical expenses (excess of 7.5% of AGI)   _____
State and local income taxes   _____
Real property taxes   _____
Personal property taxes   _____
Mortgage/home loan interest   _____
Mortgage points   _____
Charitable contributions   _____
Casualty or theft losses   _____
Unreimbursed job expenses   _____
Tax preparation fees   _____
Other   _____
Total itemized deductions   _____
Standard or Total Itemized Deduction   _____
Difference (AGI less deduction)   _____

Personal Exemptions
Number of exemptions   _____
Amount per exemption   x $2,650
Total exemptions   _____
Difference (taxable income)   _____

Tax Liability
Estimated tax (use table in Chapter 10)   _____
Credits and payments   _____
Difference (taxes due or refund)   _____

Assignment of Rights

Assignor 1's name: _____

Address: _____

Assignor 2's name: _____

Address: _____

Assignee 1's name: _____

Address: _____

Assignee 2's name: _____

Address: _____

If there is more than one assignor or assignee, the use of the singular incorporates the plural.

1. For value received, Assignor transfers to Assignee all of Assignor's rights, title and interest in the following:

   ☐ contract rights as follows: _____

   _____

   _____.

   The contract ☐ is ☐ is not attached.

   ☐ rights to receive payments: _____

   _____

   _____.

   Evidence of Assignor's right to receive payments ☐ is ☐ is not is not attached.

   ☐ rights to file a lawsuit: _____

   _____

   _____.

   Evidence of Assignor's right to file a lawsuit ☐ is ☐ is not attached.

   ☐ other: _____

   _____

   _____.

2. This assignment is subject to the following terms and conditions:

   _____

   _____

   _____

   _____

   _____.

3. This assignment takes effect on: _____.

_____   _____
Assignor 1's signature   Date

_____
Print name

_____
Location _[city or county where signed]_

_____
Address

_____   _____
Assignor 2's signature   Date

_____
Print name

_____
Location _[city or county where signed]_

_____
Address

_____   _____
Assignee 1's signature   Date

_____
Print name

_____
Location _[city or county where signed]_

_____
Address

_____   _____
Assignee 2's signature   Date

_____
Print name

_____
Location _[city or county where signed]_

_____
Address

Notice to Terminate Joint Accounts

_____

_____

_____

[name and address of creditor]

Names on account: _____

Account number: _____

To Whom It May Concern:

Please be advised that as of the date indicated below, the above-captioned account is to be closed. I am requesting that you "hard close" the account so that absolutely no new charges can be made.

If you will not hard close the account, please be informed that as of the date indicated below, I will not be responsible for any charges made on this account.

Please let me know the outstanding balance on this account. Furthermore, please acknowledge receipt of this notice by signing the duplicate of this letter and returning it to me in the enclosed stamped, self-addressed envelope.

Thank you for your assistance.

_____   _____

Signature   Date

_____

Printed or typed name

_____

Address

_____

Address

_____   _____

Home phone   Work phone

- -

Receipt acknowledged by:

_____   _____

Signature   Date

_____

Printed or typed name

_____

Title

Outstanding balance:_____ As of: _____

Notice to Stop Payment of Check

_____

_____

_____

[name and address of financial institution]

Re: Stop payment of check

To Whom It May Concern:

This letter is to confirm my telephone request of _____ *[date]* that you stop payment on the following check:

Names on account:_____

Account number: _____ Check number: _____

Payable to: _____

Date written: _____Amount of check:_____

   Please acknowledge receipt of this notice by signing the duplicate of this letter and returning it to me in the enclosed stamped, self-addressed envelope.

   Thank you for your assistance.

_____

Signature

_____

Printed or typed name

_____

Address

_____

Address

_____   _____

Home phone   Work phone

- -

Receipt acknowledged by:

_____   _____

Signature   Date

_____

Printed or typed name

_____

Title

Request for Credit Report

_____

_____

_____

[name and address of credit bureau]

To Whom It May Concern:

Please send me a copy of my credit report.

Full name: _____

Date of birth: _____ Social Security number: _____

Spouse's name: _____

Telephone number: _____

Current address: _____

_____

Previous address: _____

_____

[check one]:

☐ I was denied credit on _____ by _____
_____. Enclosed is a copy of the rejection letter.

☐ I hereby certify that I am unemployed and intend to apply for a job within the next 60 days. Enclosed is a copy of a document verifying my unemployment.

☐ I hereby certify that I receive public assistance/welfare. Enclosed is a copy of my most recent public assistance check as verification.

☐ I hereby certify that I believe there is erroneous information in my file due to fraud.

☐ I live in _____.
I am requesting my annual complimentary credit report. Enclosed is a copy of a document identifying me by my name and address.

☐ I am not entitled to a free copy of my report. Enclosed is a copy of a document identifying me by my name and address and a check for $ _____ .

Thank you for your attention to this matter.

Sincerely,

_____

Signature

Challenge Incorrect Credit Report Entry

_____

_____

_____

[name and address of credit bureau]

Date: _____

This is a request for you to reinvestigate the following items which appear on my credit report:

☐ The following personal information about me is incorrect:

Erroneous Information	Correct Information
_____	_____
_____	_____
_____	_____

☐ The following accounts are not mine:

Creditor's Name	Account Number	Explanation
_____	_____	_____
_____	_____	_____
_____	_____	_____

☐ The account status is incorrect for the following accounts:

Creditor's Name	Account Number	Correct Status
_____	_____	_____
_____	_____	_____
_____	_____	_____

☐ The following information is too old to be included in my report:

Creditor's Name	Account Number	Date of Last Activity
_____	_____	_____
_____	_____	_____
_____	_____	_____

☐ The following inquiries are older than two years:

Creditor's Name	Date of Inquiry
_____	_____
_____	_____
_____	_____

☐ The following accounts were closed by me and should say so:

Creditor's Name   Account number

_____   _____

_____   _____

_____   _____

☐ Other errors:

Explanation

_____

_____

_____

_____

_____

I understand that you will check each item above with the credit grantor reporting the information, and remove any information the credit grantor cannot verify. I further understand that under the federal Fair Credit Reporting Act, 15 United States Code §1681i(a), you must complete your reinvestigation and issue me and anyone who has requested a copy of my credit report within the previous one year (two years if requested for employment purposes) a new credit report within 30 days of receipt of this letter. Thank you.

Sincerely,

_____

Signature

_____

Name

_____

Address

_____   _____

Home phone   Social Security number

Dispute Credit Card Charge

_____

_____

_____

[name and address of credit card issuer]

Date: _____

Account number: _____

To Whom It May Concern:

I am writing to dispute the following charge that appears on my billing statement dated _____ .

    Merchant's name: _____

    Amount in dispute: _____

    I am disputing this amount for the following reason(s):

_____

_____

_____

_____

_____ .

    As required by law, I have tried in good faith to resolve this dispute with the merchant. Furthermore, this purchase was for more than $50 and was made ☐ in the state in which I live ☐ within 100 miles of my home.

    Please verify this dispute with the merchant and remove this item, and all late and interest charges attributed to this item, from my billing statement.

Sincerely,

_____

Signature

_____

Name

_____

Address

_____

Home phone

Demand Collection Agency Cease Contact

_____

_____

_____

[name and address of collection agency]

Date: _____

Name(s) on account: _____

Account number: _____

Creditor: _____

To _____ :

Since _____ *[date]*, I have received several phone calls and letters from you concerning my overdue account with the above-named creditor.

Accordingly, under 15 U.S.C. § 1692c, this is my formal notice to you to cease all further communications with me except for the reasons specifically set forth in the federal law.

Sincerely,

_____

Signature

_____

Name

_____

Address

_____

_____

Home phone

Complaint Letter

_____

_____

_____

[name and address of consumer protection office]

Date: _____

To Whom It May Concern:

I wish to lodge a complaint about the following company:

    Name:_____

    Address: _____

    _____

    Phone number: _____

    Name of person with whom I dealt: _____

The details of my complaint are as follows _[attach additional sheets if necessary]_:

_____

_____

_____

_____

_____

_____

_____.

Please investigate this matter and inform me of the results.

Sincerely,

_____

Signature

_____

Name

_____

Address

_____   _____

                                          Home phone

cc: Federal Trade Commission

    _____

    _____

    _____

    _____

Notice of Insurance Claim

_____

_____

_____

[name and address of insurance company]

Date: _____

Name of your insured: _____

Policy number: _____

To Whom It May Concern:

Please be advised that ☐ I received injuries ☐ I sustained property damage in an accident on

_____, _____, at the following location: _____

_____.

The accident was of the following nature:

    ☐ two or more motor vehicles

    ☐ motor vehicle and pedestrian

    ☐ motor vehicle and bicycle

    ☐ motor vehicle and property

        [for all motor vehicles involved other than your own, give]:

        Make, model, year and color of vehicle: _____

        License plate number and state of issuance: _____

        Vehicle identification number: _____

        Name or driver (if different from name of insured above): _____

        Driver's license number and state of issuance: _____

    ☐ slip and fall

    ☐ animal bite, claw, knockdown, etc.

    ☐ dangerous or defective product

    ☐ other (specify): _____

Please confirm in writing to the address below your liability coverage of the insured identified above. Please also advise whether your insured contends that anyone other than your insured may be in whole or in part legally responsible for accidents on or near the premises.

As requested, please respond in writing. If necessary, I may be reached by telephone at the below number.

Thank you for your prompt attention to this matter.

Sincerely,

_____   _____

Signature   Date

_____

Name

_____

Address

_____

Child Care Agreement

Parent(s)' name(s): _____

Address: _____

_____ Home phone number: _____

Work phone numbers: _____

Other contact number(s) (cell phone, fax, e-mail): _____

Child Care Worker's name:_____

Address: _____

_____ Phone number: _____

Parent(s) desire(s) to contract with Child Care Worker to provide child care for:

_____

_____ *[names and ages of the children]* at:

_____

_____ *[your address or other location where care is to be given].*

Beginning Date

Employment will begin on _____ *[date].*

Training Period

There will be a training period during the first_____ *[length of training period]*
of employment.

Responsibilities

The care to be provided under this agreement consists of the following responsibilities *[check the
appropriate boxes and provide details]:*

☐ cooking and nutrition _____

_____

☐ bathing and personal care _____

_____

☐ health and medical care_____

_____

☐ social and recreational _____

_____

☐ transportation_____

_____

☐ shopping and errands _____

_____

☐ housecleaning _____

_____

☐ ironing and laundry _____

_____

☐ other responsibilities _____

_____

Payment Terms

Child Care Worker will be paid as follows:

☐ $ _____ per hour

☐ $ _____ per month

☐ other:_____

with the following deductions and exceptions:

☐ Social Security _____

☐ federal income taxes _____

☐ state income taxes _____

☐ toll and long-distance phone charges _____

☐ other deductions (specify) _____

A salary review will occur _____.

Child Care Worker will be paid on the specified intervals and dates:

☐ once a week on every _____

☐ twice a month on _____

☐ once a month on _____

Child Care Schedule

Days and hours of child care will be _____.

Benefits

Parent(s) will provide Child Care Worker with the following benefits:

☐ meals_____

_____

☐ room and board_____

_____

☐ sick leave _____

☐ vacation days _____

☐ holidays _____

☐ health insurance _____

☐ transportation _____

☐ other _____

Confirmation of Independent Contractor Status

☐ Parent(s) and Child Care Worker agree that Child Care Worker shall perform the specified work as an independent contractor. Child Care Worker *[check appropriate boxes and provide description, if necessary]*:

☐ maintains his or her own independent business.

☐ shall use his or her own tools and equipment except:_____

_____
_____ .

Termination Policy

Either Parent(s) or Child Care Worker may terminate this agreement at any time, for any reason, without notice.

Additional Agreements and Amendments

Parent(s) and Child Care Worker additionally agree that: _____

_____
_____
_____
_____ .

Modifications in Writing

To be binding, any modifications to this contract must be in writing.

_____   _____
Parent's signature   Date

_____   _____
Child Care Worker's signature   Date

Elder Care Agreement

Person Hiring Elder Care Worker: _____

Address: _____

Home phone number: _____

Work phone number: _____

Other contact number(s) (cell phone, fax, e-mail): _____

Elder Care Worker: _____

Address: _____

Phone number: _____

Person Hiring Elder Care Worker desires to contract with Elder Care Worker to provide care for:

_____

_____ *[name of person in need of elder care]* at:

_____

_____ *[your address or other location where care is to be given].*

Beginning Date
Employment will begin on _____ *[date].*

Training Period
There will be a training period during the first_____ *[length of training period]*
of employment.

Responsibilities
The care to be provided under this agreement consists of the following responsibilities *[check the
appropriate boxes and provide details]:*

☐ cooking and nutrition _____

_____

☐ bathing and personal care _____

_____

☐ health and medical care_____

_____

☐ social and recreational _____

_____

☐ exercise and physical activities_____

_____

☐ transportation and escort _____

_____

☐ shopping and errands _____

☐ housecleaning _____

☐ light home maintenance _____

☐ ironing and laundry _____

☐ bill paying _____

☐ other responsibilities _____

Payment Terms

Elder Care Worker will be paid as follows:

☐ $ _____ per hour

☐ $ _____ per month

☐ other: _____

with the following deductions and exceptions:

☐ Social Security _____

☐ federal income taxes _____

☐ state income taxes _____

☐ toll and long-distance phone charges _____

☐ other deductions (specify) _____

A salary review will occur _____ .

Elder Care Worker will be paid on the specified intervals and dates:

☐ once a week on every _____

☐ twice a month on _____

☐ once a month on _____

Elder Care Schedule

Days and hours of elder care will be _____ .

Benefits

Person Hiring Elder Care Worker will provide Elder Care Worker with the following benefits:

☐ meals _____

☐ room and board _____

☐ sick leave _____

_____

☐ vacation days _____

_____

☐ holidays _____

_____

☐ health insurance _____

_____

☐ transportation _____

_____

☐ other _____

_____

Confirmation of Independent Contractor Status

☐ Person Hiring Elder Care Worker and Elder Care Worker agree that Elder Care Worker shall perform the specified work as an independent contractor. Elder Care Worker *[check appropriate boxes and provide description, if necessary]*:

☐ maintains his or her own independent business.

☐ shall use his or her own tools and equipment except:_____

_____

_____.

Termination Policy

Either Person Hiring Elder Care Worker or Elder Care Worker may terminate this agreement at any time, for any reason, without notice.

Additional Agreements and Amendments

Person Hiring Elder Care Worker and Elder Care Worker additionally agree that:_____

_____

_____

_____.

Modifications in Writing

To be binding, any modifications to this contract must be in writing.

_____   _____
Person Hiring Elder Care Worker's signature   Date

_____   _____
Elder Care Worker's signature   Date

Housekeeping Services Agreement

Homeowner's name: _____

Address: _____

Phone number: _____

Housekeeper's name:_____

Address: _____

Phone number: _____

Homeowner desires to contract with Housekeeper to work at:

_____.

Beginning Date

Employment will begin on _____ *[date]*.

Housecleaning Responsibilities

The responsibilities to be provided under this agreement consist of cleaning the following rooms and areas:

- ☐ Interior:_____
- ☐ living room: _____
- ☐ dining room: _____
- ☐ kitchen:_____
- ☐ bedrooms: _____
- ☐ bathrooms:_____
- ☐ family room: _____
- ☐ study or den: _____
- ☐ basement:_____
- ☐ laundry room: _____
- ☐ hallways and entryways: _____
- ☐ staircases: _____
- ☐ other rooms or interior areas: _____

_____

_____

_____

- ☐ Exterior: _____
- ☐ front porch or deck: _____
- ☐ back porch or deck: _____

☐ garage: _____

☐ pool, hot tub or sauna: _____

☐ other exterior areas: _____

_____

_____

_____

Other Responsibilities

Housekeeper also agrees to do the following types of work:

☐ cooking: _____

☐ laundry: _____

☐ ironing: _____

☐ shopping and errands: _____

☐ gardening: _____

☐ other: _____

Supplies and Equipment

Homeowner will provide all housecleaning supplies, vacuum cleaner and other equipment, except:

_____

_____ .

Payment Terms

Housekeeper will be paid as follows:

☐ $ _____ per hour

☐ $ _____ per month

☐ other: _____

with the following deductions and exceptions:

☐ Social Security _____

☐ federal income taxes _____

☐ state income taxes _____

☐ toll and long-distance phone charges _____

☐ other deductions (specify) _____

Housekeeper will be paid on the specified intervals and dates:

☐ Once a week on every _____

☐ Twice a month on _____

☐ Once a month on _____

Schedule

Dates and hours of housekeeping will be: _____ .

Additional hours of work are subject to Housekeeper's approval and will be paid at the rate of $ _____

per hour or _____ .

Benefits

Homeowner will provide Housekeeper with the following benefits:

☐ meals _____

☐ room and board _____

☐ sick leave _____

☐ vacation days _____

☐ holidays _____

☐ health insurance _____

☐ transportation _____

☐ other _____

Confirmation of Independent Contractor Status

☐ Homeowner and Housekeeper agree that Housekeeper shall perform the specified work as an

   independent contractor. Housekeeper *[check appropriate boxes and provide description, if necessary]*:

   ☐ maintains his or her own independent business.

   ☐ shall use his or her own tools and equipment except:_____

   _____

   _____ .

Additional Agreements and Amendments

Homeowner and Housekeeper additionally agree that: _____

_____

_____

_____

_____ .

Modifications in Writing

To be binding, any modification to the contract must be in writing.

_____   _____

Homeowner's signature   Date

_____   _____

Housekeeper's signature   Date

Agreement to Keep Property Separate

Partner 1's name: _____

Partner 2's name: _____

We agree as follows:

1. This contract sets forth our rights and obligations toward each other. We intend to abide by them in a spirit of cooperation and good faith.

2. All property owned by either of us as of the date of this agreement shall remain the separate property of its owner and cannot be transferred to the other person unless this is done in writing. We have each attached a list of our major items of separate property to this contract.

3. The income each of us earns—as well as any items or investments either of us purchases with our income—belongs absolutely to the person who earns the money unless there is a written joint ownership agreement as provided in Clause 6.

4. We shall each maintain our own separate bank, credit card, investment and retirement accounts, and neither of us shall in any way be responsible for the debts of the other (if we register as domestic partners in a community that makes this option available and, by so doing, the law requires us to be responsible for each other's basic living expenses, we agree to assume the minimum level of reciprocal responsibility required by the law).

5. Expenses for routine household items and services, which include groceries, utilities, rent and cleaning supplies, shall be equally divided.

6. From time to time, we may decide to keep a joint checking or savings account for a specific purpose (for example, to pay household expenses), or to own some property jointly (for example, to purchase a television). If so, the details of our joint ownership agreement shall be put in writing (either in a written contract or a deed, title slip or other joint ownership document).

7. Should either of us receive real or personal property by gift or inheritance, the property belongs absolutely to the person receiving the gift or inheritance and cannot be transferred to the other except in writing.

8. In the event we separate, each of us shall be entitled to immediate possession of our separate property.

9. Any dispute arising out of this contract shall be mediated by a third person mutually acceptable to both of us. The mediator's role shall be to help us arrive at our solution, not to impose one on us. If good-faith efforts to arrive at our own solution to all issues in dispute with the help of a mediator prove to be fruitless, either of us may pursue other legal remedies.

10. This agreement represents our complete understanding regarding our living together and replaces any and all prior agreements, written or oral. It can be amended, but only in writing, and must be signed by both of us.

11. If a court finds any portion of this contract to be illegal or otherwise unenforceable, the remainder of the contract is still in full force and effect.

_____   _____
Partner 1's signature   Date

_____   _____
Partner 2's signature   Date

Attachment A

Separate personal property of _____ :

_____

_____

_____

_____

_____

_____

_____

_____

_____

_____

_____

_____

_____

Attachment B

Separate personal property of _____ :

_____

_____

_____

_____

_____

_____

_____

_____

_____

_____

_____

_____

_____

Agreement for a Joint Purchase

Partner 1's name: _____

Partner 2's name: _____

We agree as follows:

1. We will jointly acquire and own _____
_____*[describe the property]* at a cost of $ _____.

2. ☐ We will own the property equally.

   ☐ Partner 1 will own_____ % of the property and Partner 2 will own _____ % of the property.

3. Should we separate and both want the Property, we will first jointly agree on the fair current value of the Property. Next we will flip a coin to determine who gets to keep the property. The winner, upon paying the loser the appropriate percentage of this amount (based on the loser's ownership share as set forth in Clause 2), will become the sole owner of the Property.

4. Should we separate and neither of us want the Property—or if we can't agree on a fair price—we will advertise it to the public, sell it to the highest bidder and divide the money according to our respective ownership shares as set forth in Clause 2.

5. Should either of us die while we are living together, the Property will belong absolutely to the survivor. (If either of us makes a will or other estate plan, this agreement shall be reflected in that document.)

6. This agreement can be changed, but only in writing, and must be signed by both of us.

7. Any dispute arising out of this contract shall be mediated by a third person mutually acceptable to both of us. The mediator's role shall be to help us arrive at our solution, not to impose one on us. If good-faith efforts to arrive at our own solution to all issues in dispute with the help of a mediator prove to be fruitless, either of us may pursue other legal remedies.

_____   _____
Partner 1's signature   Date

_____   _____
Partner 2's signature   Date

Agreement to Share Property

Partner 1's name: _____

Partner 2's name: _____

We agree as follows:

1. This contract sets forth our rights and obligations toward each other. We intend to abide by them in a spirit of cooperation and good faith.

2. All earned income received by either of us after the date of this contract and all property purchased with this income belongs in equal shares to both of us. Should we separate, it shall be equally divided.

3. All real or personal property earned or accumulated by either of us prior to the date of this agreement (except jointly owned property listed in Attachment C of this agreement), including all future income this property produces, is the separate property of the person who earned or accumulated it and cannot be transferred to the other except in writing. Attached to this agreement in the form of Attachments A, B and C are lists of the major items of property each of us owns separately and both of us own jointly.

4. Should either of us receive real or personal property by gift or inheritance, that property, including all future income it produces, belongs absolutely to the person receiving the gift or inheritance and cannot be transferred to the other except in writing.

5. In the event we separate, all jointly owned property shall be divided equally.

6. Any dispute arising out of this contract shall be mediated by a third person mutually acceptable to both of us. The mediator's role shall be to help us arrive at our solution, not to impose one on us. If good-faith efforts to arrive at our own solution to all issues in dispute with the help of a mediator prove to be fruitless, either of us may pursue other legal remedies.

7. This agreement represents our complete understanding regarding our living together and replaces any and all prior agreements, written or oral. It can be amended, but only in writing, and must be signed by both of us.

8. If a court finds any portion of this contract to be illegal or otherwise unenforceable, the remainder of the contract is still in full force and effect.

_____   _____
Partner 1's signature   Date

_____   _____
Partner 2's signature   Date

Attachment A

Separate property of _____ :

_____

_____

_____

_____

_____

_____

_____

_____

Attachment B

Separate property of _____ :

_____

_____

_____

_____

_____

_____

_____

_____

Attachment C

Jointly owned property acquired prior to _____ *[date of this Agreement]:*

_____

_____

_____

_____

_____

_____

_____

_____

_____

Declaration of Legal Name Change

I, the undersigned, declare that I am 18 years of age or older and further declare:

1. I, _____ [name presently used],

   was born _____ [name on birth certificate]

   in the County of _____ [county where born]

   in the State of _____ [state where born]

   on _____ [birthdate, including year].

2. I HEREBY DECLARE my intent to change my legal name, and be henceforth exclusively known as

   _____ [new name].

3. I further declare that I have no intention of defrauding any person or escaping any obligation I may presently have by this act.

4. NOTICE IS HEREBY GIVEN to all agencies of the State of _____ [state where you reside], all agencies of the Federal Government, all creditors and all private persons, groups, businesses, corporations and associations of said legal name change.

I declare under penalty of perjury under the laws of the State of _____ [state where you reside] that the foregoing is true and correct.

_____   _____

Signature, new name   Date

_____   _____

Signature, old name

[Notary Seal]

Property Division Worksheet

	Value	Ideal Settlement		Worst Deal I'll Accept		Final Settlement	
		I keep	I give up	I keep	I give up	I keep	I give up
Real estate							
Family home							
Vacation home							
Rental property							
Retirement plans							
Defined benefit plan							
Defined benefit plan							
IRA							
IRA							
Roth IRA							
Roth IRA							
401(k) or 403(b)							
401(k) or 403(b)							
Keogh							
Keogh							
SEP-IRA							
SEP-IRA							
Investments							
Stocks							
Bonds							
CD							
Mutual fund							
Life insurance							
Annuity							
Gold							
Money owed to either spouse							
Professional degrees							
Motor vehicles (including boats, planes and RVs)							

	Value	Ideal Settlement		Worst Deal I'll Accept		Final Settlement	
		I keep	I give up	I keep	I give up	I keep	I give up
Other assets							
Interest in a small business							
Copyrights, patents, trademarks							
Miscellaneous property							
Furniture							
Home furnishings							
Electronic equipment							
Computer system							
Jewelry							
Collectibles							
Animals							
Debts							
Mortgage/deed of trust							
Home equity loan							
Liens							
Car loan							
Bank loan							
Personal loan							
Student loan							
Credit card 1							
Credit card 2							
Credit card 3							
Court judgment							
Past due taxes							
Total							
Equalization payment, if necessary							

Custody and Visitation Worksheet

1. Concerns or recommendations made by a counselor, school teacher, therapist or other interested adult regarding your children's emotional, spiritual or physical well-being.

    _____

    _____

    _____

    _____

    _____

2. Each child's current relationship with each parent.
    Child 1 and me:

    _____

    _____

    _____

    Child 2 and me:

    _____

    _____

    _____

    Child 3 and me:

    _____

    _____

    _____

    Child 4 and me:

    _____

    _____

    _____

    Child 1 and other parent:

    _____

    _____

    _____

    Child 2 and other parent:

    _____

    _____

    _____

Child 3 and other parent:

_____

_____

_____

_____

Child 4 and other parent:

_____

_____

_____

_____

3. Each child's feelings, reactions or concerns about separation or divorce.

   Child 1:

   _____

   _____

   _____

   _____

   _____

   Child 2:

   _____

   _____

   _____

   _____

   Child 3:

   _____

   _____

   _____

   _____

   Child 4:

   _____

   _____

   _____

   _____

4. Changes you think are essential in each child's current relationship with each parent.

   Child 1:

   _____

   _____

   _____

_____

Child 2:

_____

_____

_____

_____

Child 3:

_____

_____

_____

_____

Child 4:

_____

_____

_____

_____

5. Changes that may be advisable in each child's current relationship with each parent.
   Child 1:

   _____

   _____

   _____

   _____

   Child 2:

   _____

   _____

   _____

   _____

   Child 3:

   _____

   _____

   _____

   _____

Child 4:

_____

_____

_____

_____

_____

6. Changes either parent would like to see in current parenting relationship.

   Me

   _____

   _____

   _____

   _____

   _____

   Other Parent:

   _____

   _____

   _____

   _____

   _____

7. Times when both parents are available to care for children:

   _____

   _____

   _____

   _____

8. Times when only **I** am available to care for children: _____

9. Times when only **Other Parent** is available to care for children: _____

10. Other adults you believe children should spend time with on a regular basis:

    _____

    _____

    _____

11. Adults or minors that children should not spend time with (or be alone with):

    _____

    _____

    _____

12. Any problems of possible violence, abuse or neglect that you believe must be confronted and planned for:

    _____

    _____

    _____

    _____

Settlement Issues	Ideal Settlement	Least Acceptable Settlement	Unacceptable Settlement	Actual Settlement
Physical custody Possibilities: • Sole/primary custody to Parent 1 • Sole/primary custody to Parent 2 • Joint custody				
Legal custody Possibilities: • Sole/primary custody to Parent 1 • Sole/primary custody to Parent 2 • Joint custody				
Visitation Possibilities for parent who does not have sole/primary physical custody: • Reasonable visitation (schedule worked out as needed) • Specific schedule, such as every other weekend and Wednesday evenings				
Child care (when parents are not available) • Who will provide • Who will pay				
Who takes tax deduction?				

Divorce or Separation Agreement

Spouse/Partner 1

Name: _____

Address: _____

_____

Spouse/Partner 2

Name: _____

Address: _____

_____

This agreement is made on _____ *[date]* between Spouse/Partner 1 and Spouse/Partner 2.

We agree that as a result of serious and irreconcilable differences, our relationship has broken down and that divorce or permanent separation is necessary. We desire to settle our affairs as amicably as possible. Therefore, in exchange for the mutual promises and acts to be performed under this agreement, we both fully agree to the terms and conditions it sets forth concerning property, support and custody issues.

1. Spouse/Partner 1 shall have exclusive rights to ownership and use of the following property, and Spouse/Partner 2 shall complete all paperwork necessary to confirm Spouse/Partner 1's exclusive ownership of such property:

   _____

   _____

   _____

   _____

   _____

   _____

   _____

   _____

2. Spouse/Partner 2 shall have exclusive rights to ownership and use of the following property, and Spouse/Partner 1 shall complete all paperwork necessary to confirm Spouse/Partner 2's exclusive ownership of such property:

   _____

   _____

   _____

   _____

   _____

   _____

   _____

   _____

3. Spouse/Partner 1 agrees to pay and to indemnify and hold Spouse/Partner 2 harmless from the following debts:

_____

_____

_____

_____

_____

_____

_____

_____.

4. Spouse/Partner 2 agrees to pay and to indemnify and hold Spouse/Partner 1 harmless from the following debts:

_____

_____

_____

_____

_____

_____

_____

_____.

5. We agree to the following concerning the custody of and visitation with our minor children:

_____

_____

_____

_____

_____

_____

_____

_____.

6. We agree that _____

[name of parent who will pay child support] shall pay $ _____ per month in child support for each child until that child reaches age 18 to _____

_____ *[name of parent who will receive child support]*. We further agree that a court may increase this amount from time to time if it is necessary and proper to do so under the child support guidelines prescribed under state law.

   We further agree that _____

[name of parent who will obtain health insurance] shall obtain and maintain in force a policy of health insurance providing major medical, dental and vision coverage for each child for the duration of the support obligation. The child's reasonable health costs that are not covered by any policy shall be paid by _____

[name of parent who will obtain health insurance, or names of both parents].

We further agree that as additional child support, _____

[name of parent who will pay child support] shall pay to _____

[name of parent who will receive child support] for child care a total of $ _____ per

month, payable in advance on the _____ day of the month, beginning on

_____ and continuing as long as child care is necessary and actually being paid.

7. Alimony/Maintenance/Spousal Support

☐ We agree to a mutual waiver of any and all rights or claims that either one of us may have now or
in the future to receive alimony, maintenance or spousal support from the other. We both fully
understand that by making this waiver we are forever giving up any right to receive such support.

☐ We agree that _____

[name of spouse who will pay alimony] shall pay $ _____ per month in alimony to

_____*[name of spouse who

will receive alimony]* until _____ *[date alimony obligation will end]*. We further

agree that alimony will terminate on this date and will not be extended for any reason.

8. Upon the entry of the final decree of divorce, _____

_____ *[name of wife]* shall resume use of the following name: _____

_____ *[wife's former name to which she's returning]*.

9. We agree to cooperate in the filing of tax returns this and next year. We also agree that any refund due
us or liability owed under a joint tax return shall be divided or paid as follows:

_____

_____ .

10. We agree to sign, deliver and submit any and all documents necessary to carry out the agreements set
forth above.

11. We agree to the following additional terms:

_____

_____

_____

_____

_____

_____

_____

_____

_____

12. This agreement contains the entire understanding between us and shall be binding on our heirs,
successors and assigns.

13. This agreement shall be governed by the laws of the state of _____ .

_____   _____

Spouse/Partner 1's signature   Date

_____   _____

Spouse/Partner 2's signature   Date

[Notary Seal]

Consent to Change Child's Name

I, the undersigned, being the legal ☐ father ☐ mother of the child currently known as:

_____ ,

do hereby give my full and free consent to the name change of my child to:_____

_____ .

_____   _____

Signature of Parent   Date

Signed in the Presence of

_____   _____

Signature of Witness   Date

_____

Title

[Notary Seal]

Demand Letter

Dear _____ ,

I am seeking redress for the following problem:

[Describe in your own words exactly what happened. Specify dates, names of people with whom you dealt and the damages you have suffered. For example, "On May 21, 199x, I took my car to your garage for servicing. Shortly after picking it up the next day, the engine caught fire because of your failure to properly connect the fuel line to the fuel injector. Fortunately, I was able to douse the fire without injury. As a direct result of the engine fire, I paid ABC Garage $1,281 for necessary repair work. I enclose a copy of the invoice. Also, I was without the use of my car for three days and had to rent a car to get to work. I enclose a copy of an invoice showing the rental cost of $145."]

_____
_____
_____
_____
_____
_____
_____
_____
_____
_____
_____
_____
_____
_____
_____
_____
_____.

Please send me a check or money order in the amount of: $ _____
on or before_____ *[specify date].*

If I don't receive payment by this date, I will promptly take this case to court unless you notify me that you are willing to attempt to resolve this dispute through mediation. In that case I am willing to promptly meet with a neutral third party agreed to by both of us in a good-faith attempt to mutually resolve this dispute without court action.

Thank you for your immediate attention to this matter.

Sincerely,

_____

Signature

_____   _____
Daytime phone   Evening phone

Request for Warranty Coverage

Dear _____ ,

I am seeking full refund of my purchase price or a replacement item under the warranty coverage provided to me by ☐ the seller ☐ the manufacturer ☐ both the seller and manufacturer, a copy of which is enclosed. Accordingly, please send me a new _____

_____ *[insert item]* or a refund check

in the amount of: $ _____ . I enclose a copy of my purchase receipt, canceled check

or other proof of purchase which shows that I made my purchase on _____ .

My reason for demanding redress is simple:

[Describe the problem and what's gone wrong. For example, "On May 21, 199x, I purchased a new pair of Doan and Javid shoes from Shoes Are All We Sell, 195 Main Street, Columbus, Ohio. I was given a one-year warranty from the manufacturer. Last week, the sole began to disintegrate, even though I've owned the shoes only four months, worn them only occasionally and have not subjected them to any extraordinary usage. The store owner has refused to refund my money or provide me with a new pair of shoes." Or, "On April 16, 199x, I purchased an Uphill bicycle from CycLeader, 3300 Sharper Avenue, Denver. In the presence of my friend Rolf Jacobs, I explained to the store clerk that I planned to use the bicycle for off-road mountain cycling throughout Colorado. The clerk, 'Mark,' assured me that the tires could handle 'any surface.' Just last week (less than a month after I purchased the bike), both tires punctured while I was cycling on a much-used mountain bike trail near Greeley. When I asked for a partial refund so as to purchase new tires, the store manager explained that no one named 'Mark' currently works at the store and claimed that this model Uphill cycle would never have been sold for off-road use."]

_____

_____

_____

_____

_____

_____

_____

_____

_____

_____

_____ .

Please process this request within 30 days. If I don't receive redress by _____ ,

_____ *[date]*. I will take further action, which may include filing a court action.

Thank you for your immediate attention to this matter.

Sincerely,

_____

Signature

_____   _____

Daytime phone   Evening phone

Accident Claim Worksheet

What Happened

Names of parties involved: _____

_____

Names of witnesses: _____

_____

Location of accident: _____

Time of accident: _____

Names of witnesses: _____

Weather condition (if outside): _____

_____

_____

_____

People Responsible for the Accident

Name: _____

Address: _____

_____

Telephone (work): _____ (home): _____

Insurance company: _____

Policy number: _____ Auto license: _____

What person did: _____

_____

_____

_____

_____

. . . .

Name: _____

Address: _____

_____

Telephone (work): _____ (home): _____

Insurance company: _____

Policy number: _____ Auto license: _____

What person did: _____

_____

_____

_____

_____

Name: _____

Address: _____

_____

Telephone (work): _____ (home): _____

Insurance company: _____

Policy number: _____ Auto license: _____

What person did: _____

_____

_____

_____

_____

Witnesses

Name: _____

Address: _____

_____

Telephone (work): _____ (home): _____

Date of first contact: _____

Written statement: ☐ yes ☐ no

What person saw: _____

_____

_____

_____

_____

_____

Name: _____

Address: _____

_____

Telephone (work): _____ (home): _____

Date of first contact: _____

Written statement: ☐ yes ☐ no

What person saw: _____

_____

_____

_____

_____

_____

Name: _____

Address: _____

_____

Telephone (work): _____ (home): _____

Date of first contact: _____

Written statement: ☐ yes ☐ no

What person saw: _____

_____

_____

_____

_____

Medical Treatment Providers

Name: _____

Address: _____

_____Telephone:_____

Date of first visit: _____ Date of most recent or last visit: _____

Person to be contacted for medical records: _____

Date requested:_____ Date received: _____

Person to be contacted for medical billing: _____

Date requested:_____ Date received: _____

Reason for treatment and prognosis: _____

_____

_____

_____

Name: _____

Address: _____

_____ Telephone: _____

Date of first visit: _____ Date of most recent or last visit: _____

Person to be contacted for medical records: _____

Date requested:_____ Date received: _____

Person to be contacted for medical billing: _____

Date requested:_____ Date received: _____

Reason for treatment and prognosis: _____

_____

_____

_____

Name: _____

Address: _____

_____ Telephone: _____

Date of first visit: _____ Date of most recent or last visit: _____

Person to be contacted for medical records: _____

Date requested:_____ Date received: _____

Person to be contacted for medical billing: _____

Date requested:_____ Date received: _____

Reason for treatment and prognosis: _____

_____

_____

_____

Other Party's Insurance Company (First Party)

Company name: _____

Address: _____

_____

Telephone:_____ Claim number: _____

Insured: _____

Adjuster:_____

Date demand letter was sent: _____

Settlement amount: _____ Date accepted: _____

Other Party's Insurance Company (Second Party)

Company name: _____

Address: _____

_____

Telephone:_____ Claim number: _____

Insured: _____

Adjuster:_____

Date demand letter was sent: _____

Settlement amount: _____ Date accepted: _____

Communications With Insurer

Date:_____

If oral, what was said: _____

_____

_____

_____

Communications With Insurer

Date:_____

If oral, what was said: _____

_____

_____

Communications With Insurer

Date:_____

If oral, what was said: _____

_____

_____

Communications With Insurer

Date:_____

If oral, what was said: _____

_____

_____

Communications With Insurer

Date:_____

If oral, what was said: _____

_____

_____

Losses

Describe damage to your property: _____

_____

Do you have photos showing damage? ☐ yes ☐ no

If Repairable

Estimates for repairs (name of repair shop and amounts of estimates):_____

_____

Actual

Repair bills (name of repair shop and amounts of bills):_____

_____

If totaled:

Value at the time destroyed: _____

Documentation of value:_____

Weather condition (if outside): _____

_____

General Release

Releasor: _____

Address: _____

Releasee: _____

Address: _____

1. Releasor voluntarily and knowingly executes this release with the express intention of eliminating Releasee's legal liabilities and obligations as described below.

2. Releasor hereby releases Releasee from all claims, known or unknown, that have arisen or may arise from the following occurrence: _____
_____
_____ .

3. In exchange for granting this release Releasor has received the following payment or other benefits:
_____
_____ .

4. In executing this release, Releasor additionally intends to bind his or her spouse, heirs, legal representatives, assigns and anyone else claiming under him or her. Releasor has not assigned any claim covered by this release to any other party. Releasor intends that this release apply to the heirs, personal representatives, assigns, insurers and successors of Releasee as well as to the Releasee.

_____   _____
Releasor's signature   Date

_____   _____
Print name   County of residence

_____   _____
Releasor's spouse's signature   Date

_____   _____
Print name   County of residence

General Mutual Release

Party 1: _____

Address: _____

Party 2: _____

Address: _____

1. We voluntarily and knowingly sign this mutual release with the express intention of eliminating the liabilities and obligations described below.

2. Disputes and differences that we mutually desire to settle have arisen between us with respect to the following: _____

   _____

   _____

   _____ .

3. The value (consideration) for this mutual release consists of our mutual relinquishment of our respective legal rights involved in the disputes described above.

4. In addition, either party will receive from the other the following:

   ☐ Party 1 will receive from Party 2: _____

   _____ .

   ☐ Party 2 will receive from Party 1: _____

   _____ .

5. In signing this release, we both intend to bind our spouses, heirs, legal representatives, assigns, and anyone else claiming under us, in addition to ourselves.

_____ _____
Party 1's signature   Date

_____ _____
Print name   County of residence

_____ _____
Party 1's spouse's signature   Date

_____ _____
Print name   County of residence

_____ _____
Party 2's signature   Date

_____ _____
Print name   County of residence

_____ _____
Party 2's spouse's signature   Date

_____ _____
Print name   County of residence

Release for Damage to Real Estate

Releasor: _____

Address: _____

Releasee: _____

Address: _____

1. Releasor is the owner of certain property (Property) located at _____
_____, which specifically consists of the following:
_____.

2. Releasor voluntarily and knowingly signs this release with the intention of eliminating Releasee's liabilities and obligations as described below.

3. Releasor hereby releases Releasee from all claims, known or unknown, that have arisen or may arise from the transaction described in Clause 4.

4. Releasor has alleged that Property suffered damage in the approximate amount of $ _____
as a result of the following activity of Releasee:_____
_____
_____.

5. In signing this release, Releasor additionally intends to bind his or her spouse, heirs, legal representatives, assigns and anyone else claiming under him or her. Releasor has not assigned any claim arising from the transaction described in Clause 4 to another party. Releasor intends that this release apply to the heirs, personal representatives, assigns, insurers and successors of Releasee as well as to the Releasee.

6. Releasor has received good and adequate value (consideration) for this release in the form of:
_____
_____.

_____   _____
Releasor's signature   Date

_____   _____
Print name   County of residence

_____   _____
Releasor's spouse's signature   Date

_____   _____
Print name   County of residence

Release for Property Damage in Auto Accident

Releasor: _____

Address: _____

Releasee: _____

Address: _____

1. Releasor voluntarily and knowingly signs this release with the express intention of eliminating Releasee's liabilities and obligations as described below.

2. Releasor hereby releases Releasee from all liability for claims, known and unknown, arising from property damage sustained by Releasor in an automobile accident that occurred on _____ [date] at _____ [location] involving a vehicle owned by Releasee or driven by Releasee or his/her agent.

3. By executing this release Releasor does not give up any claim that he or she may now or hereafter have against any person, firm or corporation other than Releasee and those persons and entities specified in Clause 6.

4. Releasor understands that Releasee does not, by providing the value described below, admit any liability or responsibility for the accident described in Clause 2 or its consequences.

5. Releasor has received good and adequate value (consideration) for this release in the form of:

   _____

   _____ .

6. In executing this release Releasor additionally intends to bind his or her spouse, heirs, legal representatives, assigns and anyone else claiming under him or her. Releasor has not assigned any claim arising from the accident described in Clause 2 to any other party. This release applies to Releasee's heirs, legal representatives, insurers and successors, as well as to Releasee.

_____   _____
Releasor's signature   Date

_____   _____
Print name   County of residence

_____   _____
Releasor's spouse's signature   Date

_____   _____
Print name   County of residence

Release for Personal Injury

Releasor: _____

Address: _____

Releasee: _____

Address: _____

1. Releasor voluntarily and knowingly executes this release with the intention of eliminating Releasee's liabilities and obligations as described below.

2. Releasor hereby releases Releasee from all liability for claims, known and unknown, arising from injuries, mental and physical, sustained by Releasor as follows:_____
    _____
    _____.

3. Releasor has been examined by a licensed physician or other health care professional competent to diagnose *[choose one or both]*:

    ☐ physical injuries and disabilities.

    ☐ mental and emotional injuries and disabilities.

    Releasor has been informed by this physician or health care professional that the injury described in Clause 2 has completely healed without causing permanent damage.

4. By executing this release Releasor does not give up any claim that he or she may now or hereafter have against any person, firm or corporation other than Releasee and those persons specified in Clause 7.

5. Releasor understands that Releasee does not, by providing the value described below, admit any liability or responsibility for the above described injury or its consequences.

6. Releasor has received good and adequate value for this release in the form of:
    _____
    _____.

7. In executing this release Releasor additionally intends to bind his or her spouse, heirs, legal representatives, assigns and anyone else claiming under him or her. Releasor has not assigned any claim arising from the accident described in Clause 2 to any other party. This release applies to Releasee's heirs, legal representatives, insurers and successors, as well as to Releasee.

_____   _____
Releasor's signature   Date

_____   _____
Print name   County of residence

Mutual Release of Contract Claims

Party 1: _____

Address: _____

Party 2: _____

Address: _____

1. We voluntarily and knowingly sign this mutual release with the intention of eliminating the liabilities and obligations described below.

2. Disputes and differences have arisen between us with respect to an agreement entered into between us on _____ *[date]*, under which we agreed to the following:

   _____

   _____

   _____ .

      This agreement is hereby made a part of this release and incorporated by reference. A copy of the agreement (if written) is attached to this release.

3. We each hereby expressly release the other from all claims and demands, known and unknown, arising out of the agreement specified in Clause 2.

4. This release additionally applies to our heirs, legal representatives and successors and is binding on our spouses, heirs, legal representatives, assigns and anyone else claiming under us. Neither of us has assigned to another party any claim arising under or out of the contract specified in Clause 2.

5. The value for this mutual release binds our mutual agreement to forgo our respective legal rights with reference to the disputes and differences described above.

6. We also agree that the contract specified in Clause 2 shall be and is hereby rescinded, terminated, and canceled as of _____ *[date]*.

_____   _____
Party 1's signature   Date

_____   _____
Print name   County of residence

_____   _____
Party 2's signature   Date

_____   _____
Print name   County of residence

Notice to Remove Name From List

_____

_____

_____

_____

[name and address of list maintainer]

To Whom It May Concern:

Please permanently remove all members of this household from all lists you maintain, sell, trade, share or use in any other capacity for direct marketing, telemarketing, credit card pre-screening or any other promotional opportunity.

_____
Name 1

_____
Address

_____

_____
Name 2

_____
Address

_____

_____
Name 3

_____
Address

_____

_____

Sincerely,

_____
Signature

_____
Print name

Notice to Add or Retain Name but Not Sell or Trade It

_____

_____

_____

_____

[name and address of list maintainer]

To Whom It May Concern:

Please ☐ add ☐ retain my name on your mailing list. ***Please do not sell, trade or share my name or address with any other company or business.***

☐ I will accept telemarketing phone calls from your company.

☐ I do not wish to receive telemarketing phone calls from your company. That is, put me on your "do not call" list.

Sincerely,

_____
Signature

_____
Print name

_____
Address

_____

_____

Telemarketing Phone Call Log

Date	Time	Company	Telemarketer's name	Product	Said "Put me on a 'do not call' list"	Followed up with letter
Example: 9/11/XX	6:15pm	AT&T	Terri	Long Distance	✔	✔

Notice to Put Name on "Do Not Call" List

_____

_____

_____

_____

[name and address of list maintainer]

To Whom It May Concern:

This letter is a follow up to the telemarketing phone call I received from _____

[name of person who placed the call to you] from your company on _____ *[date]*.

As I stated at that time, I do not wish to receive telemarketing phone calls from your company. That is, please immediately put me on your "do not call" list.

Signature

_____

Print name

_____

Address

_____

_____

Demand for Damages for Excessive Calls

_____

_____

_____

_____

[name and address of list maintainer]

To Whom It May Concern:

Since_____ *[date]*, I have received multiple phone calls from telemarketers calling on behalf of your company. I am giving your company the opportunity to settle my claim against you before I sue you in small claims court.

On or about _____ *[date]*, I received a telephone call at my home from a telemarketer by the name of _____, who stated that ☐ he ☐ she was calling on behalf of your company. I told this person that I was not interested in your company's product, and asked that my name be placed on a "do not call" list. I was assured that this would be done.

On or about _____ *[date]*, I received a second telephone call at my home from a telemarketer by the name of _____, who stated that ☐ he ☐ she was calling on behalf of your company. I told this person that I was not interested in your company's product, and asked that my name be placed on a "do not call" list. Again, I was assured that this would be done.

[Repeat the above paragraph as needed, changing the word "second" to "third," "fourth," etc.]

Section 64.1200(e)(2)(iii) of Title 47 of the Code of Federal Regulations states, in pertinent part:

> If a person or entity making a telephone solicitation (or on whose behalf a solicitation is made) receives a request from a residential telephone subscriber not to receive calls from that person or entity, the person or entity must record the request and place the subscriber's name and telephone number on the do-not-call list at the time the request is made. If such requests are recorded or maintained by a party other than the person or entity on whose behalf the solicitation is made, the person or entity on whose behalf the solicitation is made will be liable for any failures to honor the do-not-call list.

A violation of this regulation is actionable under 47 U.S.C. § 227(c)(5). That section provides that:

> A person who has received more than one telephone call within any 12-month period by or on behalf of the same entity in violation of the regulations prescribed under this subsection may ... bring in an appropriate court of that state—
>
> (A) an action based on a violation of the regulations prescribed under this subsection to enjoin such violation,
>
> (B) an action to recover for actual monetary loss from such a violation, or to received up to $500 in damages for each such violation, whichever is greater, or
>
> (C) both such actions.

In addition, treble damages are available for knowing and willful violations.

Your company clearly violated the law on _____ separate occasions. I am entitled to $500 for each violation, for a total of $ _____ . I am willing to forego my right to seek an injunction and treble damages against your company if you send me a cashier's check for the amount stated above within the next 30 days. If I do not hear from you within that time, I will seek all appropriate remedies in a court of law.

Sincerely,

_____
Signature

_____
Print name

_____
Address

_____

_____

_____
Home phone

Index

CATALOG

...more from Nolo Press

		PRICE	CODE

BUSINESS

	The California Nonprofit Corporation Handbook	$29.95	NON
⊙	The CA Nonprofit Corp Kit (Binder w/CD-ROM)	$49.95	CNP
▣	Consultant & Independent Contractor Agreements (Book w/Disk—PC)	$24.95	CICA
	The Corporate Minutes Book (Book w/Disk—PC)	$69.95	CORMI
	The Employer's Legal Handbook	$29.95	EMPL
▣	Form Your Own Limited Liability Company (Book w/Disk—PC)	$34.95	LIAB
▣	Hiring Independent Contractors: The Employer's Legal Guide (Book w/Disk—PC)	$29.95	HICI
▣	How to Form a California Professional Corporation (Book w/Disk—PC)	$49.95	PROF
▣	How to Form a Nonprofit Corporation (Book w/Disk —PC)—National Edition	$39.95	NNP
▣	How to Form Your Own California Corporation (Binder w/Disk—PC	$39.95	CACI
▣	How to Form Your Own California Corporation (Book w/Disk—PC)	$34.95	CCOR
▣	How to Form Your Own Florida Corporation (Book w/Disk—PC)	$39.95	FLCO
▣	How to Form Your Own New York Corporation (Book w/Disk—PC)	$39.95	NYCO
▣	How to Form Your Own Texas Corporation (Book w/Disk—PC)	$39.95	TCOR
	How to Mediate Your Dispute	$18.95	MEDI
	How to Write a Business Plan	$21.95	SBS
	The Independent Paralegal's Handbook	$29.95	PARA
	Legal Guide for Starting & Running a Small Business, Vol. 1	$24.95	RUNS
▣	Legal Guide for Starting & Running a Small Business, Vol. 2: Legal Forms (Book w/Disk—PC)	$29.95	RUNS2
	Marketing Without Advertising	$19.00	MWAD
	Music Law (Book w/Disk—PC)	$29.95	ML
▣	The Partnership Book: How to Write a Partnership Agreement (Book w/Disk—PC)	$34.95	PART
	Sexual Harassment on the Job	$18.95	HARS
	Starting and Running a Successful Newsletter or Magazine	$24.95	MAG
	Take Charge of Your Workers' Compensation Claim (California Edition)	$29.95	WORK
	Tax Savvy for Small Business	$28.95	SAVVY
	Trademark: Legal Care for Your Business and Product Name	$29.95	TRD
	Wage Slave No More: Law & Taxes for the Self-Employed	$24.95	WAGE
	Your Rights in the Workplace	$21.95	YRW

CONSUMER

Fed Up with the Legal System: What's Wrong & How to Fix It	$9.95	LEG
How to Win Your Personal Injury Claim	$24.95	PICL
Nolo's Everyday Law Book	$21.95	EVL
Nolo's Pocket Guide to California Law	$11.95	CLAW
Trouble-Free Travel...And What to Do When Things Go Wrong	$14.95	TRAV

ESTATE PLANNING & PROBATE

8 Ways to Avoid Probate (Quick & Legal Series)	$15.95	PRO8
How to Probate an Estate (California Edition)	$34.95	PAE

▣ Book with disk

⊙ Book with CD-ROM

	PRICE	CODE
Make Your Own Living Trust	$24.95	LITR
Nolo's Law Form Kit: Wills	$14.95	KWL
⌨ Nolo's Will Book (Book w/Disk—PC)	$29.95	SWIL
Plan Your Estate	$24.95	NEST
The Quick and Legal Will Book (Quick & Legal Series)	$15.95	QUIC

FAMILY MATTERS

Child Custody: Building Parenting Agreements That Work	$24.95	CUST
Divorce & Money: How to Make the Best Financial Decisions During Divorce	$26.95	DIMO
Do Your Own Divorce in Oregon	$19.95	ODIV
Get a Life: You Don't Need a Million to Retire Well	$18.95	LIFE
The Guardianship Book (California Edition)	$24.95	GB
How to Adopt Your Stepchild in California	$22.95	ADOP
How to Raise or Lower Child Support in California (Quick & Legal Series)	$19.95	CHLD
A Legal Guide for Lesbian and Gay Couples	$24.95	LG
The Living Together Kit	$24.95	LTK
Nolo's Pocket Guide to Family Law	$14.95	FLD

GOING TO COURT

Collect Your Court Judgment (California Edition)	$24.95	JUDG
The Criminal Law Handbook: Know Your Rights, Survive the System	$24.95	KYR
How to Seal Your Juvenile & Criminal Records (California Edition)	$24.95	CRIM
How to Sue For Up to $25,000...and Win!	$29.95	MUNI
Everybody's Guide to Small Claims Court in California	$18.95	CSCC
Everybody's Guide to Small Claims Court (National Edition)	$18.95	NSCC
Fight Your Ticket ... and Win! (California Edition)	$19.95	FYT
How to Change Your Name in California	$29.95	NAME
Mad at Your Lawyer	$21.95	MAD
Represent Yourself in Court: How to Prepare & Try a Winning Case	$29.95	RYC

HOMEOWNERS, LANDLORDS & TENANTS

The Deeds Book (California Edition)	$16.95	DEED
Dog Law	$14.95	DOG
⌨ Every Landlord's Legal Guide (National Edition, Book w/Disk—PC)	$34.95	ELLI
Every Tenant's Legal Guide	$24.95	EVTEN
For Sale by Owner in California	$24.95	FSBO
How to Buy a House in California	$24.95	BHCA
The Landlord's Law Book, Vol. 1: Rights & Responsibilities (California Edition)	$34.95	LBRT
The Landlord's Law Book, Vol. 2: Evictions (California Edition)	$34.95	LBEV
Leases & Rental Agreements (Quick & Legal Series)	$18.95	LEAR
Neighbor Law: Fences, Trees, Boundaries & Noise	$17.95	NEI
Stop Foreclosure Now in California	$29.95	CLOS
Tenants' Rights (California Edition)	$19.95	CTEN

HUMOR

29 Reasons Not to Go to Law School	$9.95	29R
Poetic Justice	$9.95	PJ

IMMIGRATION

How to Get a Green Card: Legal Ways to Stay in the U.S.A.	$24.95	GRN
U.S. Immigration Made Easy	$39.95	IMEZ

MONEY MATTERS

⌨ 101 Law Forms for Personal Use (Quick and Legal Series, Book w/disk—PC)	$24.95	SPOT
Bankruptcy: Is It the Right Solution to Your Debt Problems? (Quick & Legal Series)	$15.95	BRS
Chapter 13 Bankruptcy: Repay Your Debts	$29.95	CH13
Credit Repair (Quick & Legal Series)	$15.95	CREP
⌨ The Financial Power of Attorney Workbook (Book w/disk—PC)	$24.95	FINPOA

⌨ Book with disk

◉ Book with CD-ROM

PATENTS AND COPYRIGHTS

RESEARCH & REFERENCE

SENIORS

SOFTWARE
Call or check our website at www.nolo.com
for special discounts on Software!

🖫 Book with disk

◉ Book with CD-ROM

ORDER FORM

Code	Quantity	Title	Unit price	Total
		Subtotal		
		California residents add Sales Tax		
		Basic Shipping ($6.50)		
		UPS RUSH delivery $8.00–any size order*		
		TOTAL		

Name

Address

(UPS to street address, Priority Mail to P.O. boxes)

* Delivered in 3 business days from receipt of order.
S.F. Bay Area use regular shipping.

FOR FASTER SERVICE, USE YOUR CREDIT CARD AND OUR TOLL-FREE NUMBERS

Order 24 hours a day   1-800-992-6656

Fax your order   1-800-645-0895

Online   www.nolo.com

METHOD OF PAYMENT

☐ Check enclosed

☐ VISA   ☐ MasterCard   ☐ Discover Card   ☐ American Express

Account #   Expiration Date

Authorizing Signature

Daytime Phone

PRICES SUBJECT TO CHANGE.

VISIT OUR OUTLET STORES!

VISIT US ONLINE!

You'll find our complete line of books and software, all at a discount.

BERKELEY
950 Parker Street
Berkeley, CA 94710
1-510-704-2248

SAN JOSE
111 N. Market Street, #115
San Jose, CA 95113
1-408-271-7240

on the Internet

www.nolo.com

NOLO PRESS 950 PARKER ST., BERKELEY, CA 94710

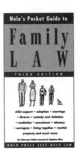
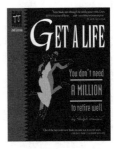

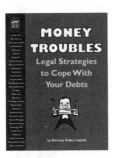

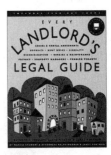

Your comments make a big difference in the development and revision of Nolo books and software. Please take a few minutes and register your Nolo product—and your comments—with us. Not only will your input make a difference, you'll receive special offers available only to the registered owners of Nolo products on our newest books and software. Register now by:

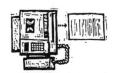

CALL	FAX	E-MAIL	OR MAIL US THIS REGISTRATION CARD
1-800-992-6656	**1-800-645-0895**	**NOLOSUB@NOLOPRESS.com**	

 *U.S. ADDRESSES ONLY. ONE YEAR INTERNATIONAL SUBSCRIPTIONS: CANADA & MEXICO $10.00; ALL OTHER FOREIGN ADDRESSES $20.00.

fold here

REGISTRATION CARD

NAME		DATE

ADDRESS

CITY	STATE	ZIP

PHONE	E-MAIL

WHERE DID YOU HEAR ABOUT THIS PRODUCT?

WHERE DID YOU PURCHASE THIS PRODUCT?

DID YOU CONSULT A LAWYER? (PLEASE CIRCLE ONE)   YES   NO   NOT APPLICABLE

DID YOU FIND THIS BOOK HELPFUL?   (VERY)   5   4   3   2   1   (NOT AT ALL)

COMMENTS

WAS IT EASY TO USE?   (VERY EASY)   5   4   3   2   1   (VERY DIFFICULT)

DO YOU OWN A COMPUTER? IF SO, WHICH FORMAT? (PLEASE CIRCLE ONE)   WINDOWS   DOS   MAC

☐ If you do not wish to receive mailings from these companies, please check this box.

☐ You can quote me in future Nolo Press promotional materials. Daytime phone number _____.   SPOT 1.0

N O L O I N T H E *N E W S*

"Nolo helps lay people perform legal tasks without the aid—or fees—of lawyers."

— **USA TODAY**

Nolo books are ..."written in plain language, free of legal mumbo jumbo, and spiced with witty personal observations."

— **ASSOCIATED PRESS**

"...Nolo publications...guide people simply through the how, when, where and why of law."

— **WASHINGTON POST**

"Increasingly, people who are not lawyers are performing tasks usually regarded as legal work... And consumers, using books like Nolo's, do routine legal work themselves."

— **NEW YORK TIMES**

"...All of [Nolo's] books are easy-to-understand, are updated regularly, provide pull-out forms...and are often quite moving in their sense of compassion for the struggles of the lay reader."

— **SAN FRANCISCO CHRONICLE**

fold here

- -

Place
stamp here

NOLO
PRESS

NOLO PRESS
950 Parker Street
Berkeley, CA 94710-9867

Attn: **SPOT 1.0**